To Maria Teresa, my wife, and to the
kids, Mariel, Carmelita, Miguel,
Lucy, and Carlos, my love and
affection.

RITUALS
OF
MARGINALITY

Politics, Process, and
Culture Change in
Central Urban Mexico,
1969-1974

Carlos G. Vélez-Ibañez

UNIVERSITY OF CALIFORNIA PRESS
Berkeley   Los Angeles   Oxford

University of California Press
Berkeley and Los Angeles, California

University of California Press, Ltd.
Oxford, England

First Paperback Printing 1991

Library of Congress Cataloging in Publication Data

Vélez-Ibañez, Carlos G.
　　Rituals of marginality.

　　Includes index.
　　1. Political participation—Mexico—Netzahualcoyotl.
2.　Marginality, Social—Mexico—Netzahualcoyotl.
3.　Elite (Social science)—Mexico—Netzahualcoyotl.
I.　Title.
JS2143.N483A78　1983　　　320.8'09725　　82-19964
ISBN 0-520-07421-1

Printed in the United States of America

1 2 3 4 5 6 7 8 9

The paper used in this publication meets the minimum
requirements of American National Standard for Information Sciences—Permanence of Paper for Printed
Library Materials, ANSI Z39.48–1984. ∞

RITUALS
OF
MARGINALITY

Contents

Foreword

NETZAHUALCOYOTL IZCALLI is not a household word in North America, and is probably unfamiliar in Ciudad de las Casas or Mazatlán. It should be, however, because it is a Mexican event of world importance. It is the migratory assemblage of upward of four million people, creating a city out of a shallow lake immediately adjacent to Mexico City. It is a major Mexican metropolis emerging next to a major world metropolis. It is a monumental urban fact, a settlement of concrete qualities daily confronting the Mexican nation. It is much more, however, because it symbolizes a human answer to the infrahuman and suprahuman processes of biological and social expansion, a solution to the problem of survival, not in primal virgin landscape of a million years ago but in the wasted, polluted, ecologically catastrophic remains of too much human occupation for too long a time. It emerged not in a world open to expanding human societies but in one already crowded by human beings, in an already existing complex national urbanized society where things necessary for survival depend not merely on what you can do for yourself but even more on what others can do for you. It is a human political answer to an ecological and organic challenge.

This book concretely parallels the significance of Ciudad Netzahualcoyotl Izcalli. Its author, Carlos G. Vélez-Ibañez, is a Mexican American anthropologist who answered the challenge of the constrictions and economic obstacles of United States society by searching out a problem of extraordinary importance, and then persisting through years of his own development to bring it to fruition. As the people of Netzahualcoyotl have developed themselves in creating their society, so Professor Vélez-Ibañez took up the challenge to develop his own abilities to be the vehicle for bringing this important and timely account to the attention of a wider public.

This book is important because it is publicly announcing that the Mexican people—and symbolically for people crowded in national societies throughout the world—will find solutions to survival, and that these solutions may not be what the planners, the designers of the lush residential areas in the Lomas de Chapultepeque or of the Pedregal, had in mind. Mexico has been the scene of some important anthropological announcements. It was there that inter-American *indigenismo* saw its early development. It was there that the *ejido* was presented as a solution to the economic suppression of prerevolutionary Mexico. It was there that Ricardo Pozas's Juan Perez Jolote raised his voice from the Chiapas highlands. It was there that Oscar Lewis's *familia Sánchez* made public the fact that urban dwellers were creating a culture of signal importance.

Netzahualcoyotl Izcalli is not the answer of a single Native American or a single family of Mexican urban poor. It is the collective response of a growing population. It is a macro-product, more like a house that has too long served as dinner for termites, or massive coral reefs composed of the collective building of uncountable miniscule creatures. One can study, decry, admire, or simply gape at the product, but one cannot stay the process without resorting to devastating destruction. What is yielded is hardly designed to please the tastes of the middle class, but rather something that is fundamentally changing the environment that the middle class has been trying to create. In decades past there was a North American saying to the effect that you could not keep sonny down on the farm once he had seen the big city; the people of Netzahualcoyotl Izcalli are telling us that if sonny is going to have to build the big city himself, he—and she—will have to do it in spite of the inadequate tools and materials that the rest of society has left for him to use. But build it they will. And if they do not announce this from the housetops, it is because the product of their efforts should be sufficient announcement in itself. But if the world is to understand, then it needs a medium of wider diffusion.

Professor Vélez-Ibañez's study is this medium. It is also considerably more. Again, paralleling the thing studied, this volume announces that Mexican Americans have expanded their own scholarly and social horizons beyond the local Chicano struggle for improvement within North American society, and that what confronts them at home is recursively in evidence in the land ancestrally related to some and collaterally to others. That the Mexican American concern is not a parochial struggle but one of hemispheric dimensions (and by extension presumably of world dimensions); that massive urban solutions are not limited to Los Angeles but are much more serious and significant in terms of the future in the Mexican homeland; these are messages implicit in Professor Vélez-Ibañez's choice of Netzahualcoyotl Izcalli as the subject of his research.

I like to think of this volume as Professor Vélez-Ibañez's first book. In fact, because of various reasons, it may be his second. But the physical appearance of another study does not alter the fact that this book is the author's first attempt to wrestle with the difficult problem of translating intricate and heretofore not well understood phenomena into a meaningful communication that will alert potential readers to the importance of the subject. I am pleased to have been asked to prepare this Foreword because I am confident that Professor Vélez-Ibañez is giving us a work of major substantive importance for understanding the immediacy of Mexican life, and even more to the nature of the human process of expansion. He is not predicting the future; he is describing it. And in so doing, I would suggest that he is incidentally also describing the emergence of an important anthropologist.

Austin, Texas   Richard N. Adams
September 1982

Acknowledgments

I WOULD LIKE to acknowledge the generosity of many persons in Ciudad Netzahualcoyotl who must remain anonymous. Especially to Julieta, Arturo, and Roberto—*mil gracias.* I hope I left a tenth of what they provided me. For theoretical insights, Professors F. G. Bailey, Neal D. Houghton, and especially Marc J. Swartz were very important to my early conceptual understandings of politics. Professors Richard N. Adams, Robert V. Kemper, and Eric R. Wolf were intellectually significant in the formation of the final theoretical framework that structures the ideas in this book. Professor Adams's willingness to comment critically on the various versions of this work contributed greatly to its broad emphases. In addition, Professor Kemper's perceptive stylistic and substantive observations strengthened the structure of exposition in major ways. Professor Wolf's critical assessment of the work's potential contribution was extremely supportive. I owe them all a great debt.

Nevertheless, Dr. Arturo Madrid is the person most responsible for the financial and moral support that allowed me to complete the graduate study and conduct the fieldwork necessary for this work. He, as national director of the Graduate Fellowships Program for Mexican Americans, Native Americans and Puerto Ricans (1974-1981) and as president of the Board of Trustees of the National Chicano Council on Higher Education, devised the structures by which the Ford Foundation provided fellowships. This support not only provided opportunities for many Chicanos to earn graduate degrees but also helped some of us earn tenured positions through continued support for our research. Dr. Madrid's leadership will be appreciated by many cohorts to follow.

Portions of chapter 6 were previously published under the title "Youth and Aging in Central Mexico: One Day in the Life of Four Families of Migrants," in *Life's Career—Aging: Cultural Variations in Growing Old,* ed. B. Myerhoff and A. Símic (Beverly Hills and London: Sage Publications, 1978). Their permission to publish these parts is acknowledged.

C.G. V.-I.

Introduction

THIS IS A WORK of political ethnography that depicts the ways in which men and women with very few material resources were able to generate sufficient energy and power to confront those in opposite circumstances. This is an analysis of the processes of political conflict between "marginalized" populations of Ciudad Netzahualcoyotl Izcalli, the fourth most populous city in the Mexican republic, and political elites in control of resources and power. The significance of the elites will be seen in how they affected the ability of local populations to articulate their goals, as well as in how they prevented those goals from being fulfilled. The analysis will show that in the end, elites seldom "lose" and local populations seldom "win" such conflicts. In fact, elites gain much more in such conflicts than do local populations.

Local populations, however, do gain a collective sense of autonomy and social power from an experience of political action which can never be erased. This collective sense of autonomy emerges from political action itself, but it derives also from the fact that such action eventually leads to the establishment of social relations based in nonpolitical contexts such as friendship, residence, marriage, and fictive kinship. Yet all such relations are given a special referent, genesis, and rationale for continuation by the struggles shared in political activity. Among the most radical changes a population can undergo are the changes generated by a

1

collective experience that provides them a sense of historical relationship and identity, and thus molds them into a specific cultural
cohort. This work will detail the political and social processes that
made such a cohort possible between 1969 and 1974 in Ciudad
Netzahualcoyotl. Such cohorts, it will be argued, are important
portents of future cohorts in much of urban Mexico.

The key idea in this work, however, is that the development of
such cultural cohorts very much contradicts the meanings, forms,
and relations by which elites maintain what I term *rituals of marginality* with local populations. Elites are part of economic and
political sectors that make up the dominant parts of Mexican
social structures. These "formal" sectors control public and private resources and make up classes of persons with similar interests, relationships, and goals. The social and economic gaps that
develop between such formal sectors and classes and local "informal" sectors and classes without influence and control of their
own labor and production are crosscut by various types of relations. These relations are expressed in repetitive forms such as
patron-client relationships, brokerage, political friendships of convenience, and other favor-producing exchanges. These I have
termed *rituals of marginality*. The development of cultural cohorts
in political action, however, contradicts rituals of marginality in
that a collective sense of social autonomy and social power arises.
Such contradiction threatens the forms used to express dominance
as well as the relations of dominance the forms express. This work
details the process by which small networks of men and women
coalesced to the point that rituals of marginality became dysfunc-
tional politically and sentimentally. This process is indicative of
"microcultural" change at the local level.

Such microcultural change is to be understood within the adaptive strategies that urban populations employ for survival. Such
change is the result of limited access to formal sectors; hence, reliance on socially autonomous networks does not necessarily
emerge because of a cultural tradition. The greater the access to
resources within formal institutional sectors, the lesser the reliance
on reciprocal networks for survival. The lesser the access to formal
sectors, the greater the reliance on reciprocal networks for sur-

vival, such as among the "marginalized" populations of Ciudad Netzahualcoyotl Izcalli.

This work emphasizes four important processes: first, it elucidates the manner in which local populations organized politically. It will be shown that the Congreso Restaurador de Colonos[1] ("Congress for Settler Restoration," or CRC) emerged from the locality but eventually became a resource for elites. The CRC became entangled in domains of influence and power controlled by elites, public and private. Because of the features of Mexican social structure, this entanglement occurred even before the political structure coalesced. Second, the work analyzes the manner in which political activities eventually led to the formation of multiple social relations based on reciprocity. Such relations provided persons with a sense of collective identity and a local context suitable for the emergence of self. Collective identity and local context have specific features and qualities, which include not only the acceptance of reciprocal relationships of various sorts but the inclusion of women and children in political activities, the use of violence for defensive and offensive purposes, and an accumulated understanding of the myths of universal access to resources and judicial redress. The third process examined here is the national "integration" of marginalized populations, the highest "achievement" of the rituals of marginality. It is argued that the public sector is the most important mechanism through which such populations become additional resources for the private sector in Mexico, and additional resources, too, for the political welfare of the public sector and members of the public-sector elite. The fourth process analyzed illustrates that it is advantageous to the survival of such marginalized populations to withdraw their political and social support from the public and private sectors that comprise the most important parts of the Mexican nation-state. These four processes are linked closely, and they unfolded as I began to study political activities in Ciudad Netzahualcoyotl in 1971.

In the summer of 1971, I had the opportunity to study at the Colegio de Mexico in Mexico City. While there, I was invited to attend a guerrilla theater performance that took place in what the actors privately called *"una ciudad perdida"* ("a lost city"). They said that in this place I would find "real people" and many Mexicans who spoke much as I did. (They were referring either to my working-class, southwestern U.S. Spanish, which was also spoken there, or to their own conception of "real folk" language.) In any case, at 7 A.M. on Sunday, June 12, 1971, I and twenty actors, together with their props, masks, bongos, guitars, maracas, and timbales, jammed into three cars and began a journey to what was to be my home intermittently for the next three years—Ciudad Netzahualcoyotl Izcalli ("the place where hungry coyote resides," from the Nahuatl language). It was during these three years and subsequent short field checks in 1975, and then much later in 1979, that I came to be a participant-observer in the growth of an urban center that today is the fourth most populous area in the Mexican republic.

On that morning we traveled seventeen kilometers from the center of Mexico City—the Zocalo, which is the famous plaza—to our destination. Although the drive seemed to take hours, it actually took twenty-five minutes. On highway Zaragoza, the main highway to the colonial city of Puebla, weekend drivers choked the roadway: cars were filled with families traveling toward Mexico City, and buses were packed with Sunday visitors to the many parks, leaving early to find an open space. Diesel trucks, heavily laden with finished goods and raw materials, crawled ponderously in both directions, spewing out black smoke; taxis, like multicolored beetles, switched in and out of lanes. Buzzing motorcycles carried pouting young men and miniskirted young women who rode sidesaddle; skinny racing bikes carried sometimes one and sometimes two riders, who, as they whizzed by, smirked at the drivers honking their horns at stalled autos.

The din was tremendous: the unmuffled growls of the diesel trucks and buses, the continuous honking of impatient motorists, and the shrill whistles of the police (*tamarindos*, also known as *azules*, because of their baby-blue uniforms) all combined in a cacophony elsewhere unexpected on a Sunday morning in Mexico. Yet Sunday, here, was the day that the people, in spite of the noise, were "out." They could be found even on the center divider of the highway approaching Netzahualcoyotl—"Netza," as it is called—in small group outings; in their midst, winos slept off Saturday night's fun. At the edge of the road, soccer players strutted in their once-a-week silk shorts, kicking the ball back and forth; others, walking more sedately, gestured in sweeping circles as they argued. Vendors were everywhere—young and old, women and children, mestizos and Indios—all hawking their wares of Kleenex, Chiclets, and bubble gum to passing motorists. Young girls and women, their arms wrapped around one another, walked in pairs or trios in mutual protection against the remarks and advances of black-haired rowdies who circled and followed, waiting like sharks for one of the females to give a slight, meaningful gesture. The scene resembled chaos: people and things out of place, incomplete, a sense of disorder that became even more acute once we left the main road and turned into Netzahualcoyotl. While there had been little apparent variation in the federal district environment from the highway, once we turned onto one of the three roads leading into Netza—Calle Ciudad Netzahualcoyotl—my impression of chaos increased.

I was struck by the expanse of a field behind a newly built, ten-storied Instituto del Seguro Social de Trabajadores y Empleados (ISSTE) hospital. The approximately one-square-mile field was covered by large, stagnant puddles of water; on it, mud-covered soccer players scurried back and forth between white, makeshift goal posts. Directly across the field, and parallel to it for the next three blocks, was an incomplete housing development of gray, single-storied homes from whose roofs extended both television aerials and reinforcing rods. The grayness of the homes and the grayness of the June day blended with the color of the soil, except where it was marked with dark-brown and sewage-green pools of leftover rainwater.

The drab soil and buildings contrasted only with the occasional commercial buildings that appeared around the corner from Netza Street—the Calle Central—one of three paved streets in the entire sixty-square-kilometer area of Netzahualcoyotl. Except for the city-planted poplar trees that stood dying in their youth, the street was barren of plant life.

Calle Central, at that time one of three paved east-west streets that transected Netza from the Zaragoza Highway, was, of all the streets, the most congested with business enterprises. Bathhouses, two stories high and a half-block long—black smokestacks jutting upward—contrasted with tiny makeshift booths consisting of four two-by-fours covered with sagging white sheets under which individuals sold *helados* ("ice cream"). In this instance, the *helados* consisted of the scrapings from blocks of ice poured into triangular paper cups and covered with various-colored syrups of questionable cleanliness. Other booths sold sundry foods such as tacos and *chicharrones* ("pork rinds cooked in deep fat"). There were also vulcanizing shops to repair overused tires; *loncherías*,[2] which are also fronts for houses of prostitution; medical clinics and drugstores; tortilla and bakery shops and tiny grocery stores; public offices and real estate shacks; pool halls, honky-tonks (*club nocturno*), and movie houses, all lining both sides of the sixteen-block street.

The most ostentatious buildings among the hundreds along the street were the furniture stores. In 1971, sixty-five such stores sold everything from small appliances to twenty-seven-inch Magnavox television sets to brocade-covered, stuffed living-room chairs. Prices ranged from 100 to 300 percent higher than those in Mexico City (where prices are very high by U.S. standards). In contrast, not until March 1974 was the first bookstore built.

The dense commercial activity along the central avenues of the city reflected two primary phenomena: first, increased density of population; second, newly arriving populations without the mass cultural artifacts of nation-states. In this context, the major streets were congruent with the population and with the administrative characteristics of the time: early urbanization and massive population influx.

This first journey into Netzahualcoyotl revealed the commercial aspect of the city. But behind that almost anarchistic chaos lay the where, how, and what of people's lives—their raison d'etre. The real life-core of the city was to be found in the muddy streets and behind the closed doors of the houses facing that mud.

The first visit beyond the facade took place on that cloudy summer day in a makeshift church. We had bumped and jolted over two miles of deeply rutted roads since turning southward off of Avenida Central into the bowels of Netzahualcoyotl. We had by-passed mounds of mud, running children, staring brown faces, frowning young men whose soccer game we had interrupted, and partially filled trenches of muck that were once roads, finally to arrive at a white plastered building from which mariachi songs accompanied by Caribbean drums sounded loudly from open windows.

Over the years I met many people here whom I would later know and learn to respect; others I would not know well and not like at all. I would meet Angel, the anthropologist-Jesuit priest who had renounced the priesthood to devote himself to directing a cooperative ceramic factory whose workers made busts of Marx and Lenin for university students. Here I would also meet Doña Carmen—a *"chingona"* of the CRC movement—a woman "tough as nails" and afraid of almost nothing.

But on this day I talked to the numerous women and men, young boys and girls, who were present at the mass. They all agreed that conditions were rough, that, as one of the males said: *"Todo era una chinga"* ("Everything is fucked"). I noticed that the legs of many of the young women were covered with rashes, that children's noses ran, that others coughed, and that mothers held listless babies in their arms. These were first impressions, but a panoramic view of the area was the first order of business if I was to establish a structure for my observations. With this in mind, that first summer was spent getting to know the nooks and crannies of the city, even though they would be continuously changing over the 1971-1974 period. But even though the "face" of Netzahualcoyotl and parts of its social and cultural "content" would change, parts would stabilize, as would the lives of some of the persons living in this area.

It is here, then, that my exposition of an ethnographic journey of a city and its people begins—a changing social and cultural mosaic over a period of three years, 1971-1974. But it was not the mosaic per se that I became interested in. I did notice also on that first summer that upon the gray walls of buildings, on the concrete electrical poles, and on the few sidewalks were scrawled the initials

"CRC." Other markings included phrases such as "No Paguen—
Huelga, Huelga" ("Do Not Pay—Strike, Strike"); "Abajo Con Los
Fraccionadores" ("Down with the Land Developers"); and finally,
"Viva Zapata." Thus, my attention came to be focused on the pop-
ulation's protest activities.

As my attention turned to inquiry, I found myself involved in
processes that transcended political protests: these processes included political activities that had nothing to do with the politics
of confrontation or of persons seeking a better life. These processes involved the basis of face-to-face relations—the cultural
strategies employed systematically in order to deal with the reality
of others more powerful and with the struggle for equality. These
processes involved also the mobilization of resources and relationships in order to ensure daily psychic survival.

PROCESSES IN URBAN SITUATIONS:
METHODS AND TECHNIQUES

In a recent article on new research strategies for urban situations
such as exist in Ciudad Netzahualcoyotl Izcalli, Walton (1976:53)
argues that "what is crucial in explaining local phenomena is extra-
local in origin." This observation is essential to an understanding
of the methods and techniques of analysis employed here. From
my point of view, the locus of the urban strategy is processual
rather than geographical. The unit of analysis, in this case, is the
process of political emergence of the Congreso Restaurador de
Colonos between 1969 and 1974. The analysis focuses on the population of Ciudad Netzahualcoyotl and the processes leading to
their residence in the city, the environmental contexts in which
they live, the CRC itself, the networks of men and women involved, and the various local and formal sectors involved. A consideration of all these components is necessary to understand the
processes involved in the emergence of the CRC as a local power
structure and its demise, and to account for microcultural change
among its networks of men and women.

More specific operational terms should be defined, however.

The "processual orientation" to political life [regards] politics [as] "events which are involved in the determination of public goals and/or the differential distribution and use of power within the group or groups concerned with the goals being considered" (Swartz 1972:9). The analysis of such events must begin by identifying a particular set of public goals (since political activity is purposive). This is done in a later chapter on the CRC. The analysis must then attempt to inquire into the means by which such goals are met and resources utilized, the equivalences of culture used, and the environmental and demographic characteristics important in the determination of public goals. In the case of competition over public goals, the analysis of the way in which support is marshaled, reputations attacked, settlements achieved, and alliances made and/or broken is crucial. Such a processual approach is central to the analysis of the way in which public goals "work out" for individuals and groups engaged in political activities, and I take such an approach in my analysis of the CRC.

Processual analysis in urban situations is especially appropriate in heterogeneous settings where high levels of conflict occur (see Cohen 1969; Gluckman 1965; Nicholas 1968; Turner 1957; Swartz et al. 1966; and Van Velsen 1967); it begins with the selection of an event as a starting point, and from that event the analysis traces decisions, maneuvers, resources, relationships, and cultural constructs used. Unintended consequences and unpredicted spiraling effects on other events are especially considered. It is from such analysis that the tracing of actors and their roles in an event is made possible; thus, in this study, the entanglement of the leadership of the CRC in domains of elites above them can be traced to the two vertical extremes: the bottom and the top. Without the analysis of those "up" and those "down," there is no way to trace the locus of the major figures who wield power and control resources in a political system; nor is it possible to trace the consequences of such power for populations (Adams 1975:19). Therefore, a major part of this work will focus on the manner in which the CRC rose "from the bottom," touched the domains of power in elite sectors "at the top," and the way in which the "top" responded.

This processual analysis of the CRC in Ciudad Netzahualcoyotl Izcalli facilitates a detailed understanding of the principles of social action that generate legitimacy to organizations. Such an analysis provides us with an understanding of the cultural systems of urban Mexicans (Adams 1975:32) and of how local cultural and social systems are part of domains of power in ways unrecognized by those in such systems. This "political" analysis will provide an understanding of the central social principles to which urban Mexican populations must respond and the contradictions generated in those responses. The responses of those members of the population in Ciudad Netzahualcoyotl Izcalli who participated in the CRC provides insight into the characteristics and features of their collective identity.

There is also an important methodological question that such an approach effectively solves. While the analysis of these data can be conducted at an "external distance," serving the researcher's needs, such an analysis removes the researcher from the experience of events and the processes in which real persons are engaged (Levine 1979:171). The "contradictions" just mentioned are as much abstractions of external behavior as are the units of opposition: "local levels of the informal sector" and the "elites of the formal sectors." This method allows the inclusion of the behavioral and phenomenological manifestations of such contradictions and the inclusion of the persons engaged in such contradictions.

I employ this methodology by focusing on the conflicts suffered by Arturo Valenzuela Cisneros (pseudonym), a man at the crossroads between the local population he represents through the CRC and the formal elite sectors that seek to enmesh him and the organization. The experiences of Arturo Valenzuela Cisneros are illustrative of many of the most important cultural and ideological constructs that enter into the creation of local level political structures in urban central Mexico. Arturo Valenzuela exhibits many of the ambivalences, conflicts, struggles, and contradictions shared by mass "marginalized" populations. He not only participates in the processes important to the emergence, development, maturity, and demise of a local political *structure*—the Congreso Restaurador de Colonos—he is also affected by the forces operating between those he represents and the domains of power above him.

This is not a biographical account of political leadership and its demise, but rather an analysis of the way in which political relationships that contradict the basis of social rewards on the local level can behaviorally affect the psychological well-being of a person who participates in the manipulation of those relationships.

TECHNIQUE OF EXPOSITION

The book is divided into three parts. Part I, "The Marginality of Ciudad Netzahualcoyotl Izcalli," develops the theoretical, quantitative, and ethnographic contexts for the discussion of the four major foci of this work. In Part I, chapter 1—"The Use of Myth in Marginality"—various theoretical and methodological issues pertinent to an understanding of "marginalized" populations and their relationship to elites in Mexico are explicated. Chapter 2— "Marginality in Quantitative Terms"—provides statistical and numerical data that substantiate the theoretical and methodological assertions made in chapter 1. Chapter 3—"The Ethnographic Context"—provides the description of the physical, environmental, and general social characteristics of Ciudad Netzahualcoyotl Izcalli. These characteristics, together with the statistical data, set the context for the emergence of the political processes described in Part II.

Part II, "The Human Dimension in the Politics of Marginality," examines the social, economic, and political processes crucial to the development of the Congreso Restaurador de Colonos and to the formation of a collective identity for the networks of women and men who participated in that political structure. Chapters 4 and 5 detail the rise of the CRC and focus upon the personalities, issues, goals, and techniques of formation important to its emergence between 1969 and 1972. These chapters illustrate that entanglement in domains of elites is a necessary and sufficient condition for even local-level groups to thrive. Chapters 6 and 7 describe the familial contexts and social networks of Valenzuela, and the manner in which such contexts and networks are the primary basis of social identity for him. These contexts and networks emerged from political action and formed the essence of the collective identity of the cultural cohort.

Part III, "The Structure of Marginalized Politics," analyzes the underlying "national integration" ritual of marginality, which structures relations between the locality and elites. Chapter 8— "The Myth of Political Integration: The CRC"—describes the important differences between the social and political relationships that emerge within a local context and the social and political relationships that emerge within political elites. We show that such elites develop strategies of enmeshment that eventually "integrate" individual political leaders from the local level and thereby accentuate and improve elite domains. The rest of the population is left in structurally worse condition. This chapter analyzes such processes between 1973 and 1974. Chapter 9—"Local-Level Rituals and Rituals of Marginality"—analyzes and describes the inherent contradictions and oppositions between political structures based on local symbolic and social support and political structures defined and allocated from elite domains. The resolution of such contradictions and oppositions results in "microcultural" change for the networks of local men and women. Chapter 10—"Conclusions"—elaborates the sociocultural dynamics behind the examples of microcultural change and the adaptive consequences of the withdrawal of social and political support from national institutions.

METHODS OF DATA COLLECTION AND USE

Ethnographic fieldwork was carried out in Ciudad Netzahualcoyotl between 1971 and 1974: during the summers of 1971 and 1972, and for twelve months during 1973 and 1974. I briefly visited the area in 1975, and again in 1979, to verify and update previous findings. I spent a total of twenty months in the field during these years. For statistical information about the population, I relied on three main sources: (1) the 1970 Mexican government census data, which, at the time, was not yet published and was derived from unpublished census data sheets; (2) *Encuesta Definitiva en Ciudad Netzahualcoyotl,* a statistically representative sample of 1,026 heads of households; and (3) *Estudio de Factibilidad Técnica, Financiera, Economía, y Social Para La Instalación de Las Obras de Alcantarillado en El Municipio de Netzahualcoyotl.*

Ethnographic fieldwork for this study included participant observation, oral histories, interviews, and reviews of available records, notations, and letters of participants in the CRC movement. I have tried to combine short-term fieldwork with a more longitudinal approach. The summer of 1971 was used to understand the basic political and economic structures that were important in the area, as well as to collect as much demographic information as was available. It was most propitious that I was in the field during that first summer, since much of the overt and covert strategy of the CRC was becoming apparent. This provided me with an opportunity to become known by participants, and many conversations later I was accepted as a *"réplica de Mexicano, imitación gringo"* ("replica of a Mexican and an imitation American"). Since I had participated in political activities during the Vietnam War era and had engaged in Chicano protest activities, I was legitimately a person of *confianza* ("mutual trust") as well as a "native son."

The following summer, in 1972, I continued my analysis but began to concentrate more attention on household inventories, household histories, and the networks of relations that persons seemed to be building through their political activities. In the year 1973-1974, I lived in Ciudad Netzahualcoyotl with one of my main informants, who had been a CRC participant and still maintained many social relations with key persons within the CRC. It was in the daily experience of trying to survive the economic and environmental hardships within the household that I came to understand most acutely the necessity of *confianza* and the necessity of reciprocal relationships. The intimacy afforded me within the households of Netzahualcoyotl permitted me to visit, celebrate, laugh, and cry with relative ease. I witnessed demonstrations, sit-ins, physical confrontations between police and the population, as well as conflict between members of the CRC. I witnessed rituals, cooperation, drastic changes in the relationships between persons and in their perceptions of themselves and others, and the establishment of a type of security found only in social interdependence. Only the ethnographic method can provide this heterogeneity of experience.

I have tried to protect the identity of persons who were engaged in the activities described in this work by giving them pseudonyms and by slightly altering events. Nevertheless, all events are real and verifiable. I have not been able to change the official titles of some public officials who were engaged in these events, since they are part of the public record, and it would have been impossible to mask their participation. Thus, the offices of the mayors of Netzahualcoyotl, the governor of the state of Mexico, and the director of the Federal Agrarian Department (DAAC) could not be fictionalized. The participants are, however, given pseudonyms. All other contemporary names, offices, organizations, and, in some cases, relationships have been changed or slightly altered. Historical names and organizations have not been changed.

PART I

The Marginality of Ciudad
Netzahualcoyotl Izcalli

1

The Use of Myth in Marginality

THERE IS A substantial theoretical, empirical, and political literature in opposition to the use of "marginality" as a heuristic, theoretical, or descriptive idea.[1] Perlman (1975) has been most persuasive in this regard by showing that the notion of marginality
consists of a series of myths used to describe persons in "squat-
ments" (Leeds 1969) who are economically exploited and politically repressed. Such myths, Perlman has asserted, are empirically
false and analytically misleading. Since I use the term *marginality*
to describe the economic and political conditions of persons in
Ciudad Netzahualcoyotl, it is necessary to discuss this term in
order to clarify the way in which it is used in this work and to
understand the various processes central to the formation of this
idea.

From Perlman's point of view, persons in shantytowns, migrant
communities, or squatter settlements like those forming a large
part of Ciudad Netzahualcoyotl Izcalli are not *"marginal* but integrated into society. . . . [They] *are not economically and politically marginal but exploited and repressed; not socially and culturally marginal but stigmatized and excluded from a closed social
system* [emphasis in original]" (1975:131). In addition, she argues
that such populations should not be considered as passively marginal, in terms of their cultural attitudes, but should be described
as actively *marginalized.*

The manner in which I use the term *marginality* to describe sub-

17

stantial portions of the population of Ciudad Netzahualcoyotl is in agreement with the notion that such populations, rural or urban, cannot be understood as behaviorally marginal. None of the characteristics associated with marginal behaviors can be regarded as peculiar or specific to such populations. Social anomie, rootlessness, nonadaptability, "traditionality," passivity, criminality, pessimism, and fatalism are neither necessary nor sufficient descriptors of urban populations in poverty circumstances.[2]

I would argue that populations like those in Ciudad Netzahualcoyotl are economically and politically excluded from the economic and political benefits of the nation-state and its economic system. For the most part, these populations are formed by a combination of economic and political events and conditions, including capital-intensive industrialization coupled with intensive investment in the urban infrastructure, as took place in urban central Mexico. When such processes combine with a hierarchical social structure, they produce large numbers of human beings who are not provided access to whatever benefits that accrue from such processes. Very large numbers from such populations then migrate to areas like Ciudad Netzahualcoyotl in order to better survive their exclusion.

I would also argue that such populations cannot be "demarginalized" or integrated within the present capitalistic industrial framework. The causes of marginalization and the factors preventing such populations from becoming "demarginalized" lie outside of and not within these populations. Many of the reasons lie within Mexican social structure.

PUBLIC, PRIVATE, AND LABOR SECTORS

Although all social structures are hierarchical by definition, Mexican social structure can be understood metaphorically as a "set of free-standing pyramids each of which duplicates itself hierarchically like a crystal from top to bottom" (Lomnitz 1980:1). Such a crystal is made up of layers of relationships defined horizontally by class and vertically by the "sector" in which persons function

(Lomnitz 1980:1). For persons to take advantage of any resource in Mexico, relationships of *confianza* ("mutual trust") based on reciprocity within the same class must constantly be in operation. Based on kinship, fictive kinship, friendship, or "fictive friendship,"[3] such reciprocity within class layers forms the basis of social life in Mexico. Without it the individual finds living an extremely lonely proposition.

Such horizontal class relationships are distributed according to "sectors" (McGee 1974; Lomnitz 1977). Lomnitz (1977:2) argues that the vertical dimensions of Mexican social structure are made up of two sectors: the formal sector and the informal sector. The formal sector is divided into the "public," "private," and "labor" sectors, and those not incorporated within these are considered part of the "informal" sector and thus regarded as "marginalized" populations.

The public sector includes governmentally operated institutions and concerns and the social relations comprising them; the private sector includes private business enterprises, the liberal professions, and the social relations comprising them; and the labor sector includes organized industrial workers, their organizations, and the social relations that comprise them (Lomnitz 1977:2).

STRUCTURAL FEATURES OF MARGINALITY POLITICS

Given these general features of Mexican social structure, local political groups that emerge from the informal sectors, such as the Congreso Restaurador de Colonos, generally do encounter the representatives of the formal sectors who control resources, and/or acess to those resources, needed by the local informal political group. That encounter is always accompanied by the creation of obligations and relationships that "entangle" local informal leaders. In time, those relationships limit the boundaries of success for all political activities in such a way that public and private elites of the formal sectors eventually come to control not only the leadership of the local organization but also the management of its constituents.

The entanglement of local leaders, like those of the CRC, is a consequence of Mexican social structure and is not simply a conscious formulation of elites. There is, however, a substantial literature (Anderson and Cockroft 1966; Cornelius 1975; Meyer 1977) arguing that "cooptation" is the process by which interactive networks are established between local leaders and elites in return for concessions. Eventually the local leadership provides support for elite strategies and their domains. Cooptation is part of a general strategy of the public sector, and especially the ruling governmental party in Mexico (Partido Revolucionario Institucional, or PRI), to ensure the elimination of upstart groups like the CRC.

I argue that while cooptation may in fact occur, and does frequently, in Mexico exchange networks of "political friendships" are established *before* local structures coalesce as structures. Cooptation is a strategy used by the PRI, but, more important, I argue that the hierarchical nature of Mexican social structure demands the absorption of local leaders at the edges of the domains of power in which elites control access to the resources demanded by local populations. This is not to suggest that such a process will necessarily occur immediately, but rather "end runs" through high-level, urban elites in one of the formal sectors will be made *before* actual contacts with those domains holding resources are made. It is at this point that entanglement begins, regardless of the legitimacy of the actual support at the local level.

A simple fact of social-structural life in Mexico, with its highly centralized class and sector structure, is that "what goes around gets around" (*lo que da vuelta, da vueltas*). That is, even with the most persuasively radical ideology, elites are tied to one another in a number of formal domains. These ties are based on social exchanges generated through reciprocal favors within networks of kinship, friendship, and fictive kinship. *Arreglos* ("arrangements") even between persons with ostensibly the most opposite ideologies are possible given the context of personal and familial ties and links. Therefore, when local leaders from marginalized populations seek redress, or protest a particular condition by demanding resources, entanglement with formal domains is assured by the presence of these networks of horizontal elite relationships. Their presence ensures the maintenance and expansion of elite control and power. Such relationships and their expansion are provided legitimacy by the myths specific to each part of the formal sector, as well as by the myth of "national integration."

SECTOR MYTHS AND MYTHS OF NATIONAL INTEGRATION

Each sector has a series of accompanying myths that provide its raison d'être. The public sector ostensibly expresses its existence in the form of the national state and its "universal" judicial, legislative, and executive institutions. The private sector makes itself known publicly through various voluntary associations that express the myths of universal rewards attendant to "hard work" and of the possibility of mobility for all Mexicans. The labor sector expresses its existence through the various institutionalized labor unions attached to the central government and through the myth of representation for the membership. Each myth addresses only those who are part of the formal sectors. Those outside of the formal sectors are also outside of the range of the myths that would legitimize their existence. The myth of the informal sectors of marginalized populations is that they are politically apathetic and therefore do not participate in the public sectors; they do not work sufficiently to pull themselves up by their bootstraps; and finally, they lack the skills necessary to enter into the industrial labor market, where protection, security, and high income can be earned.

There is, however, an overriding "meta-myth" of national integration that should be addressed. The myth consists of the proposition that great masses of marginalized persons can be integrated economically and politically. *The central myth in Mexico that underlies all formal sectors is the proposition that everybody in a highly stratified and hierarchical system has equal access to economic resources or is represented politically, regardless of status.* Given that Mexican social structure is layered by class and divided by sectors, what has been regarded as "national integration" of the informal sector is actually a predictable national ritual, controlled by cultural elites, expressing the myth of universal access and integration. Such a national ritual of integration expresses the myth of universal access and representativeness by denying the reality of inequality in a highly stratified and pyramidal social structure.

This can be argued not only on theoretical grounds but certainly empirically as well. If economic integration were possible in Mexico, then the resulting distribution of wealth would not result in 20 percent of families in the upper income ranges receiving 75 percent of the national income; or, at the lower level, 40 percent of families receiving one-tenth of the national income (Villareal 1977:77). If political integration were possible, then Mexico's political elite would not emerge primarily only from the middle and upper-middle classes (Smith 1977:137). On theoretical grounds, the Mexican social system (as well as the Brazilian system that Perlman [1976] studied) *is not closed to individuals* but is closed to *groups* and to the masses of marginalized populations. Thus, if any "integration" is possible, it applies only to selected individuals economically, and in the case of political participants, only to political leaders of local power structures and not the populations they ostensibly represent. Even in dependent industrializing capitalistic systems like Mexico's, individuals may become vertically mobile. Such a system assures sector and class inequality by a few selected individuals becoming mobile. Stratification and concentration of wealth and resources, as well as political domination by formal sectors, is assured by the filtering of selected individuals, even from marginal sectors, into formal domains. Vertical mobility is a process of ensuring the inequality of those not mobile. Thus, the "meta-myth" includes the proposition that not only do all have equal opportunity for such mobility but that mobility limits class and sector differences.

RITUALS OF MARGINALITY AND POLITICAL ACTION

Because of such cultural myths as equal opportunity and universal mobility, and because of the reality of scarcity and inequality that result from the divisions between formal sectors and their classes and the informal sectors and their classes of marginalized populations, a class of relations has emerged in Mexico that I call "rituals of marginality." As will be seen, even political activity follows the general pattern of such rituals that mark the relations between the formal and informal sectors.

I concur with Edmund Leach (1979) that *ritual* does not refer to symbolic representations that occur only in "sacred" situations, but rather that ritual expresses a pattern of symbols that reveal the system of "socially approved 'proper' relations between individuals and groups" (1979:15). I would add that ritual expressions of social relations are especially rich where populations are in asymmetrical relationships of dominance and subservience, or where relationships are established between sectors in which resources are in the hands of some but not in the hands of others. Such rituals form the "statement in action" (Leach 1979:13-14) of the "statement in words" of the myth of dominance.

The expression "rituals of marginality" refers to the manifestation of seemingly fixed patterns of social relations based on scarcity and inequality between individuals, groups, and organizations. The specific manner in which such rituals are organized is dependent upon culture, context, and historical period. In the Mexican case, and certainly in Ciudad Netzahualcoyotl, such rituals are expressed between formal sectors and informal sectors. These rituals are largely noninstitutionalized mechanisms such as patron-client relations, brokerage, friendships of convenience, and informal arrangements by which persons receive intermittent "favors." For Lomnitz (1980), unless such relations of marginality are institutionalized, local informal-sector populations like those in Ciudad Netzahualcoyotl will continue to be excluded from formal sectors and will continue to be exploited. My position, already articulated, is that institutionalization or integration for the large numbers of marginalized persons is theoretically and empirically impossible. Only selected individuals are integrated, and this ensures inequality for the rest.

Even when a large political movement like the Congreso Restaurador de Colonos forces formal sectors to "institutionalize" relations, the consequences for local populations are opposite to those intended. Political leaders are often entangled in the webs of formal sectors, political structures like the CRC become powerless, the basis of political leadership shifts from legitimacy to coercion, and autonomy is converted to dependence. The mass of the population is ignored. It is at this point that *individuals*, but not groups, become "integrated," whereas politically and economically marginalized populations become further victimized and "informal." Such "institutionalization" is in fact part of the larger national ritual of marginality that is repeated frequently, and with great success, by elites managing relations.

LOCAL-LEVEL REACTION

It would be a serious error to suggest that such rituals of marginality that we have described express harmony of relations. They "order" relations, but they are not "orderly" relations for the populations. Equally, it would be a serious error to regard populations that are "structurally marginalized" as behaviorally dependent and powerless. This would in fact lead to the sort of "culture of poverty" descriptions that have inspired the questioning of the marginalization hypotheses.

Such populations struggle against rituals of marginality and structural marginalization by coalescing around common concerns, even though eventually they will suffer loss of leadership, and even though formal sectors in the end may become even more concentrated. An unintended consequence of such struggle is that cohorts of people experience the reality of organized "power," a heady experience; they feel the legitimacy of leadership perhaps for the first and the last time; they know the feeling of accomplishment beyond short-range goals, and of organizing not only for self-benefit but also for the good of others; and they experience a sense of individual and social autonomy. In other words, such cohort experience does not leave the populations the same, in spite of losses, defeat, or "cooptation" of its leadership. Such populations have not participated in a static experience; instead, as in the case of the networks of men and women who participated in the CRC, they become further estranged and pessimistic about the "universalism" of formal sectors and the elites that make them up. They, in time, withdraw their legitimate support from such domains (Roberts 1978:158).

For those involved in the CRC, as part of this withdrawal and pessimism, they also came to recognize the myths of universal access used by elites to rationalize their existence. They came to recognize that the formal sectors are made up of highly particularistic networks of relationships that constitute elite social sectors in Mexico. The networks of men and women who participated in the CRC eventually recognized the inaccessibility of formal sectors and the consequences of that for selected individuals. For many men and women, the universalistic myths (Mills 1959; Cohen 1981) used by elites were recognized as empty statements of the cults of elites.

For the networks of men and women who participated in the CRC, local transformations of a microcultural sort emerged in urban central Mexico: the denial of universalistic myths used to express relations of scarcity and inequality, and the denial of support for individual leaders that support either the myths, their rituals, or the formal sectors and elites that these myths and rituals rationalize.

We begin to examine these processes in chapters 2 and 3, which provide the demographic and ethnographic contexts that form the bases of marginality in Ciudad Netzahualcoyotl Izcalli, and out of which the CRC arose.

2

Marginality in Quantitative Terms

THE OBJECT OF this chapter is to show that the marginalization of a major portion of the population of Ciudad Netzahualcoyotl Izcalli —that is, its exclusion from the economic benefits of the economic system—can be identified quantitatively by economic and occupational characteristics. The basic reasons behind these characteristics are then discussed in order to remove the possibility of "blaming the victim" and thus making behavioral characterizations of such populations the central focus, as the "culture of poverty" literature has done. This literature, including work by Oscar Lewis (1959, 1965), was an early attempt to understand the effects of poverty cross-culturally, and it included the idea that in class-stratified, highly individuated, and capitalistic economic systems, large portions of the population were not integrated into the major institutions of the larger society. As an adaptive strategy, such populations adopted what he described as a "culture of poverty," the characteristics of which are numerous but which include economic, political, social, cultural, and psychological traits such as free unions, or consensual marriages, high incidences of the abandonment of wives and children, trends toward female- or mother-centered families, low levels of social organization, extending only as far as the nuclear family, political passivity, and lack of knowledge of national political figures.

The crucial aspect of the total pattern, however, is that such traits are learned as part of systems of thought and cognition and are reinforced by existing economic and environmental conditions. Such a culture of poverty is passed on to succeeding generations until such populations acquire a sense of identification with larger groups. Such identification, or consciousness raising, then breaks the psychological and social core of the culture of poverty. The key, however, is that such populations "adapt" to poverty and behave according to the pattern partially described.

The "marginalization" idea will be used in this work very much in contrast to the way it is used in the culture of poverty literature. In addition, this discussion is also intended to discourage misplaced comparisons with other populations in entirely different historical contexts—for example, with groups in England and the United States of a hundred years ago. It will become apparent that for developmental and historical reasons, the informal marginalized sectors described in this work are the products of specific sorts of technological development very different from those in England and the United States.

For the most part, the population of Ciudad Netzahualcoyotl is made up of urban and rural migrants. They have concentrated in the area as a result of processes that have taken place throughout the Third World and that have produced similar populations. These groups are products of the increased social complexity of capitalistic social systems forged in the processes of capital-intensive industrialization. These processes have created populations worldwide characterized by mass poverty, overpopulation, cultural delocalization, surplus labor, rising expectations, technological displacement, and the search for work (Houghton 1969; Acedo Mendoza 1973; Vélez-Ibañez 1978b).

Although found in rural and urban areas, these marginalized populations are most evident in urban concentrations. In Latin America alone there are about 20,000 urban marginalized settlements (Portes and Walton 1976:71). Ciudad Netzahualcoyotl is one.

There are a number of basic explanations for the appearance of populations like that in Ciudad Netzahualcoyotl. In Mexico, governmental policies since 1950 have supported capital-intensive technologies. These policies have resulted in the creation of such technologies and the simultaneous displacement of older and smaller firms. Such displacement reduced the overall rates of new industrial jobs (Eckstein 1977a:18). This non-labor-absorbing policy was one aspect of a two-part strategy in Mexico. The first was the strategy of "import substitution," which developed self-sufficiency in industrial goods; the second part was the strategy of "export substitution," which developed industrial goods for export (Eckstein 1977a:18). Such a policy, however, encouraged the substitution of capital for labor and an increase in capital-intensive over labor-intensive technology (Villareal 1977:76).

The available income data for Mexico suggest that the share of national income for the masses of urban and rural dwellers does *not* increase as domestic production rises (Eckstein 1977a:19). The economic and geographical consequence, directly or indirectly, for many persons in Mexico is migration to areas where there may be possibilities of employment. Ciudad Netzahualcoyotl is one such area close to possibilities of employment in the federal district of Mexico.

There are, however, other sources for the creation of such populations in Ciudad Netzahualcoyotl and similar areas around Mexico City. For the most part, capital-intensive industry emerges within the contexts of already-existing material scarcity, and it is superimposed upon an urban social structure (Portes 1976a:27). Such superimposition exacerbates the gaps between the formal and informal sectors by creating larger populations that cannot be absorbed by industry.

In addition, capital-intensive industries concentrate mostly in urban centers and areas in which there are already-existing political and economic institutions. In time, the need arises to spend public moneys on new "urban infrastructures" (transportation, energy, consumer markets, financial institutions, political structure, and administration). Such expenditures reduce the amount of public funds available for social benefits, but, more important, the investment of new public moneys induces "locational decisions" by major capital-intensive industrial enterprises in order to make use of such publicly provided infrastructures. This is what has taken place in the "urban metropolitan areas of Mexico City" (Garza and Schteingart 1978:63-67).

Such locational decisions then escalate land values in urban areas within the federal district and its surroundings. Domestic capital invests in urban land markets, and this leads to further increases in land prices based on the anticipation of larger earnings if industries locate there. This rise in land values then results in the movement of marginalized populations from the city to areas where land values are relatively low, such as in Ciudad Netzahualcoyotl. Furthermore, populations from rural and small-town areas are also stimulated to move by the lack of occupational opportunity stemming from underinvestment of capital in rural areas. They also move to areas where land values are relatively low (as they are in Ciudad Netzahualcoyotl), and where job possibilities may exist nearby (as they do in the federal district).

These populations, both urban and rural, are the creation of governmental policies supporting capital-intensive technologies, and Ciudad Netzahualcoyotl Izcalli is made up of persons who cannot be absorbed by such technologies. In the state of Mexico, where Mexico City is located, the demographic consequences have been impressive. While population in the urban metropolitan areas of Mexico City has increased 5.4 percent annually, that in the state of Mexico has increased by 22.5 percent. In this manner, 16 percent of the urban metropolitan population of the city grew because of immigration, whereas 75 percent of the state of Mexico's population growth resulted from immigration (Garza and Schteingart 1978:70). It is ironic that such populations should select an ecological area as wasted and unwanted as Ciudad Netzahualcoyotl Izcalli for settlement.

ENVIRONMENT

Located in the eastern part of the state of Mexico and to the northeast of the federal district, Ciudad Netzahualcoyotl Izcalli is limited on the north by the municipality of Texcoco, Atenco, and Ecatepec de Morelos; on the east by the municipality of Chimalhuacán and Reyes la Paz; on the south by the municipality of Los Reyes and by the federal district; and on the west by the federal district.

Between the months of July and September, the daily rainfall may reach as high as 32.5 millimeters, and since the soil is composed of saltpeter, the city rests on a plateau and former lake bed that form a natural bathtub with no possibility of runoff of accumulated water. This collection of water during the rainy months contributes to three main problems: first, widespread stagnant pools; second, the pollution of collective wells used by 50 percent of the population in 1971-1973 as a water resource for all purposes other than drinking; and third, the breakdown of existing sewage and water systems. In addition, two other types of problems emerge from environmental conditions. First, few persons in the *municipio* had garbage service between 1971 and 1975, and because of the enormous population increases year after year through 1979, the municipal garbage systems installed were quickly overwhelmed. As a consequence, most persons were forced to dump waste along the streets, and during the dry season they burned waste in empty lots adjoining their property. Both dumping and burning, however, contributed to fly infestations and other disease carriers.

Since many persons use dogs as guardians for their homes, large numbers of these animals populate Netzahualcoyotl. The multiplying dog population generally feeds on the dumped waste, and hence contributes further waste by defecation. In addition, the federal district's sewage system and the system in Netzahualcoyotl both use Lake Texcoco as the dumping area for treated and untreated sewage; thus, odors emanating from that source create unpleasant evenings when easterly prevailing winds flow over the city. The combination of 4,600 tons of pollutants from the urban metropolitan areas of Mexico City that are pushed into the atmosphere combine with dust from the former lake bed of Texcoco to create a mixture called "smost" (smoke-dust) (Garza and Schteingart 1978:75). From 1971 to 1974, these were the most common ecological conditions to which persons in the city had to adapt, and it was not until a 600-million-peso public-works program was launched in 1974 that the physical environment began to improve in the oldest section of the city.

SETTLEMENT HISTORY

Ciudad Netzahualcoyotl is one of a number of "mushroom" cities that have grown up around the Mexico City urban area. The area, now comprising sixty-four square kilometers, began to be populated in 1946 largely by displaced persons from Mexico City who "squatted" there. Before this period, the area was largely unpopulated—a dust bowl resulting from extensive drainage operations begun before 1930, when more than half of the southern part of Lake Texcoco had been drained so that it could be put under cultivation. The rest of the lake had been dammed for watershed purposes, thereby creating an ecosystem consisting of cultivated land, waterfowl, and fish, and connected by a series of canals for marketing products.

By 1957, 10,000 persons, largely urban poor, had moved into this area. In the meantime, the state of Mexico initiated a plan of colonization and land development by the Colonia Mexico, Colonia del Sol, Estado de Mexico, and Colonia Maravillas, under the jurisdictional authority of the San Juan Chimalhuacán. Lots sold during this period ranged from three to five pesos a square meter, without potable water, sewage services, electricity, and roads. For the most part, squatters in the area relied on tank trucks for water service, but during the rainy season, the area turned into a quagmire of mud, making the transportation of water impossible.

Because of this situation, the government of the state of Mexico authorized the creation of a financial organ to bring water- and sewage works into the area. This organ—Aguas y Construcciones S.A.—sank the first water well in the present Colonia Oriental region and extended two waterlines and sidelines to other interior colonias: Romero, Evolucion, and Atlacomulco, which had been settled by both buyers and squatters by 1957 (Monroy 1969:4).

In 1959, the Law of Development (Ley de Fraccionamientos) was passed by the state legislature, requiring land developers to

install water, light, and sewage services and to develop roads into
the *colonias*. But, as is true in most of Mexico, legal codes are not
usually followed, and few services were, in fact, provided by land
developers who had managed to acquire legal title to portions of
this area. In 1960, the Council of Cooperation (Consejo de Coop-
eradores) was organized to initiate a water and sewage system,
and four new water wells and pipelines were established (Monroy
1969:4).

The ever-increasing influx of population, however, continued to
overwhelm the limits of services established. For the most part, the
history of Netzahualcoyotl has been one in which its residents
have continually battled land developers, municipal authorities,
and governmental officials for services through voluntary associations of various kinds. By 1960, 30,000 new urban and rural poor
had settled in the area, and through such voluntary associations as
the Association of Settlers (Asociación de Colonos), the Association of Parents and Teachers (Asociación de Padres de Familias y
Maestros), the Federation of Parents (Federación de Padres de
Familia), the Small Businesses Association (Frente Unico de
Comerciantes en Pequeño), the Board of Improvement (Junta de
Mejoramiento), the Council of Cooperation, the Delegation of
Teachers (Delegación de Maestros), and the Chamber of Commerce (Camara de Comercio), they joined together in a common
front, the Unión de Fuerzas Vivas ("Union of Active Forces"), to
pressure the state legislature for political autonomy from San Juan
Chimalhuacán and for the creation of a political municipality
separate from Chimalhuacán. On April 3, 1963, the *municipio* of
Ciudad Netzahualcoyotl Izcalli was politically incorporated by the
ninety-third decree (*decreto número* 93) (*División municipal de las
entidades federativas* 1969:20).

BASIC DEMOGRAPHICS

The increase in population has continued, and by 1971 Ciudad
Netzahualcoyotl had become the fourth largest city in population
in Mexico, after Mexico City, Guadalajara, and Monterrey ("Pan-

orama económico" 1971:42). In 1980 the population was estimated at 2.3 million, maintaining its fourth-place position (Seibel 1980:8).

In 1969 the estimated increase in population was 10,000 persons per month, with a projected increase of 110,000 persons per year between 1970 and 1980 (*Estudio de factibilidad* 1969:108). Table 1 shows the 1969 estimate of population growth for Netzahualcoyotl for the 1970-1980 period.

TABLE 1

Estimate of Netzahualcoyotl Population Growth, 1970-1980

Year	Number Increase	Estimated Total Population
1970	104,600	675,000
1972	131,600	848,400
1974	155,000	1,055,000
1976	206,400	1,325,000
1978	258,300	1,663,500
1980	325,400	2,090,000

Source: *Estudio de factibilidad* 1969:114.

Fifty-seven percent of the population was born in another location. According to the 1970 census, 53.63 percent of the population was born in the federal district. More than likely, many of these persons had been pushed from federal district areas in search of cheaper housing because of rising land values and because of governmental prohibition of new residential subdivisions (Garza and Schteingart 1978:70). Of the remaining 47 percent born in areas other than the federal district, most were from the rural states of Michoacan, Guanajuato, Oaxaca, and Puebla. Table 2 shows the total population, by place of birth and sex, according to the 1970 census.

Using the same data source, the breakdown of the population from other areas, by place of birth, is shown in table 3. What is important to note is that of people coming from other areas in 1970, 95,011 had been in the city for less than one year; 40,615

TABLE 2

POPULATION CENSUS OF 1970

	Population Total	Men	Women
Netzahualcoyotl	580,436	295,078	285,358
Born in Netzahualcoyotl	251,932 (43%)	128,870	123,062
Born in another place	327,974* (57%)	165,934	162,040
Born in another country	530	274	256

Source: ""Censo de población" 1970.
*In the table that follows, this sum is given by federal entity.

from one to two years; 63,063 from three to five years; 78,679 from six to ten years; 32,519 more than ten years; and 32,786 did not indicate place of origin ("Censo de población" 1970:Q-18). Therefore, of the over 341,000 persons born in areas other than Netzahualcoyotl in 1970, one-third had been in Netzahualcoyotl less than one year. This shows the massive in-migration to the city during that period.

Reasons for leaving their points of origin were basically economic. Of 1,026 families sampled, 71 percent cited economic pressures, 17 percent familial reasons, and the rest other reasons such as having no place to live. Table 4 shows responses given as reasons for leaving the birthplace.

The selection of Ciudad Netzahualcoyotl as a residence may be both social and economic. Although only males sometimes move into the area from rural or urban environments, families usually soon follow them. The initial selection of Ciudad Netzahualcoyotl by most persons from other areas, however, is primarily because of the availability of relatively cheap land, its proximity to the federal district, and the possibility of building a shack with little capital.[1]

In the case of urban migrants, the process of moving into Netzahualcoyotl entails maintaining an urban residence in the federal district and constructing a *jacal* ("shack") in the new location. Netzahualcoyotl provides a relatively inexpensive place in which to

TABLE 3

POPULATION OF NETZAHUALCOYOTL BORN ELSEWHERE

Birthplace	Number	Percentage of total
Aguascalientes	1,854	0.54
Baja California	554	0.16
Baja California T.	212	0.06
Campeche	46	0.01
Coahuila	770	0.23
Colima	568	0.17
Chiapas	1,168	0.34
Chihuahua	798	0.23
Federal District	183,707	53.76
Durango	933	0.27
Guanajuato	24,452	7.16
Guerrero	7,493	2.19
Hidalgo	11,926	3.49
Jalisco	7,728	2.26
Michoacan	27,463	8.04
Morelos	3,149	0.92
Nayarit	197	0.06
Nuevo Leon	568	0.17
Oaxaca	21,256	6.22
Puebla	20,383	5.96
Queretaro	3,125	0.91
Quintana Roo	57	0.02
San Luis Potosi	3,070	0.90
Sinaloa	274	0.08
Sonora	256	0.08
Tabasco	450	0.13
Tamaulipas	1,059	0.31
Tlaxcala	5,618	1.64
Veracruz	8,112	2.37
Yucatan	775	0.23
Zacatecas	3,723	1.09
Total	341,744*	100.00

Source: "Censo de población" 1970.
*This total does not coincide with the sum that appears in table 2 and is, in fact, greater by a considerable amount. The state of Mexico, where Netzahualcoyotl is situated, is not included.

TABLE 4

REASONS FOR LEAVING POINT OF ORIGIN

Reasons	Number	Percentage of total
To change one's life *(Por cambiar de vida)*	214	20
There was no work *(No había trabajo)*	327	32
Left with parents *(Salieron con sus padres)*	83	8
To earn more *(Querían ganar más)*	175	17
Wanted better education for children *(Deseaban mejor educación para hijos)*	72	7
Other reasons *(Otras razones)*	109	11
No answer *(No contestaron)*	57	5
Total	1,026	100

Source: Tamayo 1971:7.

meet family needs, and therefore, for most, is the point of destination primarily for economic reasons.

Basically, in-migration has consisted of whole families moving into the area. With the addition of those who established residence since 1946, the median family size, although the figures vary, is considerably higher than the national median of 5.6 (*Estudio de factibilidad* 1969:24). Representative family size in Netzahualcoyotl, by contrast, is 6.2, 7.6, and 8 members per family, according to different sources (*Estudio de factibilidad* 1969:2; "Censo de población" 1970:11, Q-12; "Resumen de la investigación" 1970). Assuming that the census figures are accurate, it is clear that subsistence needs, with little to spare, will be the primary concern of the residents in the city, especially in the light of median income, underemployment, and unemployment.

Nevertheless, families comprise the basic social unit within the city, with only 0.5 percent of the population living alone. Slightly more than 11.5 percent of the heads of households were women out of the total of 103,679 family heads in 1970, i.e., 12,009 women ("Censo de población" 1970:3, Q-5). In comparison, 91,670 males were heads of households, indicating a continuation of the patri-centered family.

Significantly, among all families in Netzahualcoyotl, 22,632 persons, or 5 percent of those living in the same housing unit, were related by other than nuclear family bonds; an insignificant number of persons (0.5 percent) lived in the same residence without consanguine or affinal bonds. The 5 percent figure, however, must be considered in the context of the domestic developmental cycle. Some persons included in that figure may be persons who are only temporary visitors from other areas; it may not necessarily be true that such persons were permanent extended kin living in the household. Those who make up the 5 percent figure are largely elderly parents who either migrated into the area with their children or joined them afterward. Nevertheless, up to their deaths they are included as part of the domestic developmental cycle. There are also different types of nucleated family units other than that of husband, wife, and children. Eldest or youngest brothers may assume care of a younger or older sister who has children. In such situations the brother becomes a kind of consanguine *pater*, and he expresses similar relationships of distance and role authority toward his sister's children.

Like Kemper (1971:93) and Lomnitz (1977:97), who report a low incidence of consensual unions, I found this same pattern existing in Netzahualcoyotl. The form of marriage service for persons twelve years and over indicates that most of the men and women were married in both a religious and a civil service. This indicates an observance of traditional ritual beliefs in the marriage bond. Slightly less than 65 percent were married in both civil and religious services, 17.45 percent were married in a civil service only, and 5.85 percent were married in a religious service only. Free unions accounted for 12.48 percent of the total of the persons living together (Tamayo 1971:9). The census shows much the same pattern as table 5 illustrates.

The basic demographic material shows that, for the most part, economic reasons are behind the moves of persons from their birthplace; social and economic reasons are shown to be important for selecting Netzahualcoyotl as the point of destination. For the most part, the population is made up of persons who have followed conventional means of generating familial ties through tra-

TABLE 5

FORM OF MARRIAGE SERVICE OBSERVED BY PERSONS TWELVE YEARS AND OVER

| | Single | Married | | | | Free Union |
		Total	Civil	Religious	Religious and Civil	
Men	68,266	81,692	16,251	5,377	60,064	11,437
Women	53,150	84,809	16,952	5,750	62,107	12,314
Total	121,416	166,501	33,203	11,127	122,171	23,751

Source: "Censo de población" 1970:3, Q-7.
NOTE: Of the total single and married population persons widowed, divorced, or separated accounted for 2.8 percent, 0.33 percent, and 1.2 percent, respectively.

ditional ritual forms, and who have maintained the nuclear family structure as the preferred form of living arrangement. There are few persons living alone, and most persons are part of intact social units. Therefore, in contrast to the culture of poverty literature, which stresses free unions or consensual marriages, a trend toward female- or mother-centered families, and a lack of ritual bonding through traditional marriage services (Lewis 1959), these economically poor populations are not part of a "culture of poverty." As the next section shows, they *are* economically poor and economically marginalized, but they are not culturally poor.

ECONOMIC MARGINALIZATION: OCCUPATIONAL

Economic marginalization can be characterized along occupational lines. Eames and Goode (1973) have distinguished between formal labor-market sectors and the informal labor market. In the informal labor market, work activities lack extended agreements, unions, or labor cooperatives, and the demand for such labor is low. When such labor is used, wages are low and "high inputs of time and/or energy on the job in relation to income" are required (Eames and Goode 1973:115).

These characteristics of the informal labor market are in keeping with the description of "peripheral" or "secondary" labor market occupations in urban ghettos or barrios in the United States (Cain 1976; Freedman 1976; Moore 1979:27-34). Such occupations lack occupational stability, security of employment, and above-average earnings (Ginzberg 1976). Most of these occupations are tied to "peripheral firms," such as sweatshops that rely on casual labor, high turnover, low skills, and an overabundance of labor.

The informal labor market and the peripheral, or secondary, labor market are synonymous with McGee's (1974) and Lomnitz's (1977) descriptions of the occupational structure of marginality. They state that such occupations include jobs of low productivity, jobs that require few or obsolete skills and little resources, and jobs that are little in demand because of an oversupply of labor or obsolescence of the task.

Specific occupations cited cross-culturally by Eames and Goode (1980:282) as marginal occupations are: nonmechanized construction, dockwork, pedicab drivers, porters, domestics, janitors, scavengers, street vendors, watchmen, and many of the self-employed. They state that in all of these jobs the return is small, intermittent, and unpredictable. In fact, the "most appropriate social unit within which the urban anthropologist might study the impact of poverty is one based upon occupation or participation in the secondary labor market" (Eames and Goode 1980:283).

Lomnitz (1977:12-13) describes marginal occupations as consisting of unassociated manual labor, unpaid family labor, and small self-employed activities. These include such occupations as construction work, housemaids, house repair, waiters, barbers, gardeners, janitors, street vendors, and those involved in obsolete craft and trade occupations. The two key elements in all of these occupations, according to Lomnitz, are that they are not part of the formal urban industrial process of production, and all such occupations suffer from chronic insecurity (1977:13).

Whether referred to as "marginal occupations," the "informal labor market," or the "secondary labor market," populations that participate in such sectors work intermittently, irregularly, and in uncertainty. They lack vertical mobility because of the occupational structure in which they are engaged, but, more important, they lack the basic ingredients of any formal, primary, or nonmarginal labor market. These characteristics include income above the minimum, job protection, and occupational security through association or contract.

The vast majority of people in Ciudad Netzahualcoyotl (or in such places as the urban barrios and ghettos of the United States) find themselves in such labor markets not because of a lack of achievement motivation or an inability to delay gratification. Data on the use of rotating credit associations shows that such populations save and delay gratification in the midst of the most stressful economic conditions (Lomnitz 1977; Kurtz 1973; Vélez-Ibañez 1983). Such populations are dependent on uncertain and insecure occupations. The issue is not economic parochialism, lack of motivation, or lack of work ethic. Rather, economically marginalized populations like those in Netzahualcoyotl participate in a very limited opportunity structure created by industrializing capital-intensive technologies.

Occupationally marginalized populations, then, can be characterized by specific categories of labor. In Netzahualcoyotl, 51.8 percent of working fathers were in the laborer-commerce activity (obrero-comerciante) category; 61 percent of working mothers were in domestic service-labor (servicio doméstico, obreras-empleadas) occupations (Tamayo 1971:12). In addition, as table 6 indicates, of 862 working fathers who were sampled, 20.3 percent were self-employed; of 109 working mothers, 20 percent were self-employed. Largely, the self-employed participate in lottery-ticket vending, street hawking of Kleenex or figurines, selling of tacos and sandwiches, and other small-scale, marginal selling activities. Thus 72.1 percent of working fathers and 81 percent of working mothers were engaged in marginal occupations. Thus, of the occupations of fathers and mothers in the sample, 77 percent were engaged in the informal, marginal labor sector.

There are, however, other significant details that should be considered in table 6. First, for 66.7 percent of male heads of households, the federal district, not Netzahualcoyotl, is the work location. This verifies the proposition that Netzahualcoyotl's proximity to the principal areas of employment is of prime importance

TABLE 6

OCCUPATIONS AND WORK LOCATIONS

	Fathers (N = 862)			
Occupation	Percentage of Total	Percentage in Netzahualcoyotl	Percentage in Federal District	Percentage in Other Areas
Laborer	41.5	8.9	30.8	1.8
Commerce	10.3	7.6	2.6	0.1
Self-employed	20.3	4.5	15.0	0.8
Bricklayer	3.5	1.8	1.6	0.1
Urban labor	0.9	0.3	0.4	0.2
Agriculture	0.3	0.2	0.1	—
Bureaucrat	3.6	0.8	2.6	0.2
Iron worker	0.3	0.2	0.1	—
Electrician	1.3	0.7	0.5	0.1
Professional	4.7	1.6	3.0	0.1
Carpenter	0.7	0.1	0.5	0.1
Other	12.8	3.2	9.3	0.3
Total	100.0	29.9	66.7	3.9

	Mothers (N = 109)			
Occupation	Percentage of Total	Percentage in Netzahualcoyotl	Percentage in Federal District	Percentage in Other Areas
Laborer	13.0	2.0	9.0	1.8
Self-employed	14.0	5.0	8.0	0.9
Commerce	20.0	17.0	5.0	—
Domestic servant	28.0	25.0	2.0	—
Professional	6.0	3.0	3.0	—
Seamstress	5.0	4.0	0.9	—
Bureaucrat	4.0	0.9	3.0	—
Other	10.0	3.0	7.0	—
Total	100.0	59.9	37.9	2.5

Source: Tamayo 1971:13.

in the selection of this city as a place of residence. Furthermore, although very recent (1974) attempts have been made to provide the city with an industrial base, the area will continue to be a "bedroom" community rather than an area with its own opportunities for employment. Second, as table 6 shows, working mothers within the sample work in a variety of occupations centered mostly in Netzahualcoyotl. Of these women, 59.9 percent are employed in Netzahualcoyotl, with one-fourth of them working as domestics. These women generally wash, iron, or clean for slightly more affluent persons, or act as babysitters for the 38.9 percent of the women working in the federal district.

For male children sampled, most follow occupational patterns similar to their fathers', including searching for work in the federal district. For example, of 447 sons who were economically active, 50.2 percent worked in self-employed commerce (*Obrero emple-ado-particular comerciante*), with 70 percent of these working in the federal district and 28 percent employed in Netzahualcoyotl. Thus, for fathers and for children, Netzahualcoyotl is "home base" and the federal district is the resource generator for economic activities, as table 7 shows.

An examination of table 7 shows that of the 477 children listed, the occupational categories in which they are employed do not differ appreciably from those of their parents: 43.35 percent were laborers, 24.42 percent were self-employed, and 5.8 percent were in commerce. These three categories accounted for 74 percent of the sample. The differences, for all categories, are slight between parents and children, with only one category (commerce) showing reduced rates among children. This points to the continued marginalization of the second generation of Netzahualcoyotlans.

For most families in Netzahualcoyotl, however, one source of income is insufficient for subsistence. In fact, in all 1,026 families sampled in the *Encuesta* (Tamayo 1971), children played a major role in providing income for their families. The following figures verify that statement: 922 fathers had at least one job; 460 of 2,046 children living with parents had at least one job; 81 mothers had at least one job; relatives or persons living with these families accounted for 89 other jobs (Tamayo 1971:11). Our ethnographic information provides verification that a single source of income for most families is insufficient for a large portion of the population. Young men, especially those going to school, constantly search for any employment they can find in Netzahualcoyotl or in the federal

TABLE 7

OCCUPATIONS AND WORK LOCATIONS FOR CHILDREN IN ECONOMICALLY ACTIVE FAMILIES
(477 CHILDREN IN 1,026 FAMILIES)

	Percentage in Federal District	Percentage in Netzahualcoyotl	Percentage in Other Areas	Percentage of Total
Laborer	31.5	11.4	0.45	43.35
Self-employed	18.7	5.5	0.22	24.42
Bricklayer	0.44	1.3	—	1.74
Bureaucrat	1.1	0.44	—	1.54
Urban worker	0.67	1.78	—	2.45
Commerce	2.9	2.9	—	5.80
Professional	3.8	0.89	0.45	4.69
Electrician	0.89	—	—	0.89
Domestic (male & female)	—	0.44	—	0.44
Seamstress	1.78	0.45	0.22	2.23
Carpenter	—	0.67	—	0.67
Other	8.2	1.78	—	4.98
Total	70.00	28.00	2.00	100.00

OCCUPATIONS AND WORK LOCATIONS OF PERSONS ATTACHED TO THE NUCLEAR FAMILIES
(81 PERSONS IN 1,026 FAMILIES)

	Percentage in Federal District	Percentage in Netzahualcoyotl	Percentage in Other Areas
Laborer	30.8	4.9	3.7
Self-employed	13.5	3.7	—
Commerce	0.12	8.6	—
Professional	3.7	0.12	0.12
Bureaucrat	4.9	—	0.12
Other	11.1	6.1	0.12
Total	65.00	26.00	9.00

Source: Tamayo 1971:13.
*All figures rounded to the nearest 10th.

district, and young women gravitate toward domestic or clerk's work.

One important fact found in the ethnographic study but not discovered by any sampling studies so far conducted in the *municipio* is that many younger persons perform free services for possible employers. That is, under the guise of apprenticeships, young men and women provide free labor to their prospective employers.

This provides employers with significant control over job seekers even before they are hired. Since competition among largely unskilled and untrained persons is so keen within the federal district, this method of employment is highly profitable for the employer and coerces the prospective employee into a totally asymmetrical relationship—one in which employee rights are usually laid aside.

Young men and women, however, usually enter such an arrangement only if influence (*palanca*)[2] cannot be utilized as a tool for employment. Furthermore, the asymmetrical arrangement continues even after an unskilled person is hired, since a portion of his income is kicked back to his immediate superior. Although the amount may vary, usually from 10 to 15 percent of this type of employee's earnings are, in fact, absorbed by his superior. In many ways this is like chattel slavery, but persons must accommodate their values to what is rather than what should be. If a person does not *ponerse bien* ("place himself well") by graft, then the probability for maintaining employment is small. But it is not just young men and women who are subject to this type of systematic exploitation: anyone who does not have proper access may have little or no choice but to enter into such a relationship. Informants provided numerous examples of employees being shifted from one job responsibility to another, or given a late shift, or finally fired for not following the dictates of their immediate employers or superiors. In fact, promotion is usually couched within the context of some sort of payoff to someone, either in direct financial remuneration or future support. For the most part, this population of employees is subject to coercion in many ways, both subtle and obvious.

ECONOMIC MARGINALIZATION: INCOME

Economic marginalization can be characterized by referring to income. Minimum wages or below can be used as a standard to denote "marginal" income (Lomnitz 1977:13-14). Income generated by persons in Netzahualcoyotl engaged in the range of occupations discussed was at the minimum or slightly above for most.

In 1970 the minimum legal wage was 32.50 pesos ($2.60) per day or 975 pesos ($28) per month. Sixty-two percent (85,132) of persons twelve years or older declaring income in Netzahualcoyotl earned less than 999 pesos per day. Another 33,225 persons earned between 1,000 and 1,499 pesos. Table 8 shows the income distribution in Netzahualcoyotl. Nevertheless, these figures indicate only those who were economically active at the time the census was taken and do not reflect periods of unemployment or under-employment. As one authoritative economic journal suggested, "Mexico does not enumerate either unemployment or under-employment" ("Panorama económico" 1971:8).

TABLE 8

INCOME DISTRIBUTION (N = 135,376)

Declared Income in Pesos	Persons Declaring Monthly Income
0 to 199	6,351
200 to 499	15,464
500 to 999	63,317
1,000 to 1,499	33,225
1,500 to 4,999	15,642
5,000 to 9,999	732
10,000 and above	645

Source: "Censo de población" 1970:15, Q-28.

By referring to our ethnographic information, and by noting the number of persons participating in the Social Security Health System (Seguro Social),[3] which is an indicator of participation in the formal sector and is associated with more secure employment since persons must pay a fee for family health protection, we conclude that unemployment in the population of those twelve years and over would comprise a minimum of about 32 percent. Those without the health plan would not be eligible for protection unless they were employed in a concern on a permanent basis. Thus, "economically active" figures do not realistically reflect the actual economic conditions for large portions of the population in 1971-1974.

By occupational structure, income generated, and the unemployment figures cited here, large parts of the population of Netzahualcoyotl could be characterized as "economically marginalized." They do not comprise, however, a "culture of poverty" sector, regardless of the informality of their labor characteristics. Certainly, their literacy and educational characteristics are not too different from those of the overall nation, as the next section illustrates.

Literacy and Educational Characteristics

The population of Netzahualcoyotl has above-average literacy rates compared with both state rates and the national average. According to the 1970 census, 83.2 percent of Netzahualcoyotl's population is literate compared to the state's 75.1 percent and the nation's 76.5 percent average.[4] It is below the federal district's rate of 90.9 percent (335,305,499). Of the total population ten years or over who know how to read and write (298,062), slightly more than 30 percent had not completed either first and second grade or had any formal instruction whatsoever; another 25 percent had completed only grades one or two ("Censo de población" 1970:6, Q-15).[5] Thus, 55 percent of those claiming the ability to read and write had little or no formal instruction; this would make suspect the quality of the reading and writing ability of a large segment of the population.

Yet the trend toward increased educational participation is clear, as greater numbers of the population, especially those under the age of fifteen, are attending primary and secondary schools, and at a greater rate than did their parents. In fact, children between the ages of ten and fourteen have achieved a rate of schooling second only to the population between ages twenty and twenty-nine. This trend will be of importance in determining expectations of future goals.

A total of 108,359 children between ages six and fourteen attend primary schools either in Netzahualcoyotl or in the federal district. Those who attend schools in the federal district, according to my informants, do so for two primary reasons: first, parents perceive that schools in Netzahualcoyotl are inferior to those in the federal district; second, parents perceive gang activity as less formidable in the district than in the city.

Regardless of the place of instruction, however, of the 108,359 school-age children between six and fourteen who attended primary school in 1970, 56,408 were male and 51,951 were female. Through grade six (prior to the secondary level) there was little decrease in the rate of females attending school ("Censo de población" 1970:16, Q-17). There is a correlation between age and grade because of the high number of children who drop out of school as they become older, but this does not preclude nine- and ten-year-olds from attending the first and second grades. More than likely, pressures to seek employment encourage decisions to discontinue schooling. School population figures for males between ages eight and thirteen, according to their academic levels, suggest a dropout rate of nearly 50 percent between grades one and six. The shaded figures in table 9 illustrate this.

At the secondary level and beyond, men outnumber women by slightly more than two times in all categories except postprofessional training. Table 10 illustrates this. What is particularly striking about these figures for ages eleven through nineteen—the ages within which most secondary-school attendance occurs—is that only 11,453 persons of both sexes have attended or are attending secondary schools. This small number, when compared to the secondary-school-age population of 112,748 persons, seems quite insignificant.[6] Thus, the great majority of persons in this age group will be competing for the same minimum-skill positions, as do their fathers and mothers. Furthermore, present population trends indicate that this age group will continue to grow rapidly, thus increasing stress on the institutions and the environment in which they live.

FECUNDITY CHARACTERISTICS

As has been stated, the median family size in Netzahualcoyotl is 7.6, according to the 1970 census, compared to the national

TABLE 9

School Population Figures (ages 8 to 13)

Male Ages						
Grades	8	9	10	11	12	13
One	2,356	1,169	576	221	169	87
Two	2,959	2,123	1,265	602	398	183
Three	1,751	2,507	2,096	1,189	797	406
Four	375	1,401	2,162	1,677	1,323	750
Five	—	291	1,172	1,647	1,714	1,209
Six	—	—	294	868	1,434	1,296

Female Ages						
Grades	8	9	10	11	12	13
One	2,258	1,093	542	225	155	67
Two	2,757	1,954	1,142	588	374	169
Three	1,680	2,457	1,980	1,174	786	361
Four	366	1,343	1,989	1,572	1,277	709
Five	—	297	1,048	1,459	1,493	1,096
Six	—	—	275	750	1,306	1,237

Source: "Censo de población" 1970:16, Q-17.

median of 5.6. Although the figures cited in table 11 are cross-sectional and should not be used to form long-range conclusions, these data do suggest that family size may not diminish until the present cohorts of ages twenty to twenty-four decide not to have children at the same rates as those cohorts of ages twenty-five to twenty-nine. Nevertheless, table 11 does suggest that childbearing and child rearing start early and extend late into the life-cycles of women.

Furthermore, a consideration of fecundity characteristics of women twelve years and over illustrates that women between ages twenty-five and fifty seem to have a minimum of five to six children; that is, between those ages the rate of childbearing increases up to six children. It is not until the sixth child that the birth rate drops (between ages thirty and fifty), as table 12 illustrates.

TABLE 10
Participation in Secondary Education and Beyond

Male Ages	Secondary Schools	Preparatory/ Vocational	Professional with Secondary	Professional with Preparatory	Professional with University Training	Postuniversity
11-14	4,038	63	3	—	—	—
15-19	3,355	1,311	173	7	122	—
20-29	601	480	119	20	396	5
30-39	103	42	22	4	77	2
40 and over	66	19	2	3	28	1
Total	8,163	1,915	319	34	623	8
Female Ages						
11-14	2,587	40	9	—	—	—
15-19	1,473	406	304	4	46	—
20-29	227	107	74	13	117	5
30-39	40	6	10	3	57	2
40 and over	37	4	3	4	43	4
Total	4,364	563	400	24	263	11

Source: "Censo de población" 1970:16, Q-16.

TABLE 11
Fecundity Characteristics

	12 and over	12-14	15-19	20-24	25-29	Female Ages 30-34	35-39	40-44	45-49	50 and over
Population total	161,352	21,131	27,568	25,028	15,938	17,141	15,111	10,087	7,258	16,658
Have not had children	64,218	20,906	23,054	9,219	3,449	1,823	1,349	961	767	2,813
Have had children	97,134	225	4,514	15,809	18,044	15,318	13,762	9,126	6,491	13,845
Total number of children	523,246	447	7,800	41,897	74,239	85,669	93,869	69,483	49,165	100,677
Median number of children per woman	5.4	2.0	1.7	2.7	4.1	5.6	6.8	7.6	7.6	7.3

Source: "Censo de población" 1970:12, Q-20.

TABLE 12
Mother's Age Relative to Total Number of Children

Number of children	Total 12 years and over	12-14	15-19	20-24	25-29	30-34	35-39	40-44	45-50	50 and over
2	12,080	76	1,215	4,589	2,505	1,085	726	478	411	995
3	11,694	73	310	3,633	3,272	1,452	901	560	450	1,043
4	11,176	—	122	2,029	3,570	2,000	1,240	625	476	1,114
5	10,334	—	72	884	3,190	2,290	1,438	753	536	1,171
6	8,998	—	64	326	2,000	2,400	1,648	840	552	1,168
7	7,504	—	48	154	1,058	2,092	1,625	867	512	1,148
8	6,273	—	27	67	479	1,468	1,602	911	559	1,160
9	4,938	—	—	69	188	833	1,330	869	569	1,080
10	3,930	—	—	38	80	457	1,042	763	527	1,023
11	2,684	—	—	32	37	211	643	622	384	755
12	2,499	—	—	23	22	122	483	577	394	878
13 or more	3,701	—	—	10	80	139	506	837	752	1,377

Source: "Censo de población" 1970:12, Q-20.

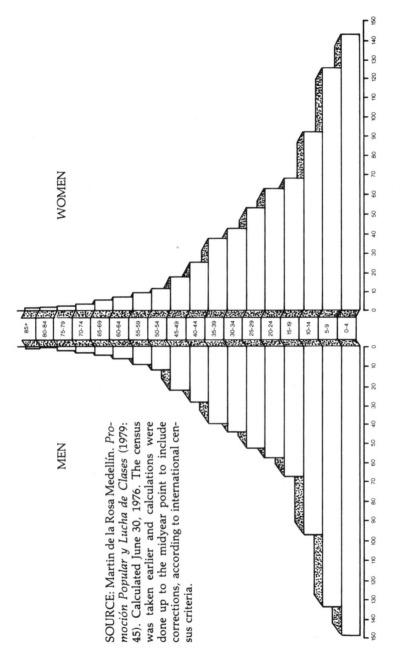

WOMEN

MEN

SOURCE: Martín de la Rosa Medellín. *Promoción Popular y Lucha de Clases* (1979: 45). Calculated June 30, 1976. The census was taken earlier and calculations were done up to the midyear point to include corrections, according to international census criteria.

Fig. 1. Population Pyramid, Ciudad Netzahualcoyotl: 1976.

Given that the population in 1971 under thirty years accounted for 77 percent of the populace of Netzahualcoyotl, the youthful population slant cannot be expected to change for the foreseeable future. An extremely pointed population pyramid resulted in 1976, as figure 1 illustrates.

THE LOCUS OF MARGINALITY: SUMMARY AND IMPLICATIONS

I have argued that Ciudad Netzahualcoyotl and large parts of its population are marginalized. The area is contaminated, swept by dust and windstorms, and is a repository for disease and waste. Yet it is a site to which great numbers of persons have moved. Such populations, I have argued, are largely economically marginalized, even though nonmarginalized populations also live in Ciudad Netzahualcoyotl. Marginalized populations are part of what Adams (1975:37-68) has described as the social "waste" that emerges when societies organize into more complex social structures. Such social "waste" in Mexico is created by governmental policies that have favored capital-intensive technologies at the expense of labor-intensive industries, as well as by undercapitalization of the rural sector. Therefore, large segments of Mexican society become useless and redundant to the larger economic and political system. Among other implications, such populations have little choice but to leave areas where their survival is no longer tenable or to move to areas where a slight "edge" on survival may be enlisted. For rural migrants, the former is usually true; for urban migrants, an "edge" can be gained by seeking lower costs for housing.

Both rural and urban migrants, as has been shown, have migrated from their points of origin for economic reasons. Seventy-one percent cited economic reasons for moving from their former residences. Such persons participated largely in the informal economic sector and earned marginal incomes. Seventy-seven percent were engaged in such occupations, and 62 percent earned incomes at the minimum level or below. The trend continues as following generations enter into similar occupational niches (74 percent).

Such marginalized populations, however, express social and cultural values little different from other populations, contrary to the culture of poverty literature. They place high value on traditional ritual marriage bonding, patri-centered families, and home ownership (77 percent owned their own home). Literacy characteristics are above the national norm and not far below that of the federal district; large numbers of children in these populations attend schools. The high fecundity figures and large family sizes are not the result of differences in culture or adherence to a culture of poverty pattern but rather to the fact that children provide essential economic assistance to their economically marginal families. Lomnitz (1977) has pointed out that marginalized families must rely on the contribution of moneys by children, unpaid child labor, and the assistance of children in emergencies. This is true also of those marginalized families in Ciudad Netzahualcoyotl Izcalli.

The population of Ciudad Netzahualcoyotl is also a "wasted" population in the sense that it is a population whose potential has not been realized. It is not a population *of waste* but one unfortunately *wasted by* the industrial forces responsible for its creation; waste is not entropy. Such a "wasted" population has exhibited the energy to invest in generating political power structures, and at one time they made elites tremble. Environmental conditions pushed these populations into action.

The Ethnographic Context:
The Parameter for Marginality

CIUDAD NETZAHUALCOYOTL IS the product of spontaneous settlements, land invasions, and clandestine subdivisions by both marginalized populations and nonmarginalized populations. The latter comprise about 20 percent of the population, since 23 percent of the working men and women apparently have jobs in the formal economic sector. Yet both marginalized and nonmarginalized families have been engaged in attempts to acquire land and home.

While it is likely that nonmarginalized persons have not participated in land invasions and spontaneous settlements but purchased their land from clandestinely developed subdivisions, nevertheless, like their marginalized counterparts, even persons in the formal sectors have participated in land invasions. Both populations, in any case, have sought to fulfill one basic need: the acquisition of home ownership.

The processes involved in acquiring land largely define not only the potentialities for community organization but also the types of risks involved in land acquisition. Ciudad Netzahualcoyotl can be classified as a type of *colonia proletaria*—a "proletarian colony" or "municipality." Yet its formation resulted from populations organizing and taking risks in order to acquire their "place in the sun." While 60 percent of 1,026 family heads sampled (Tamayo 1971:30) bought their lots from land developers, such land was in fact part of a subsystem of land holdings known as *fraccionamien-*

tos clandestinos ("illegal" or "clandestine subdivisions"), in which owners receive pseudolegal land titles.

According to Ward (1976:334), the arrangement is "illegal where either the vendor (subdivider) does not have legal title to the land, or alternatively, he defaults on the provision of services." As will be shown, even with the purchases of land and homes by nonmarginalized populations, their contracts were usually defaulted by land developers through lack of services, or their titles were subsequently deemed questionable. Both populations, then, can be considered part of clandestine subdivisions.

The other 40 percent of the 1,026 family heads sampled in the *Encuesta Definitiva* (Tamayo 1971:30) indicated that they settled into their lots before purchase or before initiating any legal measures to take possession of the lots on which they eventually built their homes. This figure is fairly accurate according to the best estimates that I have been able to make from interviews with public officials and by my own accounting of land invasions by squatters, based on recent maps and verified by public-works officials.

The combination of land invasion and acquisition of land and home through clandestine subdivision provides Ciudad Netzahualcoyotl's people with its potential for community organization, and certainly with a willingness, among large parts of the population, to engage in political-protest activities, as later developments will show. It is not true that these populations are better or worse off than other populations in different types of urban concentrations, in economic or occupational terms. In other types of urban concentrations, such *ciudades perdidas* ("lost cities"), static slum universes where most of the population rents at exorbitant prices, there is little incentive to take risks (Ward 1976:342). Because of the risks of losing rental status in a crowded market, and because of the lack of personal investment in the duration of a location that can be bulldozed away without tenure rights, persons living in *ciudades perdidas* can hardly be expected to take additional risks by organizing political activities around living conditions or rent gouging (Ward 1976:342-343). Such was not the case for the people in Ciudad Netzahualcoyotl.

Of seventy-eight neighborhoods that made up Ciudad Netzahualcoyotl in 1974, twenty-one were occupied by participants in massive land invasions, six others were partly occupied in this manner, and the rest were probably settled by persons who purchased their lots. The last group, however, made purchases with questionable tenure rights and/or with services in default. There are no accurate figures other than those given by Tamayo (1971), and gathering such information is extremely delicate, given the struggle many of these persons have experienced. In fact, a group from the Public Works Department was surrounded and menaced in 1970 when such information gathering was attempted. Nevertheless, the process of moving in usually took place in different phases according to whether those moving in were squatters or persons who had purchased their lots. For the most part, squatters initially built their *jacales* from whatever materials were available —usually secondhand boards, corrugated tin, a mixture of concrete blocks, and cardboard. In contrast, those who had purchased their lots from land developers were required by contrast to build their homes of either brick, concrete block, or similar hard-surfaced materials, and were forbidden to use wood, cardboard, corrugated tin, or other temporary materials.

Thus, two initial processes occurred: squatters built their *jacales* from whatever was available, whereas the others were required initially to build permanent structures. This difference resulted in areas of contrasting construction. But those who had squatted, if economic circumstances allowed, eventually built permanent additions to their *jacales*. Those with a previously built shelter, if it had been constructed at the rear of their lot, added adjoining rooms toward the front; if the first construction had been built toward the front of the lot, second stories were sometimes added. This second phase also resulted in a potpourri of construction.

Purchased lots averaged 98 pesos per square meter, and with most lots measuring 162 square meters, the average total price was 15,974 pesos, without the inclusion of construction costs (Tamayo 1971:30). Indeed, 60.6 percent of the sampled population who had not finished paying for their lots paid between 8,000 and 16,000 pesos. In addition, 56 percent of this group paid between 4,000 and 16,000 pesos for the construction of their homes. Those persons who had squatted paid similar amounts to build their homes, but it was not until 1974, when the Fidecomiso provided legal title to their lands, that they began to pay a similar amount for their lots. Netzahualcoyotl, however, is clearly not an area in which expenditures by its population are verifiable, and even census figures are highly suspect since those persons interviewed during the census did not, in fact, indicate their squatter status. In fact, 77 percent of those sampled stated that they were paying for or owned their own homes (Tamayo 1971:22).

Such data for persons in various legal and extralegal statuses in the *municipio* are immaterial to a consideration of the proposition that for the most part, persons settling in Netzahualcoyotl have an overriding desire to own and control their own homes, regardless of the manner in which it is done. As will be suggested in a later portion of this study, much of the political-protest activity resulted from this overriding motivation, as well as from the search for economic stability.

Yet there were costs in 1971, and to some extent through 1975, in terms of the overcrowding, unsanitary living conditions, and debts to land developers. As the 1970 census figures show, even though undercounted, 580,436 persons occupied 90,338 dwellings, which suggests that overcrowding is a major problem. As table 13 illustrates, over 81 percent of the population lived in dwellings with three or less rooms in which to cook, raise children, sleep, study, fight, love, whatever.

One of the major ills that was observed in 1971 and that continued, to some extent, in Netzahualcoyotl's eastern half in 1974, was the lack of potable water and sewage services. According to the *Estudio de factibilidad* (1969) 60.7 percent of the families in the city had waterlines to their homes, with 22 percent of the families having inside running water and 38 percent having outside running water located just inside the lot. This study also shows that 39 percent of the population had no water and had to rely on community water holes for drinking, bathing, and cooking. (The 1970 census, however, indicates that 63.93 percent had no water service, a considerable disparity in figures.) These figures have changed for the better since 1970, and although no accurate figures

TABLE 13

OCCUPANTS AND ROOMS PER DWELLING

Rooms	Dwellings	Percentage of Total	Occupants	Percentage of Total
1	32,081	35.51	182,776	31.49
2	30,206	33.44	196,782	33.91
3	13,926	15.41	97,289	16.76
4	7,812	8.65	55,790	9.62
5	2,984	3.30	22,645	3.90
6	1,606	1.78	12,034	2.07
7	770	0.85	5,832	1.00
8	405	0.45	3,195	0.55
9 or more	548	0.61	4,093	0.70

Source: "Censo de población" 1970:19, Q-32.

presently exist, recent (1974) massive public-works projects initiated by state authorities have increased the availability of potable water services to the population. Nevertheless, for reasons that will be described, such water services are largely contaminated by the environment.

Related to such contamination is the fact that sewage services for the population were extremely limited. In fact, 59 percent of the families that had inside toilets did not have sewage service, and 70 percent that had outside facilities did not have sewage connections in 1970 (Tamayo 1971:26b). Thus, in 1971, and in the western part of the city in 1974, raw sewage, coupled with contaminated water, combined to create an unhealthy situation for a substantial number of persons in the area.[1] Such conditions were made more difficult by the nature of the soil, rainfall, and lack of drainage in this area.

An overhead view of Ciudad Netzahualcoyotl as it appeared during the months of June through October 1970 is shown in figure 2. The city is laid out as an irregularly widened rectangle from which right-angled chunks have been removed. The northernmost edge of the city is bordered by a rough embankment that serves as a roadway—Avenida Xociaca (fig. 3)—and a dike against the

Fig. 2. Overhead view of Ciudad Netzahualcoyotl Izcalli.

Fig. 3. Avenida Xociaca.

sewage waters of Lake Texcoco (fig. 4), shown as dark and light blotches. For the most part, Avenida Xociaca is used by few persons except those traveling in buses, which often veer precariously close to the embankment. It is used also by some persons who walk along the embankment to a road that bisects the middle of the lake bed. Here persons have "fished" for worms, which thrive in the treated and untreated sewage. The *tequesquite* worms are raked in by the thousands and allowed to dry on the sides of the lake-bed embankments. Once dried, they are packaged and shipped out for processing as birdseed for the U.S. market.

The Colonia del Sol, the uppermost neighborhood jutting out from the rest of the area at the extreme northwestern corner of figure 2, and shown in figure 5, is the most environmentally depressed of all the sections of the city. Although this section was established in 1957, it is the most dispersed in its settlement patterns. It is surrounded on the east by the sewage overflow from the city, on the west by the sewer canal from Mexico City, on the north by the accumulated sewage in the lake bed of Texcoco, and

Fig. 4. Lake Texcoco.

Fig. 5. Colonia del Sol during rain.

Fig. 6. A *colonia* after rain.

on the south by the city of Netzahualcoyotl itself. It is in this *colonia* that persons most marginalized and unable to afford lots in other areas of Netzahualcoyotl settle. The rainy season plays particular havoc in this area since there is neither sewer service nor natural drainage. This particular *colonia* was without vegetation through the 1971-1974 period. Life consisted solely of humans, dogs, vermin, rats, and abusive police.

The area along Avenida Xociaca to the eastern boundary of the city changed little from 1971 through 1974, either in the havoc the rains play on the road or on the quality of the ecology bordering the avenue (fig. 5). To the north of the embankment-road section of Avenida Xociaca, ninety-five blocks are bordered by *agua negra* ("black water") spewing out from five drainage pipes along this route, contributing to the constant nauseating smell in those areas immediately bordering this stretch (and, at certain times, for all of Netzahualcoyotl) (fig. 6). On the southern side of the Avenida Xociaca, which borders Netzahualcoyotl itself and extends along ten additional *colonias* (see map 1),[2] both in 1971 and three

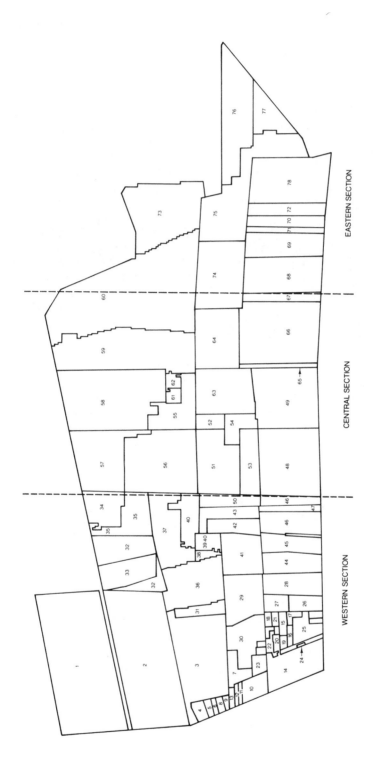

Map 1. City of Netzahualcoyotl (1974), showing neighborhoods and subdivisions.

1. el sol
2. estado de mexico
3. maravillas
4. el barco I
5. el barco II
6. el barco III
7. netzhualcoyotl I
8. netzahualcoyotl II
9. netzahualcoyotl III
10. porvenir
11. perete
12. volcanes
13. martinez de llanos
14. xochitenco
15. juarez pantitlan
16. nueva juarez pantitlan I
17. nueva juarez pantitlan II
18. nueva juarez pantitlan III
19. angel veraza
20. san mateito
21. aurorita
22. formando hogar
23. joyita
24. amipant
25. mi retiro
26. pavon
27. pavon secc. silvia
28. mexico I
29. mexico II
30. mexico III
31. central

32. tamalipas
33. tamalipas secc. virgencitas
34. tamalipas secc. las flores
35. tamalipas secc. el palmar
36. agua azul grupo a super 4
37. agua azul grupo c
38. agua azul grupo b super 4
39. agua azul grupo b super 23
40. pirules
41. las fuentes
42. porfirio diaz
43. modelo
44. romero
45. atlacomulco
46. metropolitana I
47. san lorenzo
48. metropolitana II
49. metropolitana III
50. evolucion poniente
51. evolucion super 24
52. evolucion super 43
53. evolucion super 22
54. evolucion
55. ampliacion evolucion
56. aurora sur
57. aurora I
58. aurora II
59. aurora III
60. aurora oriente
61. aurora section a
62. aurora romero

63. ampliacion villada super 43
64. ampliacion villada super 44
65. ampliacion villada poniente
66. vicente villada
67. ampliacion villada oriente
68. las aguilas
69. ampliacion las aguilas
70. constitucion de 1857
71. sta. martha
72. manantiales
73. loma bonita
74. la perla
75. reforma b
76. reforma a secc. I
77. reforma a secc. II
78. esperanza

years later, mounds of mud and paper from three to six feet high were piled from leftover excavations. Refuse, blown in both from the lake bed and from the city, was also part of the scene. Mud and refuse meet and adhere along this stretch to form modern obscene pyramids from which, occasionally, *pepenadores* ("garbage pickers") collect their goods to sell, and from which children jump and play.

Toward the city, between these mounds and the first houses of the *colonias* bordering Avenida Xociaca, are open spaces of sixty to seventy square meters that are used as soccer fields. By 1974, however, three of these fields had been allocated as sites for electrical transformers, to relieve the city from the constant blackouts experienced during the rainy season. Even with these transformers, light showers and small electrical disturbances blacked out large sections of the area as recently as 1974.

The outermost fringes of the city, however, were not representative of the city itself. Between 1971 and 1974, Netzahualcoyotl was in a continuous state of urbanization and transition. Thus, for example, in 1971 the *colonias* shown in map 2, numbered 4 through 30, could be considered somewhat stabilized in terms of population, services, and recreation. They were settled by persons who purchased their lots from developed tracts and who had relatively easy access to bus lines, schools, and hospitals in the federal district. Moreover, the developed tracts were provided with sewer and waterlines by the early land developers. Therefore, persons in these sections during the 1971-1974 period had a relatively stable environment in which to live. In addition, they had been part of a settled population for at least five years: in- and out-migration had largely ceased except for those purchasing existing homes. As a result, during the political-protest activities of much of the city, this area was the most "conservative," contributing few protestors since there was little to be gained from such participation. These areas, then, except the Colonia del Sol in the western part of the city—the first *colonia* to be developed (1946)—are the most stable in the city, both in population and in services.

Netzahualcoyotl is, nevertheless, not an evenly developed city. Of the seventy-nine primary schools operating in 1971 in Ciudad

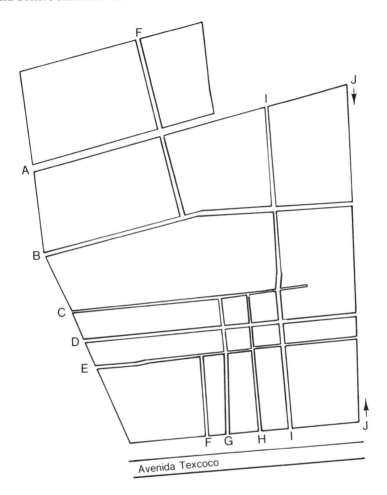

WESTERN SECTION

E-W Streets   N-S Streets

A. Xociaca   F. Vicente Palacio
B. Chimalhuacan   G. Cauhtemoc
C. Perules   H. Allende
D. Pantitlan   I. Netzahualcoyotl
E. Juarez   J. Central

Map 2. Western section of Netzahualcoyotl.

Netzahualcoyotl, the majority were built in *colonias* 1 through 50, excluding *colonias* 2 and 32 through 35 (see map 2). In the period 1971-1974, additional schools were built in other areas, especially after the protest activities of the CRC movement of that time; nevertheless, those areas in the western part of the city, except for those excluded, were in the main considerably urbanized in terms of population density, stability of settlement, and basic social and environmental services. While this was true in the 1971-1974 period, the introduction of massive public-works projects in 1974 turned this area into a morass of mud similar to that found in the less urbanized areas: sewer and waterlines turned the most environmentally stable area into one as unpassable and depressed as the developing ones in the eastern and northern parts of the city.

All parts of the city were under persistent pressures of urbanization, and such pressures created heterogeneous construction throughout the city at different periods. The type of construction was related to occupation and income but consisted mostly of self-built "modular" housing. Persons from the marginalized sectors who purchased their lots built *jacales* ("shacks") of two rooms or less toward the rear of their lots during the initial stages of their residence in the city. These *jacales*, however, were permanent constructions made from either concrete block or brick. Eventually, depending on the economic success of the residents, these were superseded by constructions built toward the front of lots. Thus, throughout Netzahualcoyotl, permanent constructions at the fronts and the backs of lots appeared, depending on the economic and occupational circumstances of the occupants (fig. 7).

There is cultural significance in where persons choose to build their homes, extending from the time the first *jacales* were built to the present state of construction on the lots. The locations of homes define those who have "made it" and those who have not. For the most part, the construction of a home is the first goal in life. It represents family values, security, and shelter from the "outside." But reflective of the increasing mass-culture content of what may be termed the "pepsi-coatlization" of modern Mexico,[3] the location of the house on the lot, the number of stories, the contemporaneity of the architecture, the number of appliances, the

Fig. 7. The original *jacal* at the rear of a lot. The owner, among those who "made it," has built the front part of a new home without destroying the original structure, which is still used for a male dormitory and cooking facility.

amount of shrubbery, and whether there is an automobile hidden behind the iron gates, all have become increasingly important physical manifestations used in defining the reputations of persons living in Netzahualcoyotl.

Thus, within *colonias* such as those in the southwestern part of the city, homes exist side by side, constructed at different times, and reflecting different stages of "making it"—stages congruent with the reputations of the inhabitants. In these as in other *colonias*, symbols define the successful. Yet such symbols do not alone define the meaning of this passage.

For those "making it," the construction of the house at the front of the lot is both a ritual and a social-network event. Visitations by neighbors, friends, and kin during the process of construction is an almost daily event. Encouragement, in the form of remarks on the quality of construction, its costs, the esthetic appeal of the house, the advantage of building toward the front of the lot, the convenience of indoor bathrooms, and the constant comparison with the present home at the rear of the lot, takes place continuously throughout the building process. All the details of what "will be" as compared to what "is" are touched upon, and it is during this building process that the content of one's new status unfolds with a special, ritualistic flavor.

Expectations concerning a new status unfold with the construction of a home toward the front of a lot. They include the following: owners will have a *pachanga* ("party") to celebrate their home, replete with barbecued goat or lamb purchased in one of the surrounding countryside towns; *compadre* and *comadre* relations will be established between the owners of the home and its sponsors, who will share, ideally, both good and bad fortune. Such *compadrazgo* is usually established with persons already possessing a home built toward the front of their lot, or with those who have greater prestige as a result of adding a second floor. Nevertheless, this combination of ritual introduced into the "housewarming" celebration is a particularly Mexican synthesis of ostentatious display of consumer values and the recognition of a moral content in this graduation to a new status.

Sometimes a priest is invited to bless the home, although he does not sanction the *compadre* relations; nevertheless, the presence of the priest and his blessing of the household enhances the moral quality and "lends" a legitimacy to the *compadre* relations. At times, all who are present in the household during such housewarmings become *compadres* and *comadres*, but such bonds pertain only to the time in which the celebrations are held and do not become lasting fictive relations.

Homes range in construction from cardboard and used-plank shelters to concrete two-story buildings, depending on whether lots and homes were purchased or were part of land invasions, and depending on the *period of time* in which these land invasions took place.

Ramifications other than heterogeneous building styles were created by the different types of ownership. Endemic conflict and daily confrontations could be observed between those seeking lots without purchase, those already in illegal possession of lots and buildings, and those who had purchased their lots and built their homes, or who sought to purchase lots and buildings. Since title was always questionable in whatever way the lots or homes were possessed, many homeowners in the city would have relatives and/or friends stay in these homes when they themselves could not occupy them. In addition, some owners would contact the local power holders in order to provide "protection" for their lots. Contradictions occurred when lot owners and lot invaders used the same power holders.

Yet all faced the same daily discomforts in this environment. Land invader, lot owner, power holders, and the least powerful shared the awful seasonal changes that brought persistent and inevitable rainfall between June and October, as well as the sandstorms from the Texcoco lake bed between January and May.[4] For persons in the city, however, it is during the rainy season that it is most difficult to travel in the streets, keep clean, find uncontaminated water, keep children healthy, block rain and sewage overflow from homes—in general, to prevent daily activities from being influenced by and subjected to constant readjustments because of the side effects of daily rainfall (see fig. 8). It seemed that during the rainy season people were never quite sure whether projected activities could be carried out. Even a relatively simple task such as catching a bus was not a certainty since many times they became bogged down in the mud or crashed because of wet brakes and excessive speed. With a reduced number of buses, there were more persons per bus clamoring for space; those unable to board sought alternative means such as *peseros* ("communal taxis") or single-passenger taxis. These vehicles, in turn, face problems similar to those faced by the buses. In this manner the "urban" transportation system has become slow-moving, packed, and frustrating for those attempting to utilize it.

Frustration is not limited only to the acquisition of transportation but permeates every aspect of it: flagging down the taxi or bus, standing in the rain, cramming into an already overcrowded bus or taxi, and, in the case of women, being manhandled by males who grope in close quarters. By the time the person reaches

Fig. 8. Aftermath of the rainy season.

his destination, stress, frustration, and anger have taken their toll. Given the endemic conflict in some of the *colonias* and the additional environmental hazards, persons in Netzahualcoyotl are subject to many stresses, including the daily sources of interpersonal stress within the family unit. The uncertainty raised by ecological and economic pressures in Ciudad Netzahualcoyotl is constant, and in the rainy season the pressures increase.

The sources of stress caused by transportation problems differ in degree depending on the point of origin and the effect of the previous day's rainfall on the roads in that starting place. For example, those living in Colonia del Sol have access only to buses that travel east and west along Avenida Xociaca (A-J, map 1), since, during the rainy season, roads within the *colonia* are impassable to vehicles.[5] Thus, persons from the interior of the *colonia* must travel long distances before reaching Avenida Xociaca, and even along this avenue, vehicular traffic sometimes has difficulty maneuvering. Pedestrians may be forced to walk even longer dis-

tances to the adjoining federal district or east to Avenida Netzahualcoyotl (I, map 1). Those living in the northwestern part of
Colonia Estado de Mexico (see 2, map 2) must rely on the same
sources of transportation as those living in Colonia del Sol, with
the attendant difficulties; persons living in the southeastern and
southern part of the colonia, however, have access to both Riva
Palacio and Chimalhuacan (F, B, map 1). Nevertheless, bus service into Riva Palacio during the rainy season is also dependent on
road conditions. In fact, such conditions are endemic in most of
the colonias, especially around their central areas.

Therefore, the seasonal rainfall affects most individuals to some
degree in the city, regardless of colonia. Housewives, for example,
have one of three options in doing their marketing. First, they may
go to the local open-air market situated along Avenida Palacio (F,
map 2) in the western part of the city. The quality and prices there
are variable but are usually 30 to 40 percent more expensive than
in Mexico City. Second, they may choose the tiresome and hectic
trip to the Cali-Max supermarket in the federal district.[6] Finally,
they may rely on the small neighborhood stores that dot every
street in all colonias; but these are even more expensive than the
local open-air markets. Since there are few cars in Netzahualcoyotl and even fewer female drivers, most women would need to
use some means of public transportation for the second alternative, and depending on where they lived, some would require public transportation for the first. In any case, the choice among these
alternatives would vary with the amount of rainfall.

Another source for groceries in most sections of the city are the
tianguis, but these too are affected by the climatic conditions of
the day. Tianguis are open-air markets that move to appointed
places in different sections of the city seven days a week. They
offer goods, including fresh meat and vegetables (unrefrigerated),
at lower prices than the permanent open-air markets, and they are
quite popular. Although the tianguis are mobile, their access to the
colonias is also determined by the conditions of the roads, and
both rain and wind dictate whether they remain open. (The tolvaneras in the windy season may be so powerful that they blow
down the temporary canvas covering the various goods.)

The wet and the dry season both affect not only the daily activities of the residents of Netzahualcoyotl but also their health. The rainy season, for example, is a time when many children, regardless of *colonia* and section, become ill with colds, coughs, and most dangerous of all, pneumonia, which accounts for the death of more children than any other single cause except childbirth (*Estudio de factibilidad* 1969:1). The dry season aggravates already weakened children with an almost continuous mist of dust particles contaminated with fecal matter from drying sewage wastes. It is probable that the northwestern rather than the southwestern part of the western section has a higher rate of death caused by ecological and climatic factors, but the one study done does not have sufficient methodological rigor to validate this.[7] It is my impression, nevertheless, based on close observation, that children from the northernmost *colonias* suffer a substantially higher illness and death rate.

Inclement conditions aside, recreation and ritual activities are well attended by inhabitants in the western section of the city. Since Netzahualcoyotl boasts five movie houses, one *plaza de toros* ("bullfight arena"), three wrestling and boxing auditoriums (see fig. 9), five Catholic churches, and various churches of other denominations, both recreation and ritual needs have outlets. For most of the inhabitants in the western section of Netzahualcoyotl, recreation is available both in the federal district and in Netzahualcoyotl. Thus, inhabitants there have a greater number of alternatives than residents in other parts of the city.

Cine Lago ("Lake Movie House"), for example, serves many of the almost 200,000 inhabitants of the western section.[8] But the theater's 2,000-person capacity is insufficient to meet the recreation needs of all those living in the immediate area. Hence, during weekends, the available alternatives in the federal district, including other nearby theaters, are well patronized by persons from this section of Netzahualcoyotl.

Regardless of the section of the city, films seem to be the most popular of all forms of recreation. For most persons in Netzahualcoyotl, adventure, comedy, and simple love films seem to be the genre most enjoyed. Thus, the various "Kaliman films" appearing

Fig. 9. Hero worship after the wrestling match.

in 1974 consisted of themes centering around heroic deeds performed by superhuman, Herculean types—a masked marvel over-
coming evildoers with a series of headlocks and flying mares, or
with the magical assistance of flying horses and/or carpets. The
"Maria films" depicted a young girl from the countryside who
finds employment as a maid in a rich person's house and rescues
her employer's fortune through perceptive intervention, saves her
employer's marriage through wise counseling, and, even more
fantastic, marries the employer's profligate son whom she miracu-
lously reforms from his reckless ways. In addition, Kung Fu and
karate films were particularly well attended in 1974, with many
young persons of both sexes later attempting to imitate Bruce Lee's
actions. Generally, both the foreign-made and Mexican films
shown in Netzahualcoyotl and the federal district were low-
budget, action and/or maudlin stories that attracted large crowds.

    Entering the theaters requires a combination of pushing, shov-
ing, and squirming to get past persons from the previous perfor-

mance trying to exit. After everyone has scurried to the best available seats, the film begins. Initial quiet is soon broken by remarks, boos, jokes, plays on words, whistling, commentaries, flatus, shuffling of feet, laughter (usually at the most inappropriate times), munching, belching, name calling, and cursing at friends—all combined with the sound track of the movie. For the most part, Mexicans in movie theaters in Netzahualcoyotl and in working-class theaters in the federal district, in contrast to the rather sedate American theater audiences and middle-class Mexican ones, are loud, boisterous, and uninhibited; little is left to the imagination as to what the audience feels about the actors and the story. The performance of the audience is as important as those in the film. In addition, the odors of recently rained-upon bodies merge warmly and unpleasantly with the pungency of cigarette smoke, the sweetness of freshly made popcorn (*palomitas*), passed gas, and bad breath. At the end of the films, the exit is as frenzied as the entry, with the push-shove-squirm sequence becoming part of the effort to board the buses and taxis. Movies, generally, are the highlight of a weekend's recreation for many persons in the western section as well as in the rest of Netzahualcoyotl.

Persons attending ritual activities in the city approach these activities in the same hectic and frenzied manner as do patrons at the movie theaters. A few bourgeois women in taffeta and lace dresses compete avidly for the front pews. In contrast, the black-shawled *viejas* ("old women"), with drooped heads and slow gait, enter the doorways and shuffle into the back pews; young men, women, and families hurry into other back pews. Yet the same deference is exhibited toward the priest and the mass regardless of age or station.

Although in 1971 priests shuttled between churches administering services, giving last rites, performing weddings and first communions, by 1973, Netzahualcoyotl had achieved sufficient status to warrant its own bishop. On February 22, 1973, Magin C. Torreblanca was consecrated as the titular Bishop of Asswan and Auxiliary of Texcoco for the diocese of Netzahualcoyotl. With such auspicious developments, ceremonies for *quinceñeras*[9] (fig. 10), full white-dress weddings (fig. 11), elaborate baptisms, confirma-

Fig. 10. A *quinceñera*.

Fig. 11. Full white-dress wedding.

tions, and feast-day celebrations were introduced into the ritual services of the various churches, especially in the western section, which has the oldest standing church. This contrasts sharply with the pre-1971 era when priests were forced to give mass in the open air, covered only by a simple white swayback cloth held up by four two-by-fours, the altar made from whatever flat surface could be supported between two props (fig. 12).

Before 1971, rituals such as Easter services were elaborately acted out by "Roman" soldiers leading a scourged Christ through muddy, water-clogged or dusty, wind-swept streets (fig. 13). By 1974, however, handmade wooden swords and cardboard helmets had been replaced by gold-painted plastic objects made in Japan, and the participant-actors walked in comfort along paved roads. Even more significant was that the actors in 1974 were not the same as those who appeared in 1971. The latter had deeply lined faces and brown, leathery skin; their hands, rough from toil, held crudely hewn artifacts. Those in 1974, for the most part, had clean, clear, olive faces; their soft hands held commercially made swords and spears.

All of these activities—recreational, religious, and ritual—occurred throughout Netzahualcoyotl in varying degrees and quality. In contrast, the focus of the "power structure" of the municipality existed within the central part of the city (map 3).

The central part of the city is the focus of municipal governmental activity. Between 1971 and 1974, the facade of this section changed radically. This area faced many of the difficulties experienced by all parts of the city, but it especially was in constant turmoil, since the municipal authorities could easily be located in the municipal buildings. As in other parts of the city, demand was high on all of the fragile urban "infrastructures," including sewage, transportation, potable water, schools, and health services. In addition to the constant pressures from rain-caused interruptions of sewage, water, and transportation services, the central area, like other sections of the city, was inundated at times with raw sewage and rainwater.

The central area, however, was largely populated by buyers of lots and homes rather than land invaders; thus, their expectations

Fig. 12. Open-air mass, circa 1971.

Fig. 13. Easter procession in the rain, circa 1971.

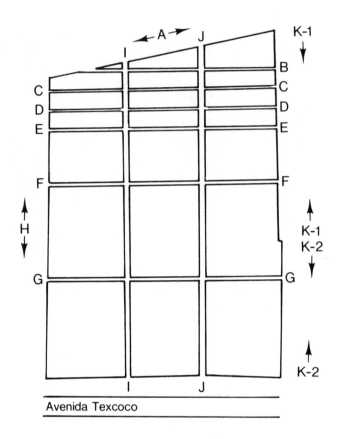

CENTRAL SECTION

E-W Streets   N-S Streets

A. Xoclaca   H. Central
B. Rancho Grande   I. Sor Juana Ines de la Cruz
C. Las Mananitas   J. Cral Vicente Villada
D. La Madrugada   K-1. Carmelo Perez
E. Rayito del Sol   K-2. Zona Federal
F. Chimalhuacan
G. Pantitlan

Map 3. Central section of Netzahualcoyotl.

for services were spelled out in purchase contracts. Compliance, however, was seldom assured, and the general perception of land buyers was that the municipal authorities often joined with land developers to assure that contractual agreements would *not* be met—either by hindering protest or by ignoring it.

For those who live in the area, the ostentatious Plaza de las Armas ("Arms Square"), also known as the *pasto de borregos* ("sheep's pasture"), and the Palacio Municipal ("Municipal Palace"), also known as the *"palacio de coyotes"* ("coyote palace") or the *"palacio de lobos"* ("Wolf Palace"), stand as physical manifestations of the abuses and hardships they suffer. The *"palacio de coyotes,"* a white stucco building with an adjoining jailhouse, is fronted by a half-city-block asphalt square, and at each of the four sides of the square, a concrete pyramidal bridge stands. The complex is a constant reminder of the political authorities' connection with and protection of land developers. This connection is particularly striking when city residents are drawing buckets of contaminated water from public wells in front of the Municipal Palace while the municipal president leaves the building arm-in-arm with one of the leading land developers in the city. Indeed, the supreme irony for those who have purchased their lots is that land invaders are provided protection and assistance by council members within the municipal government because of political and/or economic considerations. For those who live in this region, that knowledge reinforces their loss of faith in legal recourse.

There are other reminders of the many issues that people would like to resolve but that seem incapable of resolution. It is from the Palacio that the *mordelones* ("biters"—officials) exit daily in the cars they won as part of the spoils of office. These spoils are known to be part of the rewards at that level of political authority. In a sense, the rewards of the office become part of the rights and duties of the occupants, even though they always come at the expense of someone else. Persons throughout the city recognize this. It does not require much insight to perceive the relationship between the holding of political office and the rewards accrued in that office—for example, a third councilman's move from a humble *jacal* to a three-story modern home less than a year after taking office. Such obvious displays reinforce the sense of alienation felt by local populations toward political domains controlled by others.

Residents throughout Netzahualcoyotl are reminded that the acquisition of the "good life" by politicians contrasts sharply and obscenely with *their* struggle "to make it." In this sense, all persons living in the city, especially those living near the "palace of coyotes and wolves" bitterly resent those in authority and the monuments they build to themselves.

Nevertheless, thousands of persons daily pass through the blue iron doors of the Municipal Palace, hoping to ease the burdens of their lives. While the municipality is a constant reminder of what is not, it is also the place where the struggle may be lightened. The Municipal Palace is where one pleads for the release of someone from jail, is granted a construction license, makes a connection with someone who will write a letter to the Public Works Department recommending a construction permit, legalizes ownership of a lot, or serves a writ (*amparo*) against a municipal or state decision.[10] Yet the expectation of the thousands of persons who troop in and out of the Municipal Palace, regardless of weather, is that somehow, somewhere, someone will lose.

Ask a male where he is going when he goes into the Municipal Palace, and many times he will respond: *"A ver si me chingan"* ("To see if I can get fucked"). Such expectations are usually fulfilled, unless, of course (and then not positively), arrangements have been made with one of the many middlemen or brokers,[11] or unless the calling card of a state or federal official has been obtained requesting that the person be helped. But regardless of the arrangements, one can never be sure that the request will not be turned down because arrangements on the case have already been made.

Influence peddling has far-reaching ramifications for the quality of political relationships existing between the populace in the city and the political authorities at the municipal, state, and national level. These ramifications will be discussed specifically in a later chapter, but suffice it to say here that all expectations of political relations are coercive. This is the essence of "political marginalization."

The central section of the city also houses quarters for the police —in reality, the locus of coercion. The most obvious coercion takes place between the police and the local inhabitants, and it extends to all parts of the city. Nevertheless, the presence of the police (*azules*) in the central section, generally ill trained, low paid, aggressive louts, is felt most acutely.[12]

For example, in 1971, especially during the wet season when streetlights were often burnt out, workers returning home expected to be harassed by police. Workers who lived near the jailhouse, next to the Municipal Palace, had to agree to pay a bribe or they would be beaten, arrested, and jailed (figs. 14 and 15). Even after massive demonstrations in 1972 and 1973, when some police-community relations changed for the better, police reputations remained suspect.

The central section of the city, then, is distinct from other sections in that the administrative and governing bodies of the municipality are in its midst, and negative attitudes toward them are

Fig. 14. Paying the police.

Fig. 15. Familial intervention.

therefore heightened. In addition to the Municipal Palace and the city jail, one of the city's first elementary schools adjoins the west portion of the Municipal Palace,[13] and to its west is a prenatal-care clinic and a kindergarten. The significance of the positioning of these service-connected centers is that part of the spoils system of office permits the wife of the mayor and the wives of councilmen to establish such centers next to their husband's sinecure, with the rationale of maximizing the protection and/or education of their children. Unfortunately, these are another means of siphoning off considerable municipal funds into the pockets of the mayor, the councilmen, and their spouses.

In many ways the street that fronts the Municipal Palace is the setting of power and the place where the different domains of power connect with one another. Calle Chimalhuacan (see B, map 3) provides the observer a glimpse of the distinctiveness of this section, and in 1979 it had become the elite street in the city in terms of politics, business, and social pretensions—the place where future major arrangements are made.

On this street, directly across from the Municipal Palace, the PRI headquarters of the federal deputy and his *suplente* are situated in a two-story building with the deputy's name painted in large red letters over the portion of the facade with no windows.[14] This street is the site also of the Netzahualcoyotl Chamber of Commerce, whose president, an ex-mayor of Netzahualcoyotl, takes his friends and associates to lunch at a newly constructed (1974) restaurant located across the street from the Municipal Palace.

Within a two-block distance west on Chimalhuacan is the head-quarters of the third councilman—the principal protector and supporter for illegal land invasions in *colonias* 63, 64 and 66 (map 2). East on Chimalhuacan are the headquarters of the Movimiento Juvenil of the CRC, built with forced contributions from three furniture-store owners in the area.[15] One block east of the juvenile headquarters stands the headquarters of subcommittee 21 of the CRC, as well as the building in which one of the city's municipal judges sat in chambers. This judge was, in 1974, one of the political righthand men of the third councilman. He extended judicial protection to land invaders in those *colonias* mentioned and also to those in *colonias* 32-35 (map 2) in the eastern section. Finally, on Caballo Bayo, a street adjoining the western section of the pre-natal clinic and located one-half block north of the palace, a formerly powerful political group has its headquarters.

In 1974 the social security system was in the process of building a block-square administration building on the corner of Chimal-huacan and Central (F, H, map 3), which is only a half-block from the Municipal Palace. This addition reflects the national attention Netzahualcoyotl has attracted, since few projects worth 80 million pesos are begun in Mexico unless political elites in formal sectors have had their political attention stimulated.

Centers of power and quasi control, however, are not the only distinctions that contrast the central section to the rest of the city. I have stated, further, that Chimalhuacan became the elite street of the city. In addition, indications of incipient bourgeoisification had already begun. It was in the central section of the city that the syntheses of mass-cultural artifacts and native Mexican ones were blending, as expressed in the construction and content of two recently opened restaurants, which differed remarkably from those of the immediate past.

These differences could be seen in such things as the white table-cloths covering custom-made Mexican-style furniture and the decorative Mexican tile floors. Furthermore, the primary purpose of these restaurants is to serve food, in contrast to many of the luncheonettes (loncherías), which are fronts for houses of prostitution. Other differences of note include the prices for drinks and food—prices that are considerably higher than those in other places in Netzahualcoyotl—and the four-person rock bands that blare out poor imitations of British and American hard rock over the cacophony of passing buses. Customers attracted to these spots are mostly males who can afford to eat and drink in rather ostentatious surroundings. They include not only the local políticos and members of the Chamber of Commerce but also "swingers" in mod outfits. For males, the dress consists of platform shoes; bell-bottom trousers; open, wide-collared white rayon shirts worn underneath short bolero jackets; all topped with pseudostyled, razor-cut long hair. For females, dress consists of even higher platform shoes; mini-, midi-, or sometimes full-length skirts; braless tops covered with dangling beads; topped off by overpainted faces and nearly clean, long hair. For the most part, except for the older males who join in rounds of drinks while discussing the day's events, both places are mainly haunts of young persons. It is remarkable that only a few years before, in 1971, at the very place where these swingers sipped on Coca-Cola, I witnessed one dog attacking another in a pool of green fetid water.

The facade of the central section in 1974 was not the same as it had been in 1971. In 1971, regardless of season, the city's appearance reflected all of the land developers' sins. In that year persons living in the immediate environs who used Chimalhuacan as a major transit route had to contend with deep ruts of mud during the wet season and wind-blown sand during the dry, since wide expanses of the central section were not yet developed. Occasionally, the sandstorms were so fierce that buses—the main means of transport—were obscured from view entirely as they traveled over the unpaved streets, adding to an already fouled environment more kicked-up dirt and oil exhaust smoke.

Not only did persons have to contend with the pollution resulting from sand and exhaust, they also suffered from noise pollution, especially if they lived within a two-block radius of the Municipal Palace. In fact, over the three-year period, neither noise nor exhaust pollution has abated. With the recent paving of the street, however, an appreciable decrease in dust pollution is noticeable.

The basic source of noise pollution has continued to be the 500 or so buses that traffic through Netzahualcoyotl without mufflers. Drivers intentionally cause buses to backfire. Noise, however, is one of the hallmarks of an urbanizing area like Netzahualcoyotl. Regardless of season and climate, except on Sunday, all sections of the city are subject to the same variety of noises, and few areas of the city are more noisy than the central section. Indeed, from 6 A.M. until 10 P.M., on weekdays, the noise from buses is added to by the voices of street hawkers selling tamales,[16] clothes, and pots and pans. In addition, the striking of hand-held brass bells by garbage men announce the collection of garbage; motorcycles and cars add a variety of sounds; and the occasional drag race makes a particularly notable contribution to the din.

Sunday noises in the central section, especially along Chimalhuacan, did not change appreciably between 1971 and 1974. Except for the call to reveille for the Netzahualcoyotl reserve army unit and the daylong barks of marching orders to the 300 or 400 young men assembled in the Plaza de Armas, Sunday's cacophony seems slightly toned down compared to the weekdays. Of course, festival days in the city, such as Independence Day, celebrated on September 16, and the celebration of the Juarez's centennial, provide added incentives to noisemakers. Politicians shouting out the Grito de Dolores and the explosion of firecrackers blend nicely with the din of street noises.[17]

By 1974 the appearance of the central section had changed considerably, but in other, more important ways it had changed little.

Except for its political distinctions, the central section had become physically much like the western section of a few years earlier. The process of stabilization in the central section had scarcely begun because of incessant political conflicts. People took what they could while they could, focusing on the stability of their own lives.

For the rest of Ciudad Netzahualcoyotl, the basic problems of environment, rainfall and sandstorms, and conflict over land ownership remained endemic. Toward the eastern parts of the city, however, rain- and sandstorms hit particularly hard because of an open expanse of plain between the easternmost section of the city and the municipality of Chimalhuacan, located three kilometers away. Therefore, most of the northern and middle areas of the eastern part of the city, from Corrido del Norte (A, map 4) to Pantitlan (F, map 4), are as depressed as Colonia del Sol, described earlier. Social conditions are such that even in one of the neighborhoods where the state Judicial Ministry annex is located, it is largely up to individuals and family networks to defend their households against the myriad dangers of street gangs, roving policemen, land invaders, and even packs of dogs (fig. 16). One informant told me that her granddaughter had been attacked by a pack of dogs during the night when she went out to urinate. Thereafter, her grandmother kept the fire going all night. She also took extra precautions by boarding up an open gate and building concrete-block walls completely around the *jacal*. It is ironic that this woman's *jacal* was worth less than the wall built to protect it.

There are groups of families in these areas that not only effectively protect their own households against intruders but also control entire square-block sections through networks of family members. For example, through an extended network of forty-seven family members, one army captain has controlled the ingress and egress for three minor streets. He is, for all intents and purposes, the *cacique* (political leader) of the area in which his network is established.[18] His power is such that when recent attempts were made by a surgical team to institute home visitations for preventive medical care, they were rebuffed by this *cacique*. It was only after pressure was brought to bear from higher domains that he acquiesced to the medical teams; however, interference continued

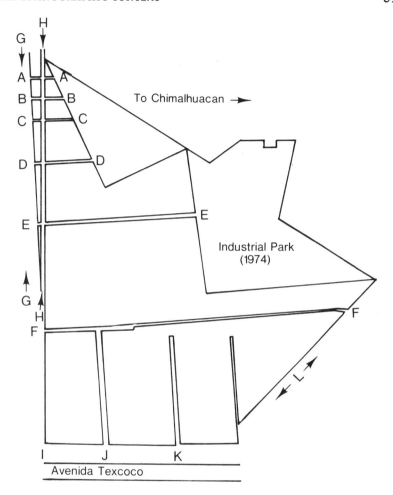

EASTERN SECTION

E-W Streets	N-S Streets
A. Corrido de Norte	G. Carmelo Perez
B. Rancho Grande	H. Zona Federal
C. Las Mananitas	I. (Perlitas: 1974)
D. Rayito del Sol	J. John F. Kennedy (Col. Aguilas only)
E. Chimalhuacan	K. Tepozanes
F. Pantitlan	L. Los Reyes

Map 4. Eastern section of Netzahualcoyotl.

Fig. 16. Gang member and dog surprised at night.

to such a degree that doctors and nurses had difficulty asking questions. If a wife of one of the *cacique's* relatives complained about a
physical condition, she was given quick notice by one of the *cacique's* male relatives that she had no business expressing her complaint.

What is most obvious in some of these areas is that neither
municipal, state, nor federal political control has been effectively
instituted. In addition, at the local level of control in these areas of
semiautonomy, petty *caciques* have various ties to persons in positions of legal authority. The *caciques* manage to prevent the imple-
mentation of legitimate political control by calling upon these ties.
They accomplish this through the utilization of legal maneuvers
such as writs or lawsuits. Some of these petty *caciques* are clients
of patrons who are in exactly those political and judicial positions
responsible for the control of the *caciques*. Thus, "losing" docu-

mentation is one "favor for friends" that patrons employ to help *caciques* remain, to some extent, in control of areas. This lack of effective municipal control is dramatically exhibited by the presence of youth gangs that gather at different spots and waylay passersby. In much of the eastern section, a great deal of political control is exercised through consanguine or peer networks rather than through formal governmental institutions.

Such semiautonomy is not peculiar to Netzahualcoyotl's eastern section but applies also to many other parts of the city as they existed in the 1960-1974 period. In fact, in sections that were illegally occupied through 1974 (2, 33-35, 63, 64, 66, 69, 72, 78, map 2), the same, basically anarchic conditions persist.

Yet the eastern section can boast of two unique attractions: the *toreo* and the industrial park. The *toreo*, called Plaza Aurora, for many years has been one of the favorite recreational sites in Netzahualcoyotl, where bullfights and wrestling matches are held.[19] The arena is located on the corner of Madrugada and Carmelo Perez streets (E, map 4), on the easternmost edge of the Colonia Aurora Oriente neighborhood (60, map 2). This recreational center is consistently filled on Sundays, especially for the wrestling matches, popular with both young and old. Like wrestling audiences everywhere, these spectators boo the villains and cheer the heroes. After bullfights, some persons go to a family-run restaurant that advertises their specialty as "typical bullfight food": soup of brains, exquisite stomach lining, and barbequed and/or fried hog skins. Needless to say, none of the above is actually "typical bullfight food," although sometimes the bull itself is served. This fare is little different from that available in luncheonettes.

The beginnings of an industrial park (map 4) make up the second attraction in the eastern section. By 1974 the area had still not seen its first industrial building; yet the park may eventually take shape. In any case, no amount of capital-intensive industrialization in this area can possibly cope with the economic needs of its citizens, because capital-intensive industrialization was precisely the economic strategy responsible for the plight of the population and the area in the first place.

SUMMARY OF PART I

In the previous chapters, I have argued that marginalized populations in Mexico are the unwanted and "redundant" masses of people created by capital-intensive industrial strategies. Such populations are made up of geographically displaced persons who are, furthermore, culturally "delocalized." They appear in urban concentrations such as Ciudad Netzahualcoyotl. I have argued, in contrast to other commentators, that such populations are not *individually* prevented from vertical mobility; instead, *selected* individuals achieve such mobility. This mobility *ensures* inequality and scarcity for the masses of such marginalized populations. I have argued, too, on empirical grounds that marginalized populations cannot be "demarginalized" or integrated. The notion of integration, I stated, was part of the meta-myth that provides a rationalization for the continuation and expansion of the cult of elites.

I argued in chapter 2 that the quantitative indicators of income and occupation define "economic marginalization," and a substantial body of work identifies such occupations as part of a "secondary labor market," or informal sector. I noted the large number of persons in Ciudad Netzahualcoyotl who participate in such labor markets and illustrated that succeeding generations seem to be destined for similar occupations and incomes. I also argued, however, that economic marginalization of this type should not be considered synonymous with behavioral or cultural marginalization, as "culture of poverty" arguments have stipulated. In fact, for the population of Ciudad Netzahualcoyotl Izcalli, the opposite is true.

In chapter 3 the emphasis was on the description of the environmental and social contexts in which many persons live. Among the important factors in this discussion was that Netzahualcoyotl was created largely by persons who purchased land and homes in "clandestine subdivisions" or who invaded land. The area has been contaminated, disowned, and unprovided with basic services, and this has made life quite difficult and dangerous. Nevertheless, both marginalized and nonmarginalized populations in the city participate in ritual, recreational, and social activities.

Among the areas most difficult to live in are those in which the population has had to interact with political authorities, either administrative or judicial. Corruption, exploitation, and violence toward the politically marginalized population are standard forms of political behavior. Acts of obeisance and supplication to get people released from jail, obtain a construction permit, or gain a writ against an administrative decision are common occurrences. This type of political marginalization entails the expectation of disadvantage vis-à-vis those who are more "connected" or who have more leverage.

I have argued also, however, that populations in such circumstances are not necessarily passive or acquiescent to their condition. Environmental, physical, economic, and political conditions in Netzahualcoyotl had been ripe for a number of years for the formation of large-scale political movements. Yet I will show that even such political movements are part of larger "rituals of marginality" in which many Mexicans participate.

PART II

The Human Dimension in
the Politics of Marginality,
1969-1974

In the discussion of the following chapters, two basic features are emphasized. The first is how Mexican social structure was primary in the development and eventual limitation of the Congreso Restaurador de Colonos. The CRC, as happens to all local political structures, eventually confronted the entangling processes of the networks of elites and became assimilated within the boundaries of the formal sector.

The second feature emphasized here are the basic social principles in operation between elites and marginalized populations and within such marginalized populations. As will be seen, *within* marginalized populations, relationships are of a *multiple-interest* type, such that affective, instrumental, and developmental activities overlap; relationships are *multiple-stranded*, such that political, economic, recreational, ritual, residential, and familial contexts bind persons involved; most relationships are relatively equal, or *symmetrical*, such that reciprocity is generally manifest; and relationships are *legitimate* and *allocated*, such that cultural symbols and meanings "glue" cohorts into what can generally be termed as "social friendship relations."

A different social principle is in operation, however, *between* elites and marginalized persons. Social relationships take shape as "political friendships," such that exchanges are largely of a *single-interest* type and political activity is paramount in importance; relationships are *single-stranded*, such that there are few contexts other than the political that bind the persons involved; relationships are unequal, or *asymmetrical*, such that the local population or local leader are subordinate and the elites dominant; and, perhaps most important, relationships are basically *coercive* and *delegated*; such that short-term concerns and immediate payoffs are emphasized and authority is "trickled down" to the local level.

In the description of events that follows, we see that when these two principles of social action operate simultaneously within the same social field, behavioral contradictions that must be resolved are created for local leaders. The resolution is inevitably in favor of the elites and includes the condition whereby coopted political leaders speak for the populations they represent at the local level but, in fact, join the formal sector or its fringes. The resolution includes the condition whereby the basis of political support for the local leaders no longer emerges from the local level but rather from within the formal-sector domain of elites. Instead of legitimate support being allocated from the bottom, coercive support is delegated from the top (Adams 1975:42-45; Swartz 1968:24, 31). Such a "resolution" transforms the basis of support from legitimacy to coercion, and relationships between leaders and supporters become culturally "delocalized," that is, stripped of their local context, meaning, and affect; institutionalized rituals of marginality expressed by patron-client relationships, political friendships, brokerage, and "favors" are established between local leaders and the elites in the formal sectors. *Individuals* become integrated, but the local populations become further pauperized and cut off. Individuals who were once legitimate political leaders become part of an illegitimate framework of relations, and they eventually acquire new class-based identities and relationships. For the rest of the population, inequality and scarcity are guaranteed.

The irony is that even though the Congreso Restaurador de Colonos arose as a partial response to basic conditions of inequality and scarcity, it eventually became one more mechanism that contributed to even greater scarcity and inequality for many in Netzahualcoyotl.

The CRC and Its Emergence:
The Nature of the Political Field

On July 17, 1969, forty persons met together in a house in the central section of the city to discuss what the leader of the group described as "the great fraud" committed by land developers in the valley of Texcoco, including the now-drained lake bed of Texcoco. According to the leader of the Frente de Afirmación Revolucionaria, Sergio Maldonado López (formerly a carpenter from the state of Veracruz), national lands had been illegally sold by land developers to the inhabitants of Netzahualcoyotl. He claimed that presidential decrees issued by President Pascual Ortíz Rubio in 1931, by President Lázaro Cardenas in 1936, and by President Miguel Alemán in 1949, all proclaimed the lake bed of Texcoco as national lands.

With this announcement, a political protest movement of major proportions was born, which, in its various manifestations, created local power structures in Netzahualcoyotl through 1974. The first version of this movement—its resources, personalities, and appeals—had a life of approximately two years, from July 17, 1969, to June 23, 1971. Even in this initial phase of the Congreso Restaurador de Colonos, however, a central pattern of development was established and became apparent. This initial appeal was based on alleged actions in domains far above those at the local level, and, as will be seen, many of the relationships that were generated reflected this initial thrust of action.

Political claims, however, were not foreign to Maldonado. In his home state of Veracruz, in the town of Talacingo,[1] Maldonado had been a "peasant's representative" in the late 1950s. He led a movement to expropriate land from a woman named Marican Carrion, and after accomplishing this, he and others took armed control of the town, resulting in the death of an opponent. He was briefly arrested, released, and then fled his bond. He settled in the federal district in the late fifties, and by 1961 Maldonado had moved to Ciudad Netzahualcoyotl.

In 1961, Maldonado purchased land in one of the neighborhoods for 17,000 pesos, which was to be paid in monthly installments. After building his *jacal*, he lived on the land for six years. During this period he paid 2,371.90 pesos toward the lot, but the payments were intermittent and he was ultimately sued for nonpayment. As a result, he signed a new contract with the land developer in 1967 for the same piece of land, and 1,837.00 pesos were returned to him. From 1967 through 1969, Maldonado continued to have difficulty making his monthly payment, and a new series of lawsuits was brought against him.

In the meantime, while supporting himself as a carpenter, Maldonado began the Frente de Afirmación Revolucionaria—an organization devised to improve social services within the city of Netzahualcoyotl. For the six-year period between 1963 and 1969, he had little success. But in October 1968, he became part of the political network of Sanchez Cárdenas, who had been campaigning for the office of federal deputy for the Partido Popular Socialista (PPS).[2] Cárdenas's campaign manager was a young man, Antonio Mondragón, who had previously been a candidate for the same party in the Texcoco district but had been defeated. After Cárdenas's election, Mondragón became a counselor to Maldonado in political organizing, and by the time of the July 17, 1969, announcement, he had organized a network of thirty-two subcommittees throughout Netzahualcoyotl. It was at this point that the Congreso Restaurador de Colonos came into existence, and with it came the claim that "land fraud" had been committed.

Maldonado's contacts with political organizations predated his association with the PPS. In his home state of Veracruz years

before, he had been an organizer for a splinter group called El
Consejo Agrarista Mexicano, and this provided him with a claim
to the patronage of the president of El Consejo Agrario, Humberto
Serrano, who was at one time the secretary-general of the Central
Campesino Independiente (CCI), a subdivision of the Movimiento
de Liberación Nacional ("Movement of National Liberation," or
MLN). This last organization developed in the aftermath of the
Latin American Conference for National Sovereignty, which was
held in March 1961, under the auspices of the World Peace Council. By 1965, however, the CCI had been coopted by the Mexican
government, and one of the resulting splinter groups was El Consejo Agrario (Johnson 1972:83, Anderson and Cockroft 1966:25).

Yet Serrano was more than Maldonado's patron in the sense of
providing him access to organizational networks. The two men
had established a *compadre* relationship in which Serrano served
as baptismal godfather to Maldonado's youngest daughter. This
integration of personalistic ritual relationships with ideological
and organizational relations became one of the resources with
which the CRC was established. What must be noted, however, is
that leftist commitment does not eliminate the form by which poli-
tical-patron relationships are established, nor does it eliminate the
patron-client structure.

This relationship provided the means through which negotiations took place and eventual entanglement with state authorities
became possible. Approximately one year after the initial
announcement of July 17, 1969, Serrano arranged for Maldonado
to meet and discuss the various issues of the CRC movement with
José G. Zuno, who was the father-in-law of President Echeverria
(1970-1976). In turn, Zuno wrote a letter of introduction to ex-
President Lázaro Cárdenas del Río, who was one of Mexico's most
respected and popular national figures.[3] In turn, ex-President Cárdenas wrote a letter of introduction to the governor of the state of
Mexico, who had recently (1970) been inaugurated. These three
contacts with members of elite domains, and the steps leading to
their establishment, illustrate the basic sequence of relations necessary to generate a local political structure, given the nature of the
Mexican social and political structure. Each contact and network

relation is termed an *arreglo* ("arrangement"), and in fact *arreglos* transcend ideology, although leftists especially deny their use. Other members of the core of the CRC also were experienced in political organizing and in the art of establishing the necessary contacts and *arreglos* with elite domains.

As mentioned previously, Antonio Mondragón, Maldonado's organizer, provided the organizing impetus for what was to become the CRC. He was aided in his efforts by the fact that he was a capable intellectual strategist, a pragmatist, and he was well read. Unlike Maldonado, who was a poor speaker, Mondragón was an eloquent, poetic speaker who could quickly capture an audience's attention with his use of extended metaphors. A short, slight, buck-toothed, fair-haired mestizo, Mondragón's ideological foundation was set while he served as an attendant to an elderly woman whose nephews owned a factory where he had been working. As a common laborer, he had quickly caught the attention of the nephews through his ability to follow printed instructions. Because their aunt suffered from cataracts, the nephews hired Mondragón as her reader and attendant. She, in turn, introduced Mondragón to the writings of Marx, Lenin, and Mao, and from that time on, he continued to study on his own until he developed a sophisticated understanding of Marxist theory. With ideology in hand, he joined the PPS, became an ardent supporter, but then went underground once he attached himself to Maldonado's clique. In time, Mondragón became Maldonado's intellectual strategist.

Besides his intelligence and the organizational training he acquired within the PPS, Mondragón's oratorical skills were second to none among those involved in the 1969 through 1971 period. As Roberto López Cobos (see chapter 6) states, Mondragón *"es chingón para la palabra"* ("is a fucking good speaker"). This resource provided the greatest impetus to the formation of the CRC. Yet Mondragón had not learned this skill in the PPS but had developed it earlier as a participant in a peasant group (of which he later became secretary-general) in the state of Hidalgo, where he was born in 1940. Like Maldonado, the rural experience provided Mondragón with an understanding of his audience in

Netzahualcoyotl, many of whom were but one generation removed from direct rural living and many others of whom had only
a decade before been landed or unlanded peasants. Mondragón
transformed the socioeconomic conditions under which his Netzahualcoyotl audiences lived to metaphorical equivalencies of his
own past experiences, with which his audiences could empathize.

In addition to Mondragón, Maldonado's resources included
others who brought suitable experiences for the positions they
were to fill in the political field. The person in charge of the
"fuerzas de choque" ("shock forces")—a group of males serving as
bodyguards and bully boys—had ample experience. He was Aris-
teo Cabezas, from the state of Oaxaca, for whom two warrants
had been issued for his arrest.[4] He was wanted for fraud, carrying
concealed weapons, aggravated assault, defamation of character,
disturbing the peace, and homicide. Cabezas became responsible
for the security of the "líderes." Angel Carbajal Morales, placed in
charge of "Honor and Justice,"[5] had been heavily involved in the
student movement of 1968 in the secondary schools, and had been
a member of one of the two strongest gangs in the city. Arturo
Valenzuela Cisneros (see chapter 6) had worked actively in the PRI
political process within the city of Netzahualcoyotl. He had been a
campaign worker for one of the mayoral candidates in 1969 and
had been rewarded with a job as a security guard at one of the
newspapers in Mexico City. Four years later, in 1973, he used this
association with the newspaper as a resource during a factional
division. Valenzuela was intimately familiar with the internal
workings of the PRI and the Confederación Nacional de Organizaciones (CNOP),[6] which provided the PRI with organizational support during election periods in Mexico. As one of the three key
organizations within the PRI, the CNOP provided both money
and bodies for the campaigns of candidates selected for the election ritual, and Valenzuela's PRI experience was utilized fully.

An additional resource brought into the field from the various
arenas was organizational knowledge. Maldonado, Mondragón,
and Valenzuela were well qualified to create networks of relations
both vertically and horizontally, and this would ensure some success in achieving their goals even before the July 17 announcement

and the creation of the Congreso Restaurador de Colonos. From most appearances, before the July 17 announcement the Frente de Afirmación Revolucionaria, of which Maldonado was president, was just another civic organization with which inhabitants in the city were familiar. In fact, thirty-two subcommittees were organized throughout the city under the Frente's banner. The subcommittees collected 6,000 payments of 118 pesos each for the installation of sewage and potable-water lines at 2,000 pesos per household. The municipality, in contrast, charged 700 pesos for the installation of water-and-sewage lines. These moneys (the equivalent of about $50,000)[7] were never accounted for but were said to have been deposited in a *financiera* ("national finance corporation"). In fact, these moneys provided financial support for the leadership prior to the actual "creation" of the political movement. The irony was that these moneys would eventually be utilized as a political resource to topple the principal leader—Sergio Maldonado López—two years later.

Personality qualifications, ease with the spoken word, organizational experience, fit of backgrounds to statuses, accumulation of moneys, creation of networks of supporters and the establishment of thirty-two subcommittees, establishment of vertical relations with national brokers, and creation of a "front" organization, although all necessary factors, were not sufficient for a political movement until after Maldonado's initiative with the July 17, 1969, announcement. Basically, the public proclamation of July 17 stated that persons living in Netzahualcoyotl had been sold property by land developers illegally, since the former lake bed of Texcoco had been declared national lands by three different presidents, and that this "fraud" perpetrated against the nation should not go unpunished. Furthermore, the federal government was asked to intervene on behalf of the inhabitants, to nationalize the lands, and to provide needed urban services that the land developers had not provided.

Insofar as the ideological content of the announcement was concerned, two aspects were important. One demonstrated the cooperation of the local, municipal, and state authorities with the land developers. It demonstrated, too, that each mayor of the city since 1953, and each governor of the state (excluding the one who took office the following year, in 1970), had conspired to defraud the nation of its national lands, protected under Article 27 of the Mexican Constitution.

This first aspect, however, demonstrated also that urban services were nonexistent because land developers and municipal and state authorities had worked closely to ensure that contracts promising sewage lines, potable water, utilities, and other urban services were *not* fulfilled. This failure to provide services is the classic problem in all clandestine developments, and was especially so for much of Ciudad Netzahualcoyotl, where few areas in the city had developed sewage, potable water, or utility lines as called for by purchase contracts.

The second aspect demonstrated xenophobic sensitivity. The surnames of the land developers were cited as proof that "foreigners," together with land developers, were responsible for conditions in Netzahualcoyotl. Appendix B provides a complete list of land-development companies and their owners. Of the nineteen owners listed, nine have non-Hispanic surnames, and hence were identified as "foreigners." Whether they actually were or were not Mexicans is moot: the fact that they had non-Spanish surnames was sufficient proof for supporters and leadership. Furthermore, as a tactic this charge was unbeatable, since denial and protest by those accused placed them in a "catch-22" situation: the more denial, the greater the propensity to conclude they were foreign.

The public goal, then, was to have the land "nationalized" and to have the federal government intervene to supply urban services, the rationale being that the land had been illegally usurped by land developers, who were foreigners, and contracts for services had been neither enforced nor fulfilled. But the public goal also had attached to it a tactic that appealed to residents: a call for a boycott of all mortgage payments, city and state taxes, license fees, water and electricity charges, and building permit fees, until the federal government intervened. This boycott of payments, introduced as a pragmatic tactic, became in time both the short-range goal and the short-range payoff. Moreover, leaders who did not adhere to this tactic lost support.

But the political field, when it was created by the announcement, was already a receptive arena. Ecological, social, economic, and political conditions, as described in previous chapters, were such that large numbers of land squatters and legal landholders were attracted by the CRC's public goals. Indeed, 40 percent of the families of Netzahualcoyotl had not purchased the lot or house where they lived (Tamayo 1971:30). These residents sought safety within an organization that could provide them protection and alliances as well as identification with some sort of political structure.

In addition, a sizable number of persons who were not land squatters joined the CRC when its public goals were announced. These people joined because, unlike land squatters, they had been denied the various services promised by land developers in the area. In particular, promises of urban services were largely unkept, and, more important, the legality of many sales was questionable. In fact, of lots purchased, I estimate that 25 percent were either sold to more than one person by land developers or were not legally registered by them.[8]

Map 5 delineates the best estimate of the pattern of legal and illegal lot holdings between 1960 and 1974. The areas on the map shaded by straight vertical lines were populated largely by land invaders; the areas shaded by wavy horizontal lines were populated approximately equally by land invaders and by lot owners with service or tenure disputes; the unshaded areas were occupied by lot owners with service or tenure disputes.

Although most parts of the city were settled by both land squatters and land buyers (the central section was predominantly settled by both), the western and eastern sections were heavily occupied by land squatters. These differences, as will be shown, had important ramifications for schisms that later developed within the CRC, and for the character of support for the resulting factions. What will become apparent is that the "illegal section" provided continuing support for what was to become the official government leadership of the CRC.

Such were the conditions in the political field when the July 17, 1969, announcement was made declaring the public goals of the

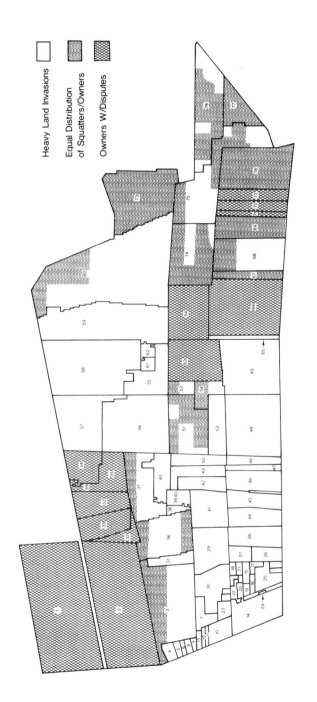

Map 5. Distribution of Legal and Illegal Lot Holdings. For identification of numbers, see map 1.

Heavy Land Invasions

Equal Distribution
of Squatters/Owners

Owners W/Disputes

CRC. Gaining support for public goals, however, is an ideological, organizational, and social process. The first sometimes leads to factionalism; the second to claims of originality of purpose and purity; the last to the disintegration of cherished relationships as well as personal alienation. These consequences will be explored in the last sections of this work. At that time, in July 1969, however, these consequences were not predicted or sought, nor could they be avoided during the heat of recruitment, the generation of organizational support, and the establishment of trust and exchange relations between those who were to form the core of the political leadership and those who were to allocate resources to them. In 1969 such processes were just beginning. An examination of the manner in which the CRC generated its support is crucial to an understanding of its synthesis as a political structure.

ORGANIZATION AND RECRUITMENT OF THE CRC

By 1973 the CRC was divided into fifty-eight subcommittees over which an executive committee provided policy and goal direction. Within the executive committee, offices were divided according to function, some having specific roles, some largely honorific. Like its component subcommittee levels, the executive committee was hierarchically organized, as shown in table 14 (see also fig. 17).

As president of the executive committee, Sergio Maldonado López held supreme decision-making power in the CRC and, in fact, was informally known as the "Líder Máximo" ("Maximum Leader"). He, like the secretary-general, was paid through a fifty-peso-per-person membership fee and whatever gifts members wanted to contribute.

The other offices varied in importance according to the personality of the individual holding it and the density of his social support. Few privileges were apparent except insofar as the individual was able to generate power by surrounding himself with a personal following. In fact, each office, except the two top ones, possessed power only according to the support awarded it. Thus, Mondragón, who was the secretary of youth action, in time

Fig. 17. Leadership of the CRC, 1971 (faces masked to preserve confidentiality).

TABLE 14

EXECUTIVE COMMITTEE OFFICES OF THE CONGRESO RESTAURADOR DE COLONOS
(AS OF SEPTEMBER 18, 1969)

President of the Executive Committee (Maldonado)
Secretary-General (Guadalupe Flores C.—begins his own organization later)
Secretary of Organization
Secretary of Acts and Promises
Secretary of the Interior
Secretary of Press and Propaganda
Treasurer
Secretary of Social Action
Secretary of Youth Action (Mondragon)
Secretary of Feminine Action
Secretary of Relations and Public Works
Secretary of Development, Culture, and Assistance
Secretary of Technical Studies
Secretary of Military Action
Secretary of the Exterior (Valenzuela)
President of the Commission of Honor and Justice
Vigilance Committee Head
Official Elder
Coordinators (4)
Assessors (3)

NOTE: These various offices were amended and reduced from eighteen to thirteen after a schism in November 1970, in which Secretary-General Guadalupe Flores C. became president of a new CRC and joined the city administration. The secretary of press and propaganda also joined this new group.

became the main figure, outmaneuvering the rest of the hierarchy. He accomplished this through the operations of his followers. Figure 17 shows the leadership in 1971.

The organizational process followed through a number of steps between 1969 and 1971, each of which focused on dispersing information to large numbers of persons without the benefit of mass-communication devices such as television or radio. Instead, a combination of mass and individual techniques were used, beginning with pamphleteering.

Every Sunday morning, persons going to church, to the city, or to visit family or friends would be met on the streets by young men passing out announcements of a meeting to be held within a particular *colonia* targeted to be "worked."[9] As Appendix C shows, the method used to gain attention was the distribution of leaflets claiming a variety of wrongs. The appeal focused first on land fraud and the attendant crimes committed; second, on the lack of urban services; third, on contaminated water, stressing that where water was available it was not fit for human use; fourth, on the contention that the Constitution had been violated; fifth, on the machinations of foreigners; sixth, on the use of false advertising; seventh, on the suggestion that neglecting payments meant less money for the enjoyment of the rich; and eighth, on the assurance that boycotting the land developers would provide for the patrimony of their children.

As each person was given a leaflet, he was told the meeting time and place and was given a quick summary of the information on the leaflet. This was to ensure that the message was relayed satisfactorily to illiterates. In any case, the meaning was clear: support was solicited by appealing to cherished values of home, children, legacy; and coercive injustices inflicted upon the city's inhabitants by the land developers were recognized. This combination of values regarding home and justice have affective spin-offs and layers of meaning specific to individuals; nevertheless, the appeal obviously generated broad affective reaction. At the same time, the message also illustrated a short-range goal for those being recruited: it introduced a possible reward in the midst of nothing.

But such a leaflet is insufficient, in itself, to evoke these responses. The necessary additional ingredients included all the verbal and polemical skills brought in from the various arenas to make the "call" felt. It is on these personal modes of persuasion that our analysis next focuses.

On Sundays, when each *colonia* was being "worked," a vanguard of persons would stake out the area where speakers would make their appeals. Generally, a central location was sought, such as a grocery store, a basketball court, a home, or sometimes even an empty lot. Usually permission for the use of the location had already been arranged through friendship, fictive kin, or kinship relations; never was municipal permission requested.

Regardless of location, each organizational event was announced by a sound truck followed by a march from one of the

central streets to the meeting place. On one occasion, a Cessna 170
airplane was used to blanket a large area with leaflets prior to an
assembly, but this occurred only once, and the pilot of the aircraft
was shortly thereafter visited by the state judicial police.[10]

Along with the speakers, guitar players, members of the
fuerzas de choque" ("shock forces"), with red arm bands, persons
from various subcommittees, the curious, and others simply out
for a stroll usually joined the march. When they arrived at the
meeting place, loudspeakers had already been set up and a cloth
banner with the CRC's crest was spanned between two seven-foot
poles implanted in the ground (see fig. 18). The importance of the
banner is that it identifies those marching, those present, and those
speaking as being in concord. In addition, other symbols legitimizing the CRC banner were also prominently displayed: the Mexican
flag; a banner with Emiliano Zapata's visage,[11] with slogans prominently imprinted on it; and a banner depicting Benito Juárez, also
with prominent slogans. The flag and the banners picturing these
two almost mythic heroes lent these meetings a type of legitimacy.

Since most such demonstrations were held on Sunday afternoons, lighting was unnecessary, but protection against sun or
rain was important. Usually a small stage was set up for the speakers and for the guitar players who preceded them. Cloth placed
between four poles provided a roof similar to that used by the
priests before churches were constructed.

With microphone in hand, a "warm-up" speaker usually cited
the reasons for the demonstration in that particular *colonia*. If the
colonia had not been previously "worked," the first speaker stated
that the group had been invited by one of the residents who had
shown interest in the goals of the CRC. For the most part, the secretary of press and propaganda made the warm-up speech. If the
colonia was one with an established subcommittee, however, then
the local president led off the demonstration. In either case, the
first speaker was usually followed by guitar-playing trios singing
corridos[12]—both local and regional ones, such as those from
Michoacan and Veracruz, Mexico. Local *corridos* were especially
pointed, relating in song the history and struggle of persons living
in Netzahualcoyotl and the CRC's role in alleviating "*los crímenes*

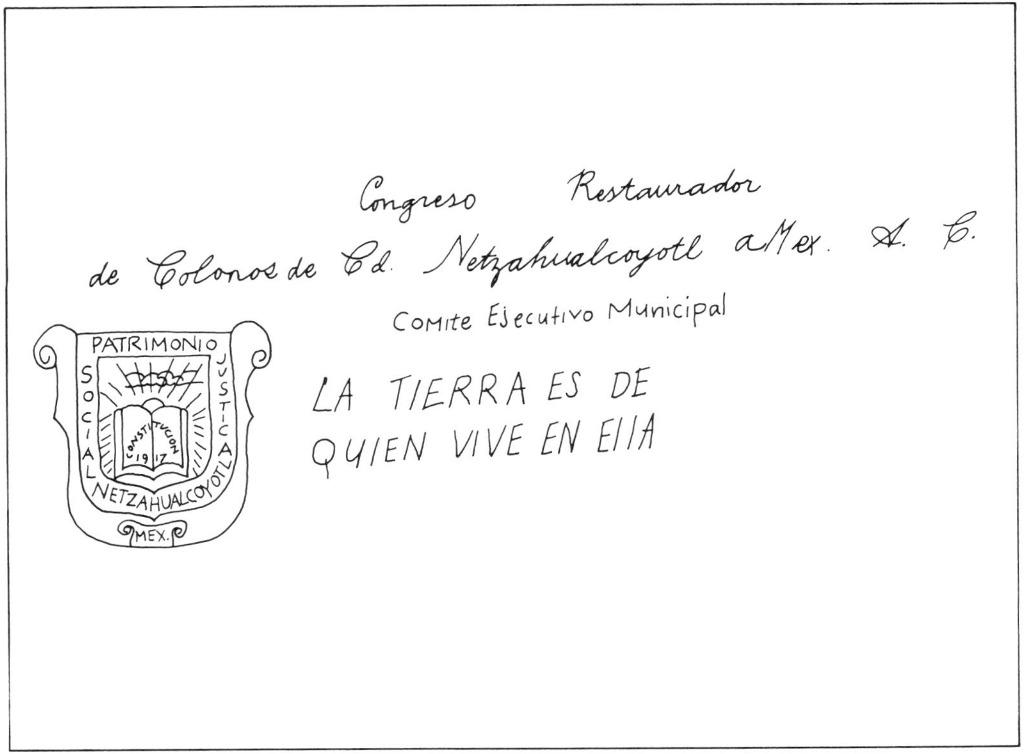

Congreso Restaurador
de Colonos de Cd. Netzahualcoyotl a/Mex. A. C.

Comite Ejecutivo Municipal

LA TIERRA ES DE
QUIEN VIVE EN EllA

PATRIMONIO
CONSTITUCION 1917
NETZAHUALCOYOTL
MEX.

Fig. 18. CRC banner with crest.

de los fraccionadores" ("the crimes of the land developers"). The songs described other issues as well, such as the student killings of 1968. For example, I recorded the following song during one of the demonstrations.

> "The Corrido of the Student"
> I am going to sing the song of the year '68.
> They killed 1,000 students in Ciudad Tlatelolco.
> The student was ready to hide in his secret mountain.
> The peasant was ready to accept his offer
> Because the people are tired of seeing their laws trampled.
> Let us give battle to these blasted bourgeois
> Let us go to Chihuahua, Let us go to Guerrero
> Let us give to the thieving government where it hurts.
> Already the bonfire is lit, like beckoning battle.
> Hooray for Genaro Vásquez, Hooray for Lucio Cabañas
> Who have made an offering of valor to my Mexican country.[13]

But the period 1969-1971 (even up to the major schism of 1973) included political demonstrations that added layers of affect to those already described. Here we would mention the variety of clothing and behavioral styles presented to audiences during this time. Although the major speakers wore straw cowboy hats similar to those worn by many in the audience, many of the younger men went hatless and wore bell-bottom trousers and knit pullovers to match many similarly dressed young men in the audience. Women with and without spouses who were CRC members were dressed as variably as the audience. Many wore what one of the women described as *"mi vestido de India"* ("my Indian dress")—a long dress down to the ankles—along with brown support hose, dilapidated shoes, a cotton blouse, and a *rebozo*. They combed their hair into braids that either hung down on each side of the head behind the ears, or were joined at the top of the head and tied together with a ribbon. For such women, this attire was worn for demonstration purposes only. Young children accompanying their mothers played while the guitars provided background music and while the warm-up speaker berated persons responsible for the ecological conditions in the particular *colonia*. The speakers, like the audience, comprised a heterogeneous sample of the population; both the singers and the speakers blended "down home" allusions into their public communications. Thus, recruitment success was partly the result of a leadership that consisted of men and women "for all seasons." This synthesis of supporters and leaders gave the political field its unique character: a combination of the rural and the urban, of folksy wisdom and trained intellect.

The speakers, too, reflected heterogeneous styles, ranging from the local subcommittee president, who alluded to local conditions, to persons like Roberto López Cobos (see chapter 7), who regaled the audience with crass double entendres to warm them up prior to the eloquence of a person like Mondragón. After the guitars had been played and the audience had cheered the *corridos* telling of the deeds of Zapata or Villa, Roberto would explain the history of the struggle against the land developers and of the municipal authorities (this was in 1970). He would be both comical and tragic, serious and joking. He referred to the land developers as *"coyotes del campo que no paran de comer de la miseria de la gente"* ("coyotes of the wild who did not stop at eating of the misery of the people"), and to the local municipal authorities as *"el grupo de viejas de la calle, pero no cobrando por lo que dan si no por lo que quitan"* ("a group of street hustlers, not charging for what they gave but for what they took").

Thus, persons like Roberto would add emphasis to leaflets and to the talks of previous speakers, repeating allegations in folksy idiom in order to reach the target population and to warm it up for later speakers. The principal speakers were usually Valenzuela and Mondragón, with Valenzuela first and Mondragón last. Maldonado seldom spoke because of a speech impediment; moreover, toward the latter part of 1971, he seldom appeared during these "working" assemblies. He spent most of his time in the Agrarian Department or in the governor's office.

Valenzuela's speech focused on the cowardly and unmanly aspects of the behavior of the land developers and municipal authorities, and he constantly reiterated his quest for social justice. Valenzuela, however, was not as good a speaker as he was an actor. He demonstrated before the audience all the signs of concern, trustworthiness, appeal, and entreaty. Appearing before the crowd, he would remove his hat, wipe his brow, and then peer from left to right. Then he would look down, place his hands on the table, if one were present, and lean over, speaking down to the ground rather than to the audience. Biting his lip, he would usually stammer out phrases that emotionally accused the federal, state, and local authorities of complicity with land developers to defraud the nation of national lands. For fifteen minutes or so he would repeat basically the same idea in different phrases and plead with those who had not yet joined to see the secretary-general of the specific subcommittee after the last speech for payment of the first *"cooperación"* ("contribution").

Then the person introducing the previous speakers would introduce Mondragón, and the last phase of the recruitment process would take place. Mondragón, hatless, would step up to the small stage—all five feet of him—tuck in his shirt, spread his feet, bend his knees, and peer at his audience for fifteen seconds or so. He would then begin his fifteen-to-twenty-minute presentation, holding the microphone closely to his lips in one hand and using the other hand to gesture. From his opening remark of *"Compañeros"* to his ending phrase, *"juntos venceremos"* ("together we will conquer"), the audience was his. The heterogeneous styles and behaviors all yielded to his persuasive speech, the rapt attention of the audience attested to by the open-mouthed stares. As one informant suggested, Mondragón was *"muy chaparro pero muy grande"* ("very short but very big").

Mondragón used the oratorical technique of extended metaphor. Thus, he would describe Netzahualcoyotl as *"un valle de lágrimas donde el patrimonio de los hijos se ahoga por las aguas de poder de las autoridades"* ("a valley of tears, where the legacy of children was drowned by the waters of power of the authorities"). The effectiveness of this type of metaphor is obvious. First, it recognized a geographical reality, in that the city was in a valley of sorts—the drained lake bed of Texcoco. Second, the location was in fact a place of sorrow, misery, and sadness, where tears were shed for a variety of causes. Third, reference to the legacy of children reflected part of the desire to "make it" among many in the audience. Fourth, the seasonal rainfall that played havoc with the daily activities of the residents was associated with the power of the authorities—a power that permitted the existing ecological conditions to persist. These layers of reference so intricately intertwined with the reality of the situation provided one of the main resources for recruiting personnel to this organization.

After each demonstration, members of the executive committee would stay to answer questions, and it was quite usual for persons not only to inquire about the goals of the organization but also to ask for relief from a particular problem. This last aspect usually was responded to affirmatively, and interviews were arranged with Mondragón, Valenzuela, or one of the other figures within the organization. Such persons were required, however, to join the organization for fifty pesos, in return for which they received a *credencial* ("membership card"). In this manner, persons were brought into the CRC organization, which continued for a year before experiencing its first serious breach.

FUSION OF THE CRC AND THE CYCLE OF COALESCENCE AND VIOLENCE

In the previous section, the description of the CRC's organizational methods shows clearly its effort to synthesize a "call" that would be effective among populations of heterogeneous styles and behaviors. The "field" as such, however, transcends city boundaries and, for that matter, city interests. By 1970 the organizational activities of the CRC had touched the interests of other domains, and hence a rapid process of entanglement with formal elite domains ensued. Nevertheless, between 1969 and 1971 the CRC began to coalesce in a manner less like a government-sponsored organization and more like a political-protest movement that encompassed areas within the city boundaries and the suburbs as well.

Within the city, the process of coalescence took two specific forms: first, the creation of primarily single-stranded relations that extended horizontally between followers and leaders and between followers and other followers. Then, in time, fictive kin, confianza, and kinship relations were created, and the single strand doubled and tripled horizontally. This can be seen in the multiplex relations between women who controlled the CRC movement during the day while the men sought work. Further discussion will elaborate this phenomenon shortly.

The second form that coalescence took concerned the parceling out of territory (to be discussed in chapter 8). By 1972 heads of some of the CRC subcommittees were dealing in the selling and occupation of lots, and were using some of the multiplex relations to hide their deeds. As will be seen, a deep schism developed between those selling and those not selling lots.

Outside of the city, the process of coalescence resulted in the establishment of patron-client relations—an aspect of the rituals of marginality—with a variety of authorities through 1971, and it terminated in the appointment of Maldonado as a "consultant" to the municipal government of the city.

Two important agents assisted in the process of coalescence. These will be described briefly so that the increasing complexity and shifts in the content of the political field may be understood. In January 1970, the new mayor of Netzahualcoyotl was installed. Prior to his election, he offered Maldonado a councilman's office within the city administration in exchange for the support of the CRC. Maldonado refused and suggested that the mayor was himself in league with the land developers. Thus began a vitriolic campaign against the mayor that utilized the offer to Maldonado as a political resource in neighborhood demonstrations.

During one of the demonstrations in which Maldonado told of the mayor's bribe, the local city police surrounded the meeting place and, after a flurry of beatings countered by rock throwing, one woman was arrested. The following week, the CRC held a demonstration in the Lyric Theater in Mexico City denouncing the mayor, demanding his removal from office, and accusing the state of Mexico's judicial police, the federal Agrarian Department, and the governor of the state of being lackeys for the land developers. That night, 500 or so followers returned to Netzahualcoyotl, demonstrated in front of the Municipal Palace, and demanded the release of María Cruz, who had been arrested in the earlier altercation.

While they were demanding the release of Ms. Cruz, a Volkswagen patrol car with two prisoners entered the side entrance to the jail, next to the Municipal Palace. As has already been mentioned, police are generally disliked. This night's demonstration had attracted both supporters and nonsupporters of the CRC who joined in the whistling and jeering at the police patrol car. When one of the policemen began to wave his pistol about, the police car was attacked, the policemen were beaten, their weapons taken, the two prisoners released, and the jail was then heavily damaged by rocks. The breach had been made, and public enmity between the CRC and the police flowed freely for the next year and a half, until June 23, 1971. As will be seen, this breach contributed to the coalescence of networks of persons within the various *colonias* that had been organized, the most significant occurring between women in the various neighborhoods.

The other coalescing agent was the election of the new state governor, who pictured himself as a concerned liberal in his two visits to Ciudad Netzahualcoyotl in late December 1969. Among the promises made in various quarters was that he would resolve the incessant problem of *paracaidismo* ("land invasions") and would establish improved urban services. In various speeches before assembled persons at the *"palacio de coyotes,"* the governor indicated that a number of irregularities would be corrected, and in so indicating, he provided political resources for the demonstrations. As he himself suggested: *"Uno tiene que ser muy hombre para vivir in Netzahualcoyotl"* ("One really has to be quite a man to live in Netzahualcoyotl").

Utilizing this rationale, the weekly demonstrations by the CRC continued to gather supporters in each *colonia*, and by January 1971 most *colonias* in large parts of the central and eastern sections of the city had been "worked." Fifty-seven subcommittees were established throughout Ciudad Netzahualcoyotl, with a few even in the western section of the city.[14] For the most part, in the older *colonias*, such as 3-29 (map 5), residents either had paid off their lots or had paid substantial portions of the mortgage. But in the case of Colonia del Sol (map 5, sec. 1) and parts of Estado de Mexico (map 5, sec. 2), local *caciques* were too well entrenched to be moved out by the CRC organizers. For these two reasons, most of the western section stayed outside of the CRC's range.

After the breach between supporters of the CRC and the police, action and reaction between the two groups continued. CRC supporters would attack passing red-and-white police cars with rocks, and the police would arrest, beat, and fine rock throwers. Such behavior, however, occurred primarily on weekends and at night, and, for the most part, was limited to men. During the week and during the day, "defensive violence" was in the hands of women.

THE COALESCENCE OF WOMEN: MULTIPLE RELATIONS AND THEIR SUPPORT FOR NETWORKS OF DEFENSE

The use of violence and confrontation was not specific to men. Since women generally worked in the household during the day, they in essence physically controlled the CRC within the various *colonias* of Netzahualcoyotl during daytime. In additon, they provided the most intense protection and assistance. The basis for such protection and participation by women were the various networks of multiple relations formed between them and articulated in communication contacts that men normally referred to as "gossip networks." From the point of view of the women, however, these communication networks were normally used to share important information about local food prices, weather conditions, health problems, schools and teachers, the availability of food supplements from governmental stores, the approach of salesmen, and posts for news about the arrival of children from school. Since there were no telephones in most homes, these communication networks were invaluable. The method, of course, was simple, since homes in Netzahualcoyotl adjoin, and most share a common wall at the rear. Communication among women was a simple matter and part of the daily processes of living.

Once the breach between the population and the police began, it was the women who basically controlled the protection of property during the day against land developers attempting to evict persons from their homes for nonpayment of utilities, and against police authorities attempting to arrest participants in the CRC. The reason is simple. During the day, most men were out looking for work or were working; but, in addition, men had not developed the kind of communication networks that existed among women.

On any given day, main "links" of women would be at home. Women such as Arturo Valenzuela's wife, Julieta, would serve as main links or relays in a communication system that would disperse information throughout the network. In this case, it merely involved Julieta peering over her back wall and calling one of the children playing in the adjoining yard. The child would then call his own mother, the two women would exchange news, and both would return to their households. The woman receiving the information from Julieta, however, would then move through her home, out the front door, and on to the adjoining households to relay the information. Children, always present in large numbers, often served as communication relays throughout the networks.

In each block there were "terminals" that not only connected one network to another but also served as "feedback stations" to the main source of information. In this case, one of the "viejas chingonas," and comadre to Julieta, would double-check times and other specific aspects of information exchanged, as well as any other "noise" in the communication that may have emerged. Like any other communication system, these networks broke down at times, resulting in shared misinformation. Nevertheless, they served a number of important political functions during the day, including the supplying of information to men about the "state" of the locality for their evening exchange. Most males were seldom either aware of the sources of their information or of the importance of these networks for the total cycle of operations and the coalescence of the CRC.

Moreover, it was in defense that such networks were especially effective. Many daytime confrontations—the battles in the larger political war—involved women, some of whom were CRC members and some not. During the day, if a policeman or a "stranger" entered any of the "worked" colonias, women, with their extensive networks of communication, could generate thirty to fifty confederates for the protection of a lot, usually within ten minutes and sometimes dressed in their "Indian" dresses.

For example, in 1971 I observed the afternoon arrival of a local municipal judge, a land developer's representative, and two policemen from the municipality, who came to serve eviction papers on a lot owner who had not made a mortgage payment since 1969. One of the comadres had used the communication network to inform the subcommittee office (in a private home). Persons there then contacted others.

Although the president of the subcommittee was at work, his wife and two female cousins accompanied the informant back to the place where the eviction was to be carried out. By the time they returned, thirty-two women with their children had gathered, as well as three adult males. Surrounding the lot's periphery and sitting in the lot itself, the women did not permit the eviction notice to be served. The judge, representative, and policemen positioned themselves across the street from the women and the lot. As soon as one of the men tried to cross the street, his way was immediately blocked by ten to fifteen women, and he was subjected to a barrage of insults. Immediately, he backed off.

During the first five minutes of activity, women continued to congregrate close to the lot, until forty to fifty stood either on the lot and sidewalk or in front of other homes next to the lot. Meanwhile, they began to taunt the land developer's representative, the judge, and the policemen, calling them cobardes ("cowards") and maricones ("sissies"), after which they would be consumed by laughter. This, of course, infuriated the male intruders, and one of the policemen took his billy club from its sheath. Ten women at the front of the group then picked up rocks and dared him to try to use it. One of the more vociferous of these comadres said: "Pero mira qué chingón contra las mujeres. Caras de papa y frijol. Que no tan machotes—no más que vengan los hombres" ("Well, just look at the fuckers, against women! Potato and bean faces. We thought you were machos—just wait until the men come home").

Of course, as soon as the women picked up the rocks, the police-men backed off. Threats of males entering the fray were unnec-essary.

Verbal confrontation, however, was usually a prelude to physi-cal violence. In the case just described, the women eventually chased the males from the street, pelting them with rocks, tearing the coat off the representative, and jabbing a stick into the anus of the judge.

Women were also utilized in other ways. One of the major tac-tics employed by the CRC during this period, and to a greater extent in 1972, was to burn down the land developers' mortgage-payment huts that were scattered throughout the city. These col-lecting centers were targets not only for nighttime firebombings but, during the day, groups of ten to twenty women would "visit" these collecting huts, loot them, throw out the workers, and, if a male were present, strip him of his clothing and throw him into one of the many nearby sewage-filled ditches.

The use of violence by women, as well as their participation in political action, has largely been ignored. It is remarkable that such activities have never been reported by social scientists like Cornelius (1975), who studied in the area at the same time these activities were taking place. One reason cited by Cornelius (1975: 12) for ignoring women in his study was based on the assumption that politics was only men's business; thus, women were left out of the sample. Findings here argue against such assumptions.

Women, however, coalesced in a manner different from men. Their activities brought them together in concert for the first time; additionally, for some of them, this was the first time they had col-lectively asserted themselves as women against men. Other more important bonds were established between these women: friend-ship (*amistad*), fictive kinswomen relations (*comadres*), and neighbor relations. In each subcommittee (fifty-eight in 1971), small networks of women bound by *confianza* ("mutual trust") became important organizational resources in the strategies of the males. But among the most important ramifications of the coales-cence of women was the emergence of a collective identity. Known affectionately as the *"viejas chingonas"* ("fucking strong women") by men and as the *"comadres"* ("godmothers") by the women themselves, their experience in confronting males or females who threatened their community's security forged them into a formidable group. The bases for such a cohort identity were the multiple-interest, multiple-stranded, symmetrical, and legitimate relations they generated over time.

Entanglement, Fission, and Reorganization of the CRC: Steps Toward Failure

In 1971 a coalescing process took place also outside of Netza-hualcoyotl. While women were tossing officials into ditches and men were risking jail daily in their confrontations with police, Maldonado was meeting with members of the governor's office, the Agrarian Department, and, through one of his leftist links, President Echeverria's executive office. In all relations and contacts established, the avenue for resolution that had been articulated in the public goals of the CRC eventually led to the newly elected governor of the state. For Maldonado, as long as he insisted upon maintaining relations with public officials, one of two things had to occur: he would either be eliminated or he would join with the public sector, which, in the state of Mexico, the governor ably represented. Maldonado opted for the latter, and on June 23, 1971, he became an official advisor to the city's mayor.

It must be understood that Maldonado had little choice but to establish relations with public-sector officials. If land-tenure problems were going to be resolved, the federal Agrarian Department was the logical agency to resolve them. If supporters needed water, sewage services, clinics, schools, and building permits, the state was similarly the logical entity to resolve such problems. But even though his political goals may have been legitimate at the outset, formal-sector entanglement eventually prevailed. Locally, Maldonado had already been approached by the mayor, and he had accepted a "favor" in a political and economic exchange with him in 1970. This favor was to persuade the prosecuting attorney for the municipality to release Arturo Valenzuela from jail after he had been arrested in a fracas outside of the Municipal Palace.

In gaining Valenzuela's release, however, Maldonado participated in a trade. He had previously acquired the deed to Valenzuela's lot and later gave it to the mayor in return for Valenzuela's release. In 1972, when the state judicial police were searching for Valenzuela, the mayor sold Valenzuela's lot to a local teacher who tried to coerce Valenzuela's wife—Julieta—into moving out. She, however, merely called upon her *comadres*, and the schoolteacher quickly left.

As a result of these events, Maldonado became entangled in arrangements that were not necessarily to his liking but that were inevitable given the web of connections necessary to accomplish the simplest task. As soon as Maldonado sought access to those resources demanded by his supporters, he was caught within a web of reciprocal but unequal arrangements in relation to domains above him. In becoming the counselor to the mayor of Netzahualcoyotl, he became a client of the official most closely identified by the CRC with the interests of the land developers. Entanglement is an enveloping process originating from above, but, as in this case, the process is inevitable and predictable regardless of professed ideology. The structure of relations, because of the limited options available to persons, like Maldonado, who approach the domains where resources are located, eventually leads to involvement in unintended arrangements. What began, in the first stage, as the politics of protest soon became the politics of marginalization, before any of the articulated public goals were achieved. This was inevitable, since, unwittingly, the public goals themselves reflected local needs versus elite control of resources.

The reaction to Maldonado's appointment as mayoral counselor was swift. For the next three weeks, in almost daily confrontations, Maldonado's home was attacked by groups throwing rocks for what was termed *otra traición* ("another betrayal"). Within what was left of the CRC, the scramble began, and a new CRC was born amid proclamations of friendship.

TABLE 15

MEMBERSHIP IN FIVE SUBCOMMITTEES OF THE CRC

Subcommittee	Total	Male	Female	Colonia Number*
22	427	348	79	58
32	262	189	73	66
16 de septiembre	187	101	86	74
Lázaro Cárdenas	122	98	24	32
8	22	14	8	36

*See map 5.

Before discussing the reconstitution of the CRC, we should establish what losses had been suffered within the organization, the supporting networks of relations, and the political field. First, three of the subcommittees left with Maldonado and joined with the CNOP.[1] This included approximately 400 persons from subcommittees 3, 10, and 17. Since accurate membership records were not consistently kept by each subcommittee, it is difficult to gauge exactly how many persons split off. A membership sample for five subcommittees randomly selected from the western, central, and eastern sections of the city in 1971 reveals subcommittee memberships ranging from a low of 22 persons in the western section, to an intermediate number of 172 persons in the eastern section, to a high of 427 persons in the central. Table 15 provides 1971 figures for total membership in the five subcommittees randomly selected from the total of fifty-eight subcommittees.

For the most part, the subcommittees that stayed with Maldonado were in the western section of the city and centered in the Colonia Estado de Mexico (map 5, sec. 2). Considering that the single largest subcommittee in Netzahualcoyotl in 1971 had a membership of 427 persons and the smallest had 22, a reasonable estimate is that about 400 supporters followed Maldonado, assuming a membership of about 250 for the largest subcommittee (3), 100 for the middle-sized subcommittee (10), and 50 for the smallest committee (17). (This approximation was verified by members of the CRC executive body, although there was no empirical, objective manner of acquiring verifiable data because of the conflict at the time.)

It should also be noted that numbers alone do not indicate the extent of the fission and the change in the complexity of the political field, as will be seen. Along with Maldonado, his wife, Teresa Artemio Reyes,[2] and her network of women also left, including a core of twelve *"chingonas"* who had multiple relations. Among males, however, no such core departed. Except for the presidents of the three subcommittees that broke away, who were supported by moneys taken in by the illegal sale of lots, Maldonado's supporters were basically self-interested persons. In fact, except for Maldonado's wife, no personnel within the core of the original executive committee joined Maldonado; thus, the original CRC leadership, as such, remained intact.

Nevertheless, this fission introduced into the political field the official power of the governor of the state and one section of the PRI: the CNOP. In entangling Maldonado, state authorities were provided some respite from demonstrations, since Maldonado himself was eventually targeted as the focus of much of the energy expended by what remained of the CRC. The fission had other ramifications. For example, various *arreglos* with functionaries within the Agrarian Department and within the governor's office, as well as links within the municipality, went with Maldonado. Although this network of *arreglos* ultimately entangled Maldonado, they had to be retained in order to facilitate requests from his supporters. The field later changed when the connecting links to supralocal and local authorities were severed. Then, even though the core leadership of the CRC did not join with Maldonado, the avenues to resolution and the resources necessary for such resolution were temporarily blocked for those still propounding the public goals of the CRC.

Other ramifications were equally important for those supporters who remained. One was Maldonado's "integration" into the municipality as an individual; another was the withdrawal from the movement of large numbers of persons who neither followed Maldonado nor continued to support the original CRC. These were people who had been willing to take the brunt of police violence but who no longer considered the CRC's mission to be a *causa justa* ("just cause"). Therefore, they left the fold of the CRC in very large numbers in the wake of Maldonado's integration. By July 28, 1971, a month after Maldonado's appointment, the best sources estimate that half of the supporters of the fifty-eight subcommittees left.[3] A variety of reasons was given, but most suggested that they were *"decepcionados y engañados por la traición"* ("disappointed and deceived by the treason"). Thus, of the fifty-eight subcommittees, totaling approximately 39,424 persons in 1971, 15,000 supporters had supposedly dropped their support by the end of July. (This is an inflated total because it is based on an inflated estimate of total membership given by subcommittee presidents. My own figures, based on an average of 213 members per subcommittee, suggest a total membership of only 12,354 persons. This number reflects a more accurate picture of the total number of persons engaged in the CRC before the fission of 1971.) By July 28, 1971, this figure had been at least halved, leaving a membership of approximately 6,177. Those dropping out were largely persons who had purchased their lots; those who remained were persons who had invaded lots in the various *colonias*, especially those in *colonias* 34-35 and 63-72. Thus, the composition of the field shifted culturally, and unless the source of support (largely invaders seeking "protection") changed, it would become rooted among those with limited, self-interested aims.

Such a consideration was discussed among the leadership of the CRC in 1971. As a result, the first strategy initiated by the core leadership was to publicize that the political leadership of what they called *"personalismo con jefe máximo"* ("personalism with a maximum chief") was the main cause for the fission within the CRC. They also reorganized the executive committee, abolishing the office of president but retaining secretary-general and the other offices comprising the organizational structure of the old CRC (see table 14). In reality, Mondragón and Valenzuela became the power figures within the organization, with Mondragón serving as secretary-general and Valenzuela as secretary of external relations. In terms of function, Mondragón oversaw the collection of fees, weekly demonstrations, and the operation of the individual sub-committees. Valenzuela saw to the establishment of relations with federal, state, and city authorities, in the continuing effort to expedite and articulate the CRC's public goals.

With this reorganization, the reconstituted CRC set out to recapture the support lost during the fission. It was not the same organization, however, and the principal change involved its decentralization. That is, members of the executive committee who were also presidents of their own subcommittees achieved a somewhat independent status. A few years later this became an important development. Of the seventeen members of the executive committee, fifteen became presidents of their own subcommittees, appointed by Secretary-General Mondragón. Whoever controlled these fifteen persons would eventually control the CRC itself, and the substance of the support from the followers of these fifteen, in the final outcome (by 1974), would be very much like the support lent to Maldonado for his "loyalty" within the PRI.

Through 1971 and into 1972, the process of reconstituting the networks of supporters and the relations with supralocal officials became the main objective for the CRC. During this period, the effort to reconstitute was affected by further changes in the political field. These changes included the extensive use of violence; the utilization of demonstrations in the federal district; the creation of alliances with communal landholders, street vendor groups, and market networks; the inclusion of taxi drivers; the membership of individuals seeking intervention for specific problems; coverage of CRC activities by periodicals and newspapers; and finally, the incorporation of the reconstituted CRC into the CNC.[4]

By the summer of 1971, the strategy to disassociate the newly reconstituted CRC from Sergio Maldonado López had been made clear. The attacks upon his political reputation employed four basic techniques: first, verbal demonstrations held outside of his home; second, violent attacks upon his household by rock-throwing persons; third, public attacks in other *colonias* during demonstrations; and fourth, an attempt to upset his vertical relations with supralocal persons. The first type of attack, however, had personal connotations beyond just stressing Maldonado's culpability in joining with the city administration and with the PRI. In arranging for demonstrations at Maldonado's home, normal politics went by the wayside. These demonstrations attacked Maldonado's family and those closest to him, either by kinship or friendship, and thus clearly attacked the basis of his legitimate support. It was not simply a matter of attacking close followers but rather the entire basis of local support.

Demonstrations in front of his home were basically the same each time: a series of speakers and then a call for Maldonado to respond appropriately. He was invited to speak, and to answer for his betrayal. Needless to say, Maldonado did not respond to the assembled crowd of 700 to 1,000 persons; instead, he sent for the police. In August 1971, I observed a confrontation between CRC followers and the police following a demonstration at Maldonado's home, with the police losing the physical battle. Using rocks, slingshots, and hardened mud clods, CRC supporters routed the fifty or so policemen, who then retreated to the Municipal Palace. Following this, CRC supporters dispersed an even larger group of police that had assembled. But the violence did not cease with the resolution of these conflicts between police and the CRC. Night raids on Maldonado's household occurred on three different occasions, resulting in serious damage to his new, two-story home. In addition, public attacks upon his reputation became part of the weekly demonstrations in the various *colonias*, and such vituperative attacks did, in fact, restore some of the lost adherents to the CRC fold. By November 1971, many supporters who had been attached to the CRC but who had dropped their membership, especially those in the *colonias* 50-65, had rejoined the CRC.[5]

Another, equally important part of the CRC strategy was to "undo" Maldonado's relations and replace them with a new network of relations between the CRC and supralocal authorities. This task fell to Arturo Valenzuela Cisneros, the secretary of exterior relations, and it was an activity that in the long run had consequences similar to but more tragic than those that befell Maldonado. In the meantime, Valenzuela's attempt to connect himself with authorities was successful, largely because of a political friendship that he established with the editor of a monthly leftist periodical. A former member of the PPS but now the chairman of a new party, Mr. X had been a schoolmate and close friend of the director of the federal Agrarian Department (DAAC).[6] The director was introduced to Valenzuela, and the director then arranged with his assistant director, Felipe Carranza, who was also a personal counselor to President Echeverria, to resolve the land-tenure problems in Netzahualcoyotl. With such impressive relations, two consequences followed: first, Maldonado's connections with federal officials were effectively supplanted, and he became "small fish" (pescadito); second, Valenzuela became involved in higher domains than even Maldonado had reached. By January 1972, Valenzuela's visits to the Agrarian Department and to the governor's office became weekly activities. Supralocal relations had been established.

With Maldonado effectively discredited, the weekly demonstrations became more aggressive. Valenzuela's arreglado ("connection into the network of influence") provided supporters of the CRC and its leadership with a sense of euphoria and power that lasted well into 1972. From the point of view of those involved in the weekly demonstrations that I observed in June 1972 and during the rest of the summer of that year, the general feeling was one of impunity and safety in numbers; this was manifested most dramatically in the violent confrontations with the police. During 1972 three massive, violent confrontations between the CRC and the police (one of which I observed firsthand) resulted in the resignation of the chief of police and his replacement by an individual endorsed by the executive committee of the CRC. Each time the police and the CRC confronted each other, the police were routed with rocks, slingshots, and anything else CRC supporters could pick up. The police continued to be routed until the state judicial police were sent in by the governor; then large numbers of CRC supporters were arrested, and Mondragón and Valenzuela temporarily went into hiding in a nearby municipality. A week later they emerged, after the national newspapers began to focus on the alleged causes of the violence. In interviews, both Mondragón and Valenzuela blamed gangs for the outbreak of violence and denied the membership of such groups in the CRC.

Meanwhile, the burning of mortgage-collection huts and the beating of their personnel, as well as the boycotting of payments of all types, continued to be employed as major strategies by the CRC into 1973. Such tactics were based on the assumption that constant pressure would force the Agrarian Department to act on the public goals of the CRC: the expropriation of Netzahualcoyotl by the federal government, the introduction of massive urban services to the municipality, and the punishment of "foreign" land developers. But Valenzuela and Mr. X knew that the director, Carranza, and the governor would expect further involvement by Valenzuela in elite domains.

Valenzuela and his leftist intermediary were quite aware at that time of the dangers of becoming involved with such functionaries as the director and Carranza. Yet the intermediary relied on his intimate friendship with the director to "set things right," and Valenzuela relied on the demonstrations by CRC members to pressure federal authorities sufficiently to react to their demands. For both Valenzuela and Mr. X, political and social friendships coupled with the actual or potential ability to unleash the coercive energy of CRC followers provided a magnificent opportunity to fulfill CRC goals. Valenzuela's denial of the involvement of CRC followers in clashes with police is simply not supported by the facts.

The state of Mexico reacted not only with state police but also by investing 30 million pesos in 1971 and 600 million pesos (borrowed from the Chase Manhattan Bank of New York) in 1972 in Netzahualcoyotl's urban services.[7] This certainly presented a clear problem for the fulfillment of one of the CRC's public goals: the nationalization of the area. The prospect of a business-conscious governor (a member of the board of directors for Volkswagen of Mexico) losing such an investment was a key element in the formation of a supralocal relationship between federal authorities and the state of Mexico. In fact, as will be shown in chapter 7, this strategy became clear once the CRC was subsequently "integrated."

Of course, Valenzuela received a number of offers of permanent employment from the Agrarian Department as well as 100 taxi certificates from the state government. This was an extraordinary bounty since each certificate can be worth up to 100,000 pesos, and for marginalized populations, the possibility of borrowing on the certificate to purchase a car, use the car as a taxi, or even hire others to drive was extremely valuable. Valenzuela did accept 20 certificates between 1971 and 1974, and this signaled his entanglement.

CRC goals were not acted upon. Given the state's investment, neither the state of Mexico nor its governor were anxious that the city be nationalized, especially in light of the state's outstanding debt. Indeed, the relations in which Valenzuela became entangled were a part of federal and state bureaucratic networks that could, upon demand, be made to resolve the minor problems of supporters. Such public sectors and their elites could be used also to pressure local municipal functionaries to do favors for Valenzuela. But it was not in the interests of the state and federal governments, nor, as will be shown in chapter 8, in the interests of the private sector, to fulfill CRC goals. Private interests had most to lose by any fulfillment of contractual obligations through provision of public services and expropriation of lots illegally sold. As will be shown, the "formal public sector" is the single most important mechanism through which economically and politically marginalized populations become further sources for exploitation by the private sector in Mexico, and the single most important mechanism for ensuring the private sector's expansion and development.

In the meantime, other external relations coalesced after the summer of 1972. Led by a group of matriarchs, communal landholders in the municipality of Chimalhuacan, three kilometers from Netzahualcoyotl, provided the CRC with three valuable resources: first, legitimate, long-standing land-tenure experience; second, a network of 1,700 kinpersons who could and would be called upon to swell the ranks of demonstrators; third, and even more valuable, the symbolic value that these women represented. The communal landholders evoked memories of a segment of the Mexican nation that had fought a revolution; and they provided proof of an elaborate mythology—a mythology that has been a basic theme in Mexican mural art—repeated in school texts, in *corridos*, in films: that is, the overthrow of land usurpers. Such a mythology was referred to in the demonstrations that took place after the alliance between the CRC and the communal landholders. The matriarchs, who represented the struggle of the communal landholders, were paraded by the CRC like newly found treasures. Their entrance into the political field legitimized the public goals of the CRC, especially those concerning the illegality of land development. Communal landholdings had been developed by land developers illegally in Netzahualcoyotl, as they had in other times and places.

The struggle against land encroachment by hacienda owners went back to the middle of the nineteenth century. The core of matriarchs who carried on the struggle in the twentieth century were the widows of men who were themselves the grandchildren of the original protestors against land incursions in the Texcoco-Chimalhuacan region. Their struggle against land usurpation by modern land developers had largely failed. But this group of elderly females and their kindred of 1,646 people extending throughout the seven *barrios* ("neighborhoods") that made up the *municipio* of Chimalhuacan had continued legally to protest the illegal division of communal land into lots in what is now the easternmost section of Netzahualcoyotl.

Although their public goals had consisted of pressuring the Agrarian Department to return the land invaded and developed by land developers and *paracaidistas*, a two-year period of courting by Valenzuela and an intimate friend finally convinced the matriarchs to join with the CRC in pressuring the Agrarian Department to settle their claims once and for all. This alliance became an important resource in the political field and provided legitimacy to the political goals of the CRC.

As I have indicated, there were other changes in the political field that further enhanced the sphere of influence of the CRC. These consisted of four massive demonstrations held illegally in the federal district: one was a sit-in of 5,000 persons at the Agrarian Department; the other three took place at the Zocalo,[8] where approximately 12,000 persons gathered unsupported by government buses or networks. In the Agrarian Department sit-in, a four-story building that houses the Agrarian Department was occupied, and it culminated in an agreement by the director to meet with the CRC and the communal landholders to resolve the illegal sale of communal lands, to provide for the indemnification of the communal landholders, to ensure fulfillment of contract obligations on the part of the land developers, and to guarantee the introduction of massive urban works.

The agreement by the Agrarian Department to discuss substantive issues must, however, be understood as an aspect of wider elite strategy. The response to CRC demands was not based on fulfilling legal codes, constitutional law, or values of justice. Instead, it was a response to potential independent power threats. The response, then, was not to the repeated demands of the communal landholders but rather to the threat of physical violence by large numbers of people. Ironically, pressure exerted from the bottom that causes men like the director to respond to the legal codes amounts to a use of power to insist that values be fulfilled. But for him and his cohorts, to respond positively would upset the balance of horizontal relations at their levels of power. They respond, therefore, only in terms of their relation to other power holders, even though the rhetoric may have been dominated by phrases like "justice and trust." It was this type of response that ultimately met the massive demonstrations held before the presidential palace. Yet for a short period, networks of people thought they were finally going to win.

There were other indications that the protestors were going to win, and the composition of the field reflected it. Increasing numbers of people were joining daily. Even at this time, however, the shift back to coercion was obvious. Those joining either individually or as groups all wanted assistance in matters with state and local authorities. Groups of street vendors (*tianguistas*), who were being prohibited by the municipality from selling, joined with 500 persons as an associate organization in order to get state authorization to sell. Market networks of women and men who had fought very hard against one of the local female *caciques* who collected fees from the market-booth owners at gunpoint joined in order to receive the support of the CRC against the state and federal authorities. Taxi drivers, who were constantly harassed by the local police, joined for mutual protection, but it was not long before they also began to ask for favors in getting taxi licenses at reduced rates from the state transit authorities.

Newspaper articles and periodicals indicated that the CRC was becoming more and more prominent;[9] so prominent, in fact, that the Confederación Nacional Campesina ("National Peasant's Confederation," or CNC) formally invited the CRC to join it as an independent organization. As part of the formal "public sector," and one of the tripartite sections making up the official government party—the PRI—the CNC declared that it was prepared to smooth the way for the resolution of all problems articulated by the CRC and the communal landholders of Chimalhuacan. By September 1972, the CRC did join the CNC, apparently for tactical reasons. Chapter 7 fully discusses the causes and implications of this decision, including the eventual cooptation of the CRC.

For now, however, this merging of political fates must be understood within the context of larger processes concerned not only with high-level political strategies but also with the strategies of daily living that formed the basis of local support: relationships based on affect and respect; meanings and equivalencies rooted in legitimacy and *confianza* ("mutual trust"). It is by analyzing these social and cultural contexts that the full range of the unintended consequences for local populations in Ciudad Netzahualcoyotl can be understood in other than just political terms. By examining Arturo Valenzuela Cisneros's living networks and supports of legitimacy, the contradictions in social principle between the local level and the domains of elites can be understood. Such an understanding must begin with careful analysis of the most primary of social contexts on the local level: the family.

6

One Day in the Life of the Valenzuela Family: Primary-Order Locality

THERE IS AN affective dimension and context from which much of Arturo Valenzuela's ability "to politick" emerges. Within the pressures and limits of economic and political marginalization, men like Valenzuela need the support of long-term relations in order to deal with the reality of the coercive effects of short-term political ones. These long-term relations for Mexican males can be found within only the most basic loci of experience: the primary locality of networks of family and friendship. The "support" from such ties provides the only secure and fairly determinate means by which to confront the indeterminacy and insecurity of political competition. This "legitimate" support, when placed in jeopardy, has far-reaching consequences for persons like Valenzuela, because these supportive relations are not only enclaves of relative predictability but also form the basis of social identity. For most Mexican males, including political entrepreneurs like Valenzuela, such an identity is very much tied to the affective content and political support provided by females. Julieta Valenzuela is one such female.

ONE DAY: 1974

For Julieta Valenzuela there is little time for television, which is really about the only pastime in the city that does not cost money.

136

From early morning until late in the evening, strangers, friends, relatives, and family members, including her husband, troop in and out of the house on Calle Cucaracha, next to the Municipal Palace in the central part of the city. As one of thirty-four brothers, sisters, half-brothers, half-sisters, and others who claim to be related, Julieta is seldom alone.[1] She is the wife of Arturo Valenzuela Cisneros—one of the *jovenes líderes* ("young political leaders")—and she is expected to attend to the many persons who come to her home seeking her husband's help, intervention, counseling, and even money. In his absence, which is usual during the day, Julieta must keep track of the various problems of those who enter her home. She must also "cover" for her husband when he has missed an appointment with someone at their home.

Surrounded by persons for most of the day and for much of the evening, seven days a week, Julieta has wondered what it would be like to have privacy. Nevertheless, she recognizes that without the many *comadres* and *amigas*, it would be very difficult to deal with the hardships she experiences: the lack of water, the illnesses of her children, the physical dangers her husband attracts, and the deep physical pains in her abdomen that confine her to bed occasionally. Without her *comadres*, friends, and relatives, Julieta has stated that she probably could not have survived Netzahualcoyotl.

Eleven years before (1963), when the family moved to Netzahualcoyotl from Mexico City, the central section of the city near the Municipal Palace was barren, dusty, and lifeless in the dry season, and equally barren, though muddy, wet, and smelly in the rainy season. Julieta, Arturo, and their children—Arturito, then three years old; Teófilo, age two; and Marco, soon to be born—together with Arturo's father, Don Teófilo, his mother, Doña Margarita, Arturo's eldest brother, Jaime, and his wife, Lucinda, all moved into a house on Calle Cucaracha to face what Julieta has described as "a horror." And it was a "horror"—without water, electricity, or sanitary facilities, and with a great many dangers to all of them, especially the children. The two eldest children have each been hospitalized three times with pneumonia and typhoid, and the eldest is thought to have contracted tuberculosis—all this within their first two years in Netzahualcoyotl. What was worse in many ways, Julieta said, was that the entire family was crowded into the small, three-room *jacal* in which Julieta, Arturo, and their children now live.

For three years, they all lived together, until Arturo and his brother Jaime one day agreed that this arrangement could not continue, especially with Don Teófilo's *borracheras* ("drinking episodes"). Jaime, his wife, their child, who had been born a year after their arrival in Netzahualcoyotl, and the *viejos* ("old people" —parents) then moved to another *jacal* a few blocks away.

HOME

Arturo and Julieta agree that their house in Netzahualcoyotl is not much to look at; but they also agree that it does serve their needs. Neither spouse is pretentious; neither is much concerned with how and where they live, although Julieta has expressed her discomfort when a dignitary visits. She has noticed the way such persons turn up their noses (especially if their wives are with them) at the chicken offal on the floor and at the furniture in the living room. But both Julieta and Arturo have stated that for his work, the home is ideal, since it is a very short walk to the *"plaza de coyotes."*

A person walking by their home will find their *jacal* little different from most. By community standards of who has "made it" and who has not, this home falls into the latter category, with only a few exceptions: two seven-foot poles stand parallel to each other at the very front of the lot. From them hangs a faded sign that reads: "Colonos Organizadores del Valle de México" ("Organizing Settlers of the Valley of Mexico"). Next to the two poles and parallel to the sidewalk is a two-foot-high rock wall built ten years earlier by Don Teófilo and now crumbling from inattention.[2] Beyond the wall, a two-foot-deep hole, into which a water pipe extends from the main in the street, is partially covered by two loose one-by-twos. It is from this source during the wet season that water is taken. When the main is clogged or the water level is too low, the *pipero* ("water tank truck") is contacted and drums are filled.

The rest of the lot, set between a two-story building to the north and a luncheonette (*lonchería*) to the south, is cluttered with left-over lumber, brick, a chicken coop, clods of burnt rubbish or piles of ash (depending on the season), two empty oil drums for water in the dry season, and a concrete washbasin for dishes and clothes. Behind the washbasin and drums is the outside bathroom: a four-foot-square concrete-block structure with a laminated cardboard roof. A dirty, flowered curtain serves as a door. Inside, a brown-encrusted seatless toilet sits on rough, gray concrete. Two large metal tubs hang by their handles on nails embedded in the un-painted walls. Next to the tubs, wash brushes, lye soap, and deter-gent powder partially fill secondhand wood shelves tacked up beneath a screenless window. A lone wire-suspended light bulb provides the only illumination, since the windowpanes are painted black.

Behind the outside bathroom, at the very back of the lot, sits the Valenzuelas' pastel-blue, three-room, concrete-block house, with its corrugated cardboard roof covered with debris. Black initials are painted over much of the surface of the walls, thus distinguish-ing this house from most others in the neighborhood.

There is yet another feature distinguishing the Valenzuela home, that is, its accessibility. Most homes, regardless of their location in the city or their location on the lot, are closed off from a front and side view. (Fences obstruct the front view and the contiguous con-struction with other homes shield the side.) But the Valenzuela home is clearly visible to all who pass by, and access is unencum-bered except by the crumbling rock wall. Not even a gate hinders a person entering, and the rock fence is in such a dilapidated state that small children can and do step over what is left of it. It is this willingness on the Valenzuelas' part to be "open" to the view of passersby—to provide unlimited accessibility to anyone, children or adults—that differentiates them and their home from the great majority of persons and homes in Netzahualcoyotl.

This "openness" extends to the inside of the home as well. Upon entering, one sees that the first room is not just the ordinary living room of an average Netzahualcoyotlian. After passing the over-hanging outside light bulb (the main source of light for night meet-ings in the yard) and entering the living room, one sees a large glass-framed photograph of Arturo and a past Mexican president. Although little natural light enters the room through the entry or through the one window in the room to the right of the entry, only the most unobservant can fail to notice this photograph.

Clearly, the room is not arranged for family privacy. Except for one small shelf with a small mirror above it, located in the extreme upper corner of the west wall, no private family utilitarian artifacts can be seen in the room. But the room is cluttered. Next to the west wall leans a roughly made, white wooden desk, its paint badly chipped. On top of the desk sits a 1940-vintage Corona portable typewriter and seven bundles of yellowing newspapers. Next to the newspapers, a microphone amplifier and loudspeakers accompany the objects on the table along the west wall. The eight-foot-long south wall, like all the walls in the house, is unpainted, but its grayness is relieved by three tacked-on posters: one pictures Benito Juárez in somber, centennial pose; the second shows a plumed Aztec warrior carrying a newly sacrificed maiden down the steps of a pyramid in Tenochtitlán; and the third advertises Superior beer. Underneath these posters and along the width of the wall, three shelves house the legal codes for national, state, and municipal government.

The photograph of Arturo and the former Mexican president hangs conspicuously on the east wall. Next to it is a collage of pictures in one large frame: Arturo, dressed in levis, cowboy boots, and hat, sitting on horseback; Arturo standing in a completely black *charro* suit with a sombrero held in his right hand;[3] and three other photographs of Arturo among groups of politicians or colleagues who are important in his present political activities.

The room is devoid of decorative objects such as curtains, flowers, or ashtrays, but two unmatched couches are positioned against the west and north walls. One couch has a large hole down to the springs, and the brown color of the fabric is largely worn away. The other couch is covered with cracking red-plastic upholstery and is missing one leg. It tilts to one side until someone sits on it and straightens it out. A wooden chair and a bench resting on two concrete blocks complete the furniture in this room, except for the naked light bulb hanging down from the open-beamed ceiling.

The bareness of the north wall is interrupted only by a hanging flowered curtain that serves as the door leading to the only bedroom of the house. It is here that we find the private area of the Valenzuela household. Upon entering the bedroom and immediately to the left of the doorway, a five-foot-high double-doored bureau with interior drawers and a clothes bar adjoins the west wall all the way to the entrance to the kitchen. On a top corner of this bureau is a fourteen-inch black-and-white television encased in a dirty white-plastic cabinet and topped by half of a rabbit-eared antenna. On the other top corner are photographs of Arturo in a *charro* suit and Julieta wearing a provincial wedding dress from the state of Oaxaca—both photographs taken sixteen years before. Recent school pictures of their children sit nearby: Arturo, age fourteen; Teófilo, age twelve; Marco, age eleven; Julieta, age nine; and a snapshot of Arturo's favorite, Felipe, age two. Between the television set and the photographs hangs a one-by-two-foot reproduction of a translucent Christ in flowing robes with arms open and beckoning. On the bureau, underneath the picture, stands a candle in a red-glass holder.

On the other side of the open doorway to the kitchen is a large trunk that holds the boys' clothes. On top of the trunk rests two orange crates, also jammed with clothing. Next to these, a bed shared by the four eldest children is propped up at each corner by concrete blocks that protect it from flooding. The bed is covered by a clean, well-worn, lime-green chenille bedspread. The mattress beneath it is swaybacked, and tufts of cotton bulge from torn spots on the sides. The bed's headboard has built-in compartments filled with prescription and nonprescription medicines and with old copies of "Kaliman the Magnificent" comic books. Over the headboard hangs a reproduction of the virgin of Guadalupe presenting flowers to the Indian, Juan Diego. Perpendicular to the children's bed is Arturo and Julieta's bed, which is also used by little Felipe. It too is covered by a well-used, lime-green chenille bedspread, but the bed does not have a headboard.

The users of both beds vary. If one or more of the older children sleep at their grandparents' home, Felipe will sleep in the bed with the other children. When Felipe sleeps with his grandparents, none of the other children sleep with Arturo and Julieta, because neither Julieta nor Arturo want the older children to become reaccustomed to doing so. In the past each child has slept with his parents until replaced by a younger child, and each time this has caused considerable jealousy. This rationale, provided by Julieta, was not quite the complete explanation. Arturo added, with a wry smile, that "I sleep better" without any of the children in bed with him and his wife. The meaning of his facial expression is obvious.

Except for light from the window on the east wall, the light from the sixty-watt bulb hanging from the ceiling, and the small amount of light that may shine through the doorway from the kitchen window, little light enters the bedroom. The one steel-sashed paneless window in the room is usually kept covered by an old door to keep out rain and dust. When the front door of the house is closed, however, the door covering the window is usually removed so that the rooster and the three chickens may enter the house. Nevertheless, the bedroom is usually quite dark, unless of course family members or close friends visit. Then the sixty-watt bulb is replaced by one with a higher wattage.

From the bedroom, the kitchen is easily accessible. It is here that much of the significant social intercourse takes place between females—not just kitchen activities but much of the private and public political worlds of Arturo are here shared between Julieta and her *comadres*. It is in the kitchen that semiritual and ritual relationships are reinforced by the women, and these have far-reaching consequences, since they are part of Arturo's political resources. Nevertheless, this area of the house is both private and public—private within a circle of *comadres* but public in consequence for Arturo.

The kitchen, measuring eight feet square, has unpainted concrete-block walls, one steel-sashed window with three of the four glass panes missing, an open-beamed corrugated cardboard roof, and a rough concrete floor. From nails embedded in the walls hang six battered aluminum pots, and four one- and two-quart-size earthen pots (*ollas*) scorched on their bottoms. All pots are neatly arranged in grid (from smallest to largest), with aluminum pots on one side and earthen pots on the other. Both metal and earthenware are used by Julieta and Doña Margarita (Arturo's mother), who spends considerable time in the household. Below the pots, a four-burner stove stands on four concrete bricks. Its oven is unusable, and its white enamel sides are badly chipped. A wooden table, with two boards underneath serving as shelves, takes up the space between the stove and the room's only window. The shelves under the table hold a box that stores eating utensils; glasses, both store-bought and empty preserve jars; a blender with attachments; dishes and bowls; and canned goods such as coffee, condensed milk (buffet size), and jars of jam and old baby food.

Like 84 percent of the households in Netzahualcoyotl, the Valenzuela home is not equipped with a refrigerator (Tamayo 1971: 33). Therefore, fresh vegetables, meat, and dairy products must be purchased daily in quantities appropriate to family size and income. But because of the large number of persons entering the house in addition to the nuclear family, larger quantities of canned goods, cereals, and dry legumes (black beans) are kept in the Valenzuela household than in homes of comparable income and size. These goods are stored under a table directly across from the stove. The table is used also as the serving and eating surface for the family, with persons sitting on a rough wooden bench positioned parallel to the table.

Next to the table and bench, three plastic and two metal pails are stacked. Both types are used to carry water from the source outside the house to the dish- and clothes-washing basin. They are used also to carry water inside to be heated on the stove for bathing purposes. In the latter case, the water is poured into one of the large metal cooking pots that normally hang over the stove. When the water is hot, it is taken to the outside bathroom and poured into one of the tubs. In this household, as in most, pails are indispensable. Equally indispensable are two four-gallon bottle containers of Electro-pura drinking water, which are held in metal tipping frames standing next to the pails. Since this household, like many, has neither interior plumbing nor a source of uncontaminated drinking water, water for drinking purposes must be purchased from companies specializing in "pure" water.[4] Not many persons in this city, however, including Julieta and Arturo, trust the water-supply company. Most suggest that such companies utilize Netzahualcoyotl sources for their "pure" water.

UNCERTAINTY IN PROCESSES

The day for Julieta begins at about the same time it does for most women in Netzahualcoyotl. But unlike others, Julieta cannot be certain that the day's activities will unfold routinely. Arturo is the focus of attention in this household, but Arturo's schedule is not firmly established. The morning's activity depends on Arturo's schedule for the day, or the previous night's meeting held in the living room or in the front part of the lot, or on Arturo's health. Julieta has remarked that "many times I do not know whether I am coming or going in the morning, with so many different responses that I have to make." In essence, then, Julieta's activity within the household is continuously affected by Arturo's activities.

Although Arturo is neither an elected nor an appointed official (though he does act as a consultant to a federal-state corporation), he (in 1974) is one of a number of mini-*caciques* and brokers in Netzahualcoyotl. Like many persons occupying such positions, Arturo has become enmeshed in national, state, and local institutions in his effort to represent the interests of clients from his network of supporters. This "job," without portfolio or salary, places great tensions and stresses on the household, on interpersonal relationships, and, as the analysis in chapter 7 will show, on the mental health of some of the family's members. Because of Arturo's political status, Julieta's household activities are seldom accomplished without some compromise or change, to say nothing about changes resulting from the unexpected machinations of two-year-old Felipe.

Nevertheless, a "typical" day begins with Julieta arising first, at 6 A.M., dressing, and then walking outside with two pails in hand. After filling both—one for washing and another for the toilet (defecation and urine are flushed away by pouring water into the commode)—she relieves herself, washes, and then brushes her teeth. Except for elimination, all activities are carried out on the open lot. Teeth brushing requires that she take a glass of water from the bottle containers in the kitchen. Face and hands are soaped and rinsed at the concrete washbasin and dried with a towel sometimes hung on a nail inside the bathroom.

By 6:20 Julieta has roused the eldest boys, who, after due protests, rise and then go through the same basic procedure as their
mother performed earlier. While they wash and dress, Julieta
warms the previous night's tortillas or rolls and heats sufficient
water for *café con leche* ("coffee with milk").[5] In between heating
water and warming food, she must also wash whatever dishes
have been left from the night before. Moving between the boys
washing their faces, filling pails with water, and trying not to step
on the now-awakened rooster requires adept coordination.

Since both boys take the bus to the western section of the city
where they attend school, Arturito and Teófilo must be out of
the house by approximately 7 A.M. Although the central section
has a secondary school, Arturo has decided that the federal *secun-
daria* in the western section is safer for the boys, in light of his various political enemies.[6] Although he feels that the dangers to them
of attending the central-section high school would be remote,
nevertheless, in the past, political enemies have attacked his home
with hails of pistol bullets and rocks, without regard for the presence of his family. This has prompted him to take some precautions.

This situation, however, places extra stress on Julieta and the
boys. For the latter, it is imperative that they take the 7:10 bus,
since many environmental factors could prevent them from arriving at their school by 8 A.M. if they left at a later time. When they
have left late, especially at times when fewer buses were available,
they have had to ride the bumpers of the bus, hanging desperately
to whatever object or person was near to them. Sometimes they
have returned home, unsuccessful in even catching a bus.

For Julieta, the stress comes from two sources: first, she must
hurry to ensure that the boys are ready on time; second, each
morning the boys argue about who is going to wear what clothes.
Since both are exactly the same size (Arturito is undersized for his
age because of illness), each wears the other's clothing. Julieta
must make sure that they do not quarrel noisily over the articles of
clothing they have selected to wear, and in so doing, awaken their
father. It is this last consideration that most concerns Julieta.

By the time Arturito and Teófilo have left for school, Marco
and little Julieta have awakened and repeat the washing and dress-

ing routine that their mother and brothers have followed. By 7:45, while Marco eats his tortilla and drinks his coffee and milk, Julieta has combed little Julieta's hair, tied it into twin braids, and then joined the braids at the top of the child's head with a red or yellow ribbon, while checking the child's head for lice. By the time she has finished with little Julieta, Felipe has awakened, and it is Marco's responsibility to help his little brother with the water pails, and to wash and dress him. While little Julieta warms her own tortilla and makes her coffee and milk, Julieta awakens Arturo (if he has told her the night before that he has an appointment the next morning). If someone calls at that hour to see Arturo, she asks the person to return later, unless the problem is urgent. If Arturo does not have to be awakened, Julieta then shifts her attention to Felipe, finishing Marco's attempts to dress him. By 8:15, little Julieta and Marco have left to walk to the elementary school next to the "zoologico" ("zoo"—another pejorative for the Municipal Palace).[7]

These morning sequences, however, may all be disrupted by illnesses, by visitations from Arturo's mother and/or father, by the availability of water during the dry season, by the flooding of the household during the wet season, by the stoppage of the sewage line to the bathroom, by the eldest boys returning home because they did not catch their bus, by the younger children requesting money for their report cards, by little Felipe awakening his father who then demands breakfast, by comadres who stop by on their way to the mercado, by an early-rising Arturo who demands special attention for a hangover, or by the stomach pains and cramps that Julieta says "twist and grab" her intestines. Most happenings in the Valenzuela home are "possibles" rather than "probables," and Julieta's certainty about her activities is equivocal, at best. She has stated that she fears each activity will not be finished or satisfactorily carried out. She says:

> Beginning in the morning, one is always in a hurry. I do not know if I can finish one thing when another begins. Each [person] asks for attention; each [person] asks for something; and there is no end. As a mother I know that the responsibility is mine, but what concerns me most is to have to be on guard constantly for the unexpected.[8]

From Julieta's point of view, nothing is certain in the early-morning routines. This is true for most persons in Netzahualcoyotl, except for those few who are fortunate enough to control disruptive interventions artificially with servants.

Julieta can, with relative certainty, count on the assistance of her *comadres*, and through a number of bad times, she has done so. For example, when she, Arturo, and the children were to be evicted from their home during the height of political activities in 1970, it was the *comadres* who surrounded the lot and for two weeks aligned themselves against the police. They supplied the family with food daily, brought clean water, cared for the Valenzuela children in their own homes, and finally, when the battle against the land developers had stalemated, they helped move the Valenzuelas back into their home. While most men stood back in fear of the police, the *comadres* faced them down. These women, Julieta has stated, are *comadres y hermanas* ("co-godmothers and sisters").

RELATIONS

Julieta expresses trust for Arturo, for his protection and affection for herself and their children, and for his nobility throughout his past struggles against the land developers. But she says: "Like all men, he is not faithful [sexually]." She states that Arturo is "a fighter, noble in many ways, and a valiant person, but faithful?— that he has never been."

In a conversation with one of her *comadres* at which I was present, Julieta states that in Oaxaca, when Arturo first started courting her, she had been fairly sure that he was not going to be like her politician-father who had more children than she could count. But soon after their elaborate wedding, when elders had gathered together and *compadres* had spoken for the other's family as they faced one another in lines to tie the families together, Arturo had *robado* ("stolen") another sixteen-year-old in the next village. But she says wearily: "I forgave him then, and now I forgive him. I know that he loves us." In other conversations with her *comadres*, she has said: "I continue to serve him [as a wife] even while he comes home drunk and even while he comes in smelling of [the woman] from Ecatepec."⁹

In interviews, Arturo has stated that he always wakes up in his own bed, even when he has been drunk the night before and totally confused as to time and place. Since 1973, I have observed that Arturo has been drunk more frequently than in the past. Nevertheless, it is true that Arturo generally ends up in his own bed even after the worst of these binges. Recently, however, his *mujer* ("woman"), as he calls Julieta, has not been sufficient to comfort him. To cure his depression he has taken up with Gloria, an old girlfriend whose husband Arturo refers to as a *pendejo* ("pubic hair"—cuckold). His rationale for this reestablished affair was to forget all that worried him. Besides, as he often points out: "Julieta is not aware of anything, since she always has been prepared to serve." Thus, Arturo implies that Julieta ceases to serve his food, clean and wash his clothes, and prepare his meals only when she suspects he is having extramarital affairs. From observation, however, this is an incorrect assumption since Arturo has never been denied her services, even during those periods before she left him to return to her native state. (These were periods when Julieta threatened divorce and actually left their home.)

From Arturo's perspective, he can count on her to bring coffee to his bed, to fix him special herb tea when he is hung over, to pour him a half glass of El Presidente brandy in the morning *para curarse* ("to become cured"), to tie garlic to his feet and place a clove on his navel when he has been sick, and to massage his body when he cannot arise from bed. All these services and more Arturo feels he can count on as long as Julieta does not suspect his involvement with other women. As Arturo sees it, he will always have Julieta to care for him, to serve him, and to respond hurriedly to his whistles when he wishes something brought to him—as long as he is discreet and Julieta does not suspect his infidelity. The irony, of course, is that she not only knows of his infidelity but knows with whom he is unfaithful.

Arturo has stated that he loves and deeply respects his *mujer* for the way she has stood by him when, except for his mother, few others did. When he first started organizing politically, five years previously (1969), few persons, including his older brother and his father, took seriously his involvement in the protest activities. When he gave up his work as a machinist to join the CRC, and his family was forced to rely on monthly contributions from the membership, most persons, including his father and eldest brother, thought him insane. As Arturo states: "Even my father and Jaime and all of the family and friends thought me crazy. Everyone thought I would get screwed—everyone except my mother and woman." His friends, father, and brother changed their minds only in 1971, Arturo states, when he began to make contact with and become friends of functionaries, middlemen who could help with problems, and clerks who could make things easier. It was only then, after it became convenient, that the family accepted his political activities. He says bitterly in 1974:

> If it had not been for my mother and woman, in that time I would have been alone [without friends and family support]. Afterward, naturally, after we "swept the ground with them," after the functionaries paid attention to us, after I became friends of middlemen, after they found out who I was at "Los Pinos" [the presidential palace in Mexico City], after it became convenient for them, then they did not pay [they joined the rent strike]. That I do not forget.[10]

By the time Arturo has washed and dressed in the morning, people usually are waiting in the living room for him. If he can, he listens briefly to them. (But early in the morning, perhaps with a headache and a hangover, Arturo is hardly in condition to do much, unless, of course, the problem is really serious or his action would mean the possible embarrassment of one of his ex-comrades who is now his enemy.) He usually gives the person a minute or two of double-talk and then dismisses him. But not all persons come for political advice or assistance. Arturo is also sometimes asked to give massages or reset bones, skills he learned as a young man in his village in Oaxaca before going with his brother in 1953 to the United States as a bracero.

Except for Saturday, when he reserves the morning for persons wishing to see him without an appointment, Arturo usually leaves the house by approximately 10 A.M. for one of his many appointments with persons in governmental institutions in the federal district, the state capital, or in Netzahualcoyotl itself. For the rest of the day, depending on whether his 1968 Renault is running, Arturo travels a minimum of thirty-five kilometers and talks with an average of eight persons.[11] Usually such contacts involve intervention on behalf of a client (or clients) with an official, and always they are couched in the language of friendship, even though afterward he may comment on a particular contact's shrewdness, avarice, or dishonesty. Regardless, his contacts are made to initiate a favor for a client or to follow up on a favor previously promised to a client. Arturo spends much of the day going from agency to agency, from official to official, from "pal" to "pal" who knows officials with whom Arturo has not yet made a connection.

While Arturo takes advantage of his *arreglos*, Julieta continues her tasks: preparing food for the young children who return home at midday for their *comida*; checking to see that Felipe, who plays in the yard, has not fallen in the water hole. Usually young Felipe occupies himself by throwing rocks at the chickens, playing with the two dogs, Coyote and Tigre, or scampering in and out of the house, until he goes to sleep after the midday meal.

Seldom, however, does Julieta prepare the meal alone. Usually her mother-in-law, Doña Margarita, walks over from the house she and her husband share with their eldest son, Jaime, his wife, and their three children. Although Doña Margarita spends much of her time caring for Don Teófilo and the grandchildren who live with her, she nevertheless visits Julieta and Felipe daily. Julieta and her mother-in-law seem to have maintained an affectionate, warm, and deferent relationship. Although Julieta addresses her mother-in-law in the second-person formal *usted*, each greets the other with close embraces and soft, affectionate kisses close to their mouths.

It is quite obvious that the two are very fond of each other, but at times a certain ambivalence is expressed by Julieta toward her mother-in-law. She has stated that her mother-in-law is *"una torre"* ("a tower"), *pero a veces demasiado cuidadosa* ("but at times unnecessarily particular").[12] Julieta has stated that Doña Margarita has been "a tower" whenever she has needed counsel in dealing with Arturo. Early in their marriage, Julieta considered divorcing Arturo, but Doña Margarita dissuaded her and took Arturo aside and scolded him like a small child. At the same time, Doña Margarita advised Julieta that all men can be expected to be unfaithful, and that Arturo, especially, could never really be made *manso* ("tamed"). Yet Julieta has left Arturo and taken the youngest children with her to "visit" relatives when she can no longer tolerate Arturo's unfaithfulness. In 1974, through Doña Margarita, she and Arturo maintained a kind of truce: she continued to serve him until the next time she thought it necessary to "visit" relatives, and he rationalized his extramarital affairs by refusing to admit that Julieta suspected them. Nevertheless, Julieta suggests that it has been Doña Margarita who has largely been responsible for maintaining their marital relationship.

Such close association has another side. Julieta has suggested that Doña Margarita's constant complaints about Don Teófilo's alcoholic excesses have become tiresome, but what bothers her most is that Doña Margarita has constantly maintained a critical attitude toward her housekeeping abilities. But in fact, as Julieta says: *"Ella puso y mantiene la loza sobre la pared en esa manera tan exacta"* ("She places and maintains the pots on the wall in that exact way"). Clearly, Doña Margarita is an exacting woman who maintains that disorder, more than anything else, drives men away from their wives. Julieta suggests that such a complaint is an "excuse" rather than a real reason for infidelity. Julieta suspects that the unkempt appearance of her home is what Doña Margarita considers the cause of Arturo's unfaithfulness, even though Arturo's extramarital affairs began long before the Valenzuelas moved into Ciudad Netzahualcoyotl and the inclement living conditions there.

Doña Margarita was the only one of Arturo's family who helped him and his wife when they were dispossessed by the land developers. This single fact, Julieta states, she will always remember. In addition, it was with Doña Margarita's help that the *comadres* were organized into self-defense groups so that they could not be thrown out of their own homes during the rental strikes of 1970-1974. Julieta says: *"Esta torre y mis comadres nos salvaron la vida"* ("This tower and my *comadres* saved our lives"). Since that time, many of the *comadres* have continued to maintain a ritual relation with both Julieta and Doña Margarita, and although they do not vehemently support Arturo as they once did, they nevertheless do not oppose him, nor have they joined with others.

By 11 A.M., at least one of the fourteen *comadres* will have come to Julieta's home for a visit of at least half an hour, drinking coffee and chatting in the kitchen. Although they range in age from thirty-four to sixty-eight years, these women have shared the same struggles since they arrived in Netzahualcoyotl. The political movement before 1973 brought them together initially only for politics. As time passed, they have become even more bound to one another, often sharing in the ritual activities of baptism and confirmation of their children and becoming *comadres de casa* by exchanging saints for the household. Moreover, the fourteen women making up this network of *comadres* provide support for one another beyond that created by the consanguine ties among them: two sisters-in-law, a mother and daughter, two sisters, and a first cousin to the two sisters.

There was a crucial difference, however, between Julieta and five of the women: these women had been abandoned by men and had been left with a brood of children. Three of the five who had never been married lived with parents or with near-relatives. Those who were married were, along with their husbands, friends of Arturo—his *compadres* and *comadres*. Some of the men, however, were also Arturo's *compadres de la botella* ("bottle compadres"—drinking pals) who sought Arturo's companionship just because he would usually pay the tab. The crucial ties, however, were not between men; they were between women, and they extended to Arturo through Julieta and Doña Margarita.

By 1 P.M., between twenty and thirty persons usually have trooped in and out of the Valenzuela home—men and women of all ages—all of them seeking assistance in resolving immediate problems. Meanwhile, with or without her mother-in-law's help,

Julieta has cooked the afternoon meal for herself and Felipe; for a *comadre*, if present; and for Marco and little Julieta, home from school for lunch. It is at this time that the front door of the house closes for a momentary respite from the outside world. Sometimes, however, persons who had not learned this cue called at the Valenzuela household, and Julieta would be forced to interrupt her cooking, serving, or eating to answer the front door. The few times I observed Julieta visibly irritated occurred as a result of such interruptions. The rest of the afternoon, until 7 P.M., Julieta spends balancing the demands of visitors with those of her family.

Depending on the day's activities, Arturo returns home usually no earlier than 8 P.M. Julieta has already fed the children; all have completed their homework; and someone will invariably be waiting to ask Arturo for a favor. Sometimes, though rarely, no one is around except for Roberto, his intimate friend, *compadre* José and his wife, his mother and father, or perhaps a combination of these. Then all will sit with the children in the only bedroom, watching them fall, scream, jump on the bed, and wrestle. Julieta will strum the guitar and Arturo will sing. All the men will drink brandy or tequila or sometimes beer—but not the women. Then jokes will be told by the men—raucous, ribald, earthy jokes—and each man will take his turn poking fun at another in the room. Everyone participates except the women, who just laugh and shake their heads at the foolishness of the men. Only Doña Carmen, a close *comadre*, banters with the men, but she is a *"chingona,"* as the men call her privately, against whose allusions no man could compete.

But even these times seldom go uninterrupted. Don Teófilo soon will have too much to drink and will have to be taken home; Julieta will have to treat the injuries of one of the boys, caused by a fall from the bed; the older boys will fight with each other and crying will begin; or one of the men will joke too aggressively and insult another. Then someone, usually Arturo, will intervene, and the evening will come to an end. The front door will then close until the next morning, and the primary locality and basis of Arturo's sense of self, determinacy, certainty, and political support will be hidden from view.

There is little doubt, from the data presented, that women, especially Julieta, Arturo's mother, and the *comadres* who form part of their network, are of great importance in Netzahualcoyotl. They are the sources for Arturo's sense of the past and present, as well as his sense of continuity. When they become endangered because of his political activities, the stress that results is manifested psychologically and physically in various hysterical episodes. As we will see, to regard familial activities and social support for political activities analytically as simply resources for the organizational activities of a political entrepreneur, limits the level of "locality" in an obvious way. The primary locality, for Valenzuela, begins with the basis for his personal identity: women and the family.

7

Broader Networks of Support and Social Identity: Second-Order Locality

IF THE FAMILIAL and friendship networks that operate within the home are primary or "basic" sources of identity and support, there are also broader networks of identity and support that are of a second order of locality. These emerge in such social contexts as in the neighborhood, voluntary associations, schools, churches, recreational activities, or the work place. And, of course, they overlap into the home and are often regarded as familial, especially insofar as they entail fictive kinship arrangements. They are also important, however, in providing a person with a sense of "public" social identity, as well as with part of the personal identity (provided mainly by women, in Arturo's case, as argued in the last chapter). But for men, other men, too, provide important aspects of personal identity. In Valenzuela's case, most of the men who provide him with a sense of public self are also those most able to provide him with information regarding part of his private self. These men are *compadres* of political struggles, but they are not "political friends" like those in the Agrarian Department, the state bureaucracy, or the municipal government.

SOCIAL FRIENDS AND EXCHANGE

Normally, if he is not sick in bed (which occurred with greater frequency during 1974 than at any other time), Arturo's day goes by

155

quickly. His numerous activities include, for example, speaking to functionaries in the Agrarian Department about the status of a land-tenure problem for a nearby municipality; traveling to the state capital to intercede on behalf of a bus line blocked from establishing service (by someone like him who has interceded in behalf of an already-established bus line); or seeing the judge of the *municipio* in order to persuade him to release a pair of clients who are in jail. Whatever the activity, the day is filled with intrigue and ploys. I have concluded, from observation and from interviews, that each meeting, each *arreglo*, inevitably results in a price to be paid by Arturo. The stress resulting from this is what he finds most exhausting.

At times, at the end of the work day, he goes to his friend Roberto's house a few blocks away from the Municipal Palace to drink beer, flirt with his friend's sister, and sometimes even play marbles with his friend's nephew. He releases, he says, "the demons of worries" with his pals. In fact, for Arturo, social friends, as opposed to "political" friends, form the secondary basis of his personal identity. Social friends are part of the "second order" of his locality, but they are characterized by frequent, intimate, and long-term exchanges of various sorts. These *confianza* relations vary in strength, but they do form another level of social relations within what comprises Valenzuela's total locality.

One central characteristic of these relationships is that many have emerged within political activities. But these relationships are *not* "political friendships," rather, they are, first and foremost, social relations of intimacy generated by common participation in the CRC and its political activities. Like the *comadres*, these males are linked to Arturo, but directly, without intermediaries. These relationships are largely egalitarian, marked by joking and unrestrained irreverence; they are multiple in interest and, given the variety of exchanges and the contexts in which they occur, partly affective and partly instrumental; and they are largely long term. Most of the males are largely in the same age cohort (twenty-seven to thirty-five), reside in the same locality, and have participated in the same political activities. Some are linked to Julieta through fictive kinship and friendship, but such links are through the spouses of the males.

THE NETWORK

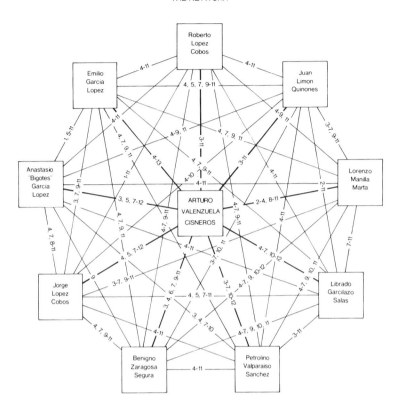

— Relations with Arturo only
— Relations with each other
1. Consanguine
2. Affinal
3. Fictive kinship
4. Friendship
5. Economic
6. Business

7. Political cohort
8. Ritual
9. Visitation and recreation
10. Indirect links
11. Residence
12. Broker-client
13. Practitioner-patient

Fig. 19. Arturo Valenzuela Cisneros's network of second-order relations.

Most of these second-order male associations have been Arturo's political cohorts; have engaged in some sort of economic relations with him; have participated in ritual activities with him; have taken part in recreational and visitation events with him; and have been cross-linked with one another through other persons and relationships. They represent the public mirroring of Arturo's social identity. They are all urban or rural migrants who have engaged in equivalent struggles for survival.

The Network

Composed of nine males, the network is made up of a variety of links and connections with Arturo and with one another. Figure 19 depicts all links, direct and indirect, with Arturo, and all links with one another. The direct links with Arturo and with one another are numbered according to type of relationship; indirect links are represented by the number 10.

As Figure 19 illustrates, there is no single person tied to another with fewer than five relations of various strengths. The key relation that all of them share is the political one, but this was merely the beginning relation, with all others generated over time. The political exchanges of the past became subordinated to other layers of relationship; nevertheless, these political relations are inseparable from the others. The political relations have provided an experiential "glue" to all others. No one in the network can forget how the group protected one another when circumstances of danger arose. This glue of political experience, like the political experience of the *comadres*, provides the network with a means of reference to the past, as well as an important basis for social identity.

The Dyads

Each person, as can be seen in figure 19, has multiple relations with Arturo Valenzuela. These provide insight into the most important sources of Arturo's public male identity, as well as his sense of social identification. As will be seen, although some of these men are rather deferent, none are Arturo's lackeys, and some even question his basic political position.

First, Roberto López Cobos is Arturo's best and most intimate friend. They met at a political demonstration in 1970 and became part of a *confianza* network through the mutual exchange of favors, attendance at rituals, visitations to the rural areas of Mexico, and sharing of a general political orientation. There are disagreements between the two, especially when it concerns Arturo's relationships with political elites. Roberto distrusts the professed ideology of the elites, and he scorns their past commitments by commenting, "What happened will happen and continue happening." By this he means that elites will always have their own interests to serve in politics. Regardless of their different points of view, however, the content of Arturo and Roberto's relationship illustrates the density of the relations between them.

Both belong to a building-materials cooperative that they formed with other members of the network. The cooperative is known as the Cooperativa Mutualista de Netzahualcoyotl and is fully incorporated, providing low-cost mortar, sand, cement, cement blocks, and steel reinforcing rods to the locality. In this context the cooperative is very important, since self-constructed housing is the most common way for persons to acquire homes, as I have pointed out in the ethnographic description of chapter 3. Most persons in Ciudad Netzahualcoyotl contract out only for major construction, and, in the main, build their homes themselves, in the stages described earlier (see chapter 3).

Roberto serves as the cooperative's secretary; Arturo is its president. In addition, Arturo generally participates in Roberto's rotating credit associations (*tandas*). Roberto generally reserves Arturo a turn close to the beginning of the cycle so that Arturo can receive cash first and pay last.[1] The two friends also borrow money from each other for personal and business reasons. Since Roberto owns a small grocery store, Arturo sometimes uses credit to buy groceries there. Frequently, Arturo charges his account for quarts of beer (*caguamas*, meaning "turtles," because of the shape of the bottle) that he then shares with his pals (*cuates*) during the nocturnal unwinding sessions following a day's political activities.

Among other economic ties, Arturo is responsible for obtaining a taxi certificate of operation for Roberto—a very valuable commodity acquired only through political pressures at the state level. This certificate is one of twenty that Arturo distributed among his pals and kin, all of whom formed part of a taxi cooperative. In part, such economic exchanges are inseparable from the long-standing political ties and mutual protection each has offered the other during the intense periods of political organizing in Netzahualcoyotl and outside of the city in the town of Chimalhuacan. Roberto, who is an expert small-town speech mimic, and who has an easy, outgoing manner and warm personality, has been Arturo's key link in expanding his political activities to more rural areas.

Among the most important political ties that have emerged are those acquired as part of a cohort of political activists who braved police beatings, intimidation, and arrest. Arturo and Roberto recount, with some glee and at times with almost mythic flavor, their apprehension by state police (*granaderos*), their beating with carbine rifle butts while in the back of a police van, and their release when CRC cohorts stopped the vehicle and threatened to overturn it. It is from such experiences that Roberto and Arturo have sealed their social friendship. When former supporters and followers of Arturo criticize his tactics, strategy, or moral reputation, Roberto quickly responds by saying, "Arturo is my friend, and if you and I are to remain friends, we had better change the conversation to another topic."

There are, however, other important ties that have been established between Arturo and Roberto. These consist of a number of direct and indirect relationships, and cues for each are repeated during the course of a visit to Roberto's home. Arturo is matrimonial godfather to Roberto's sister and her husband and baptismal godfather of their child. Arturo is addressed respectfully as *padrino* ("godfather") by Roberto's sister, Socorro, and her husband, Cándido. Their child, María Cristina, also refers to Arturo as *padrino;* Roberto's father and Arturo refer to each other as *compadre.*

Although separated by twenty-five years, the two have common migratory experience in the United States, about which they speak often. Between Arturo and Roberto, no title of deference is used. In conversation, in Arturo's presence or not, Roberto always refers to Arturo by his name and not by an honorific title of deference.

In addition, Arturo has had a romantic relationship with Roberto's other sister, Gloria (who, with her son, lives in the same household with Roberto). It is with Gloria that Arturo carries on a flirtatious relationship during his frequent visits to the household. Figure 20 illustrates the multiple ties between Arturo and Roberto.

Another pal, Juan Limón Quiñones, is referred to as *"mi compadre Juan"* by Arturo. This term of address, in even the most casual conversations, indicates an extremely intense social relation. Arturo is Juan Limón's daughter's baptismal godfather. Julieta Valenzuela is also godparent to the daughter and therefore *comadre* to both Juan Limón and his wife Estella. Since they live only three doors away from Julieta, Estella, in addition, can be counted as one of Julieta's closest *comadres* in the political activities of the neighborhood and is considered one of the *"viejas chingonas."* Julieta and Estella also provide child-care services for each other during crucial periods of political activity. Estella and Julieta attend religious activities together on important Mexican ritual days, such as festivities to the Virgin of Guadalupe, Christmas, and Easter. Neither woman, however, is a church regular.

"Compadre Juan" is also a member of the business cooperative and serves as its treasurer, and he too forms *tandas* in which Arturo sometimes participates. Occasionally the two borrow money from each other, and Arturo was especially instrumental in Juan receiving a ten percent interest loan from one of the local loan sharks. This last favor was most unusual, since money is usually lent by loan sharks at twenty cents on the dollar. For Arturo's birthday, Compadre Juan presented him with a very expensive pair of high-heeled calfskin boots, although it is most unusual for males to exchange gifts on such occasions.

Compadre Juan is important to Arturo for political advice, and his frank disagreement with Arturo over establishing intimate ties with governmental officials has been an ongoing source of conflict.

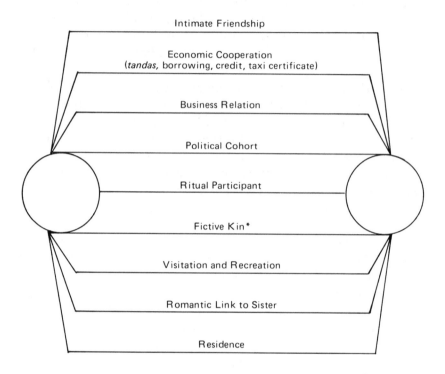

Intimate Friendship

Economic Cooperation
(*tandas,* borrowing, credit, taxi certificate)

Business Relation

Political Cohort

Ritual Participant

Fictive Kin*

Visitation and Recreation

Romantic Link to Sister

Residence

Arturo Valenzuela Cisneros   *Roberto López Cobos*

*It is important to note that although there is no direct fictive kinship between Roberto and Arturo, the fictive kinship established by Arturo with Roberto's consanguines establishes an indirect fictive-kinship relation between the two friends. Thus, when his sister or his father speak of "El Compadre" or "El Padrino," Roberto knows that it is certainly Arturo who is being referred to.

Fig. 20. Multiple ties between Arturo Valenzuela Cisneros
and Roberto López Cobos.

Juan is especially adamant about the dangers of entering formal governmental sectors. In conversations during the frequent unwinding sessions at Roberto's, Juan always points to what he calls *"revoltijo de huevos"* ("scrambled eggs"),[2] which describes the frequent attempts by elites in the government to buy out their opposition or to "integrate" the opposition in such a way as to make them ineffective. This disagreement eventually resulted in Juan

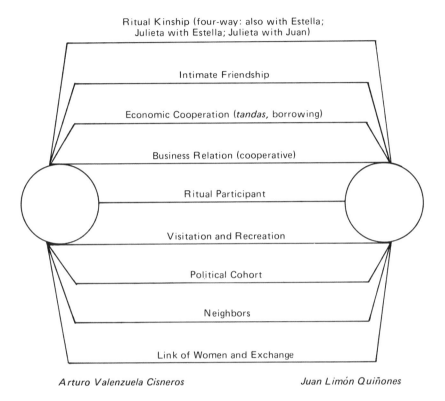

Ritual Kinship (four-way: also with Estella; Julieta with Estella; Julieta with Juan)

Intimate Friendship

Economic Cooperation (*tandas*, borrowing)

Business Relation (cooperative)

Ritual Participant

Visitation and Recreation

Political Cohort

Neighbors

Link of Women and Exchange

Arturo Valenzuela Cisneros   *Juan Limón Quiñones*

Fig. 21. Multiple ties between Arturo Valenzuela Cisneros
and Juan Limón Quiñones.

and Estella withdrawing, as direct participants, from the demonstrations organized by Arturo in 1975. Nevertheless, they remained close friends and *compadres*, and still were in 1979. Figure 21 illustrates their multiple ties.

Third, Emilio García López (nicknamed "Tlaxcala" for having been born in that Mexican state), prior to his withdrawal from the CRC in 1973, had been Arturo's intimate friend and part-time bodyguard, and had provided some of the security during public demonstrations. A former security agent for the state judicial body in Tlaxcala, Emilio earned a very modest living from raising

and selling chickens in Ciudad Netzahualcoyotl until his death in
1974. For both Arturo and Emilio, however, their shared experiences as migrant workers in Tracy, California, where both learned
English, was part of the experiential dimension that "glued" their
dense relationship.

Emilio and his brother Anastasio ("Bigotes") both borrowed
from and lent money to Arturo.[3] Both brothers are also intimate
friends of Roberto López Cobos (fig. 20). Emilio, Roberto, and
"Bigotes" have accompanied Arturo to Tlaxcala, where Emilio's
eldest brother owns a small ranch. There Arturo has often un-
wound from his political activities, riding horseback, cutting
wood, drinking, swimming, and playing the guitar into the early
morning (see figs. 22, 23, 24, and 25). Including other trips to the
countryside, Arturo has had six such outings with his pals during
the year (1974). For him, the countryside is important, and he ex-
plains that "my head explodes if I do not return to breathe the
clean air and see the fields grow."

Emilio also participates in the nocturnal sessions at Roberto's
when he is able to be away from his chicken-business responsibili-
ties, including trying to duck the city inspectors, who want to
close him down for not having a poultry license. Arturo has twice
served as an intermediary with the municipal authorities when
they confiscated Emilio's poultry. Arturo also has assisted Emilio
in legitimizing his land tenure with the local urban-development
office.

Between Emilio and Arturo, however, there is an added element. Arturo, in addition to his political roles, is a *huesero* ("bone-
setter")—a practice known primarily in village communities. He
not only manipulates muscles and sets bone fractures but at times
also prescribes herbal medicines for particular ailments. For example, between 1972 and 1974, Emilio has been Arturo's patient for
various intestinal disorders. Unfortunately, neither Arturo's prescriptions and massages, which he provided rather frequently during this period, nor regular medical care was able to prevent
Emilio's death in 1974. Figure 26 illustrates their relationship.

Anastasio "Bigotes" García López is Emilio's youngest brother
of a family of seven brothers and four sisters. Like Emilio, he was

Fig. 22. Arturo on the ranch (face masked to preserve confidentiality).

Fig. 23. Arturo cutting wood at Emilio's brother's ranch.

born in the state of Tlaxcala, and after a series of moves from village to town to Mexico City and then to Ciudad Netzahualcoyotl, "Bigotes" settled two blocks away from his brother. Except for his eldest brother, who runs the ranch in Tlaxcala that Arturo and the others visit on occasion, the partition of land among the eleven siblings forced them all to migrate eventually to Mexico City. Anastasio and Emilio jointly own the lots on which each of the brothers now lives with his family.

For Arturo, Anastasio has been his most physically ardent supporter. By this I mean that although his brother Emilio was usually in charge of security arrangements, it was Anastasio who carried out any demanding physical violence against opponents, or the police on occasion. Since Anastasio is a fine physical specimen, with unusually well-developed musculature, very good eyesight, extremely quick hand and feet reactions, and an almost fearless disposition, he is quite formidable.

On two occasions when members of the state judicial police had

Fig. 24. Emilio with a bottle of *aguardiente* at his brother's ranch.

arrested Arturo and had begun beating his followers, "Bigotes" managed to generate sufficient counterforce by either gathering together some of the "shock troops," if they were available, or by calling upon some of the local street gangs for assistance. On one occasion, "Bigotes" used members of the notorious Girafos ("Giraffes"), who had been used also by the Mexican government during the 1968 student demonstrations (then called the Halcones ["Hawks"]). Regardless of their name, they respected "Bigotes's" street reputation.

"Bigotes" has been most responsible for Arturo's physical safety, but this represents only one layer of a multiple relationship. In addition, Arturo has assisted "Bigotes" in obtaining construction permits for his jointly held lots, the legality of which are quite questionable; they have participated together in *tandas*; they have borrowed money from each other; and they have assisted each other with carpentry work, since "Bigotes's" skill was widely known throughout the area. During their association, Arturo has

Fig. 25. Arturo and Emilio toasting their friendship (faces masked
to preserve confidentiality).

massaged "Bigotes" and set a broken finger. In addition, "Bigotes"
has brought relatives and friends to Arturo for treatment. Especially when "Bigotes," Roberto, and Emilio are present, the treatment process is marked by good-natured jokes and fun. This is
particularly true when "La Negra"—one of Emilio and Anastasio's
cousins—seeks treatment. A voluptuous, beautiful, dark-skinned,
curly-haired surgical nurse, "La Negra," although massaged in the
presence of Julieta, Arturo's wife, is nevertheless the object of
double and triple entendres from both males and females present.
She reciprocates then or at a latter time, even more pointedly,
when she administers vitamin injections to Arturo.

Discussion of political events, conversations about money,
jokes about "La Negra," reminiscences of the good times at the
ranch, philosophical meanderings, and crass male-defined talk of
sex, all punctuate the frequent gatherings at Roberto's store, where
Anastasio is also present. In addition, Arturo is baptismal god-

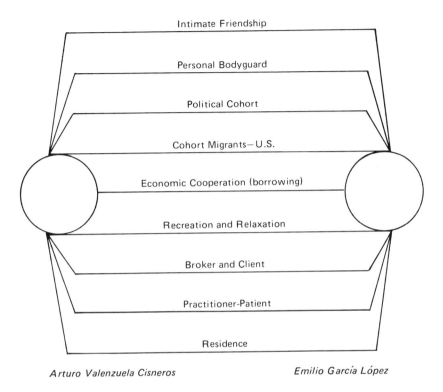

Intimate Friendship

Personal Bodyguard

Political Cohort

Cohort Migrants—U.S.

Economic Cooperation (borrowing)

Recreation and Relaxation

Broker and Client

Practitioner-Patient

Residence

Arturo Valenzuela Cisneros   *Emilio García López*

Fig. 26. Multiple ties between Arturo Valenzuela Cisneros
and Emilio García López.

father to "Bigotes's" eldest of seven children, as well as *compadre* to "Bigotes's" wife. Julieta, however, is not baptismal godmother and therefore does not have a *comadre* relation with either "Bigotes" or his wife. Figure 27 illustrates their relationship.

Benigno Zaragosa Segura is the foreman of the building-materials cooperative in which Arturo, Roberto, and Juan Limón participate. He was the treasurer of the executive committee of the CRC before its schism, secretary of Arturo's own subcommittee prior to its demise, and confirmation godfather to one of Arturo's eldest sons. Benigno's wife is therefore a fictive kin, because

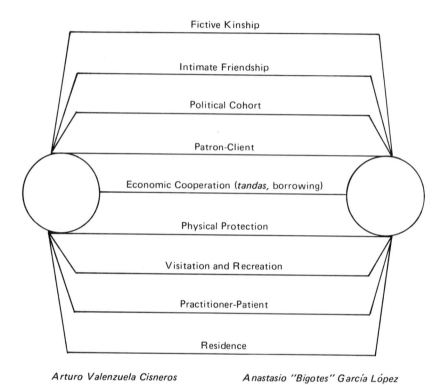

Arturo Valenzuela Cisneros   *Anastasio "Bigotes" García López*

Fig. 27. Multiple ties between Arturo Valenzuela Cisneros
and Anastasio "Bigotes" García López.

although a godmother is not required, she indirectly acquires fictive status. But confirmation sponsorship is usually regarded as
less important and less obligatory than baptismal sponsorship
(Lomnitz 1977:164).

In addition, Benigno has received one of the taxi certificates (see
chapter 5) that Arturo distributed among his male network of fictive kin and friends and to members of his consanguine family.
Benigno is one of the members of the taxi cooperative and serves
as a sort of manager, keeping track of receipts turned in by drivers
hired by the cooperative and of the 10 percent shared by all mem-

bers who are driver-owners. For the most part, the taxi cooperative's business meetings are held in Benigno's small office in the
building-materials cooperative, or in one of the taxis parked in the
street islands in the center of the city, or at one of the nocturnal
sessions at Roberto's home. Like most of Arturo's pals (cuates),
Benigno also participates in the drinking sessions at Roberto's.

Benigno can also be counted upon by Arturo and by members
of the cooperative to repair their automobiles or provide mechani-
cal guidance. It is this ability of Benigno's that has also saddled
him with the responsibility of maintaining the two vintage 1952
Chevrolet two-and-a-half tonners that are used by the building
cooperative to haul sand, cement bags, construction rods, and
cement blocks from suppliers.

Like Arturo and some of the other members of the CRC executive committee, however, Benigno went into hiding during the
most violent periods of confrontation between the CRC and city
and state judicial authorities. It was during this period that Benigno introduced Arturo to his compadres in Ecatepec,[4] who hid
them both from the police at different times during 1971 and 1972.
Later, Arturo would seek refuge in a household here for other than
political reasons, for he had fathered a child of a compadre's eldest
daughter. Even after she had married and moved from the household of Arturo's compadre, "the woman from Ecatepec," as Julieta
called her, would rush with her child to her parents' home when
Arturo visited. Arturo did not know that he was the child's father.
The true paternity of the child was known to Benigno, his compadres, and Roberto, and it was probably the most intimate secret
shared between them. Figure 28 illustrates the multiple ties between Arturo and Benigno.

Among the most formalistic relations of confianza in Arturo's
network are those he shares with Lorenzo Manilla Marta. At one
time, the former secretary of exterior relations for Arturo's subcommittee within the CRC, Lorenzo functioned as Arturo's subcommittee broker with a few local merchants and businessmen.
Manilla, also from the state of Oaxaca, where Arturo and his wife
were born, had learned massage and bonesetting techniques from
the same curer who taught Arturo. In fact, it was Manilla who

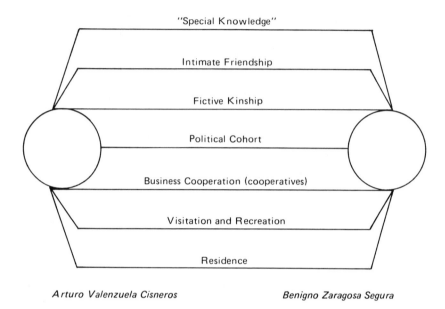

"Special Knowledge"

Intimate Friendship

Fictive Kinship

Political Cohort

Business Cooperation (cooperatives)

Visitation and Recreation

Residence

Arturo Valenzuela Cisneros   *Benigno Zaragosa Segura*

Fig. 28. Multiple ties between Arturo Valenzuela Cisneros
and Benigno Zaragosa Segura.

introduced Arturo to Don Teófilo, whom Arturo still visits once a
year to receive "brush-up" information on new herbs, massages,
or bonesettings. In addition, Julieta and Arturo, accompanied by
Manilla, have sought Don Teófilo's professional advice for various physical and emotional ailments, and especially for Arturo's
occasional paralysis.

Manilla is Julieta's second cousin (paternal) and *compadre* of
confirmation to Jorge López Cobos, Roberto's youngest brother.
In addition, Manilla, Roberto, Gloria, one of the taxi drivers, and
Arturo travel to Roberto's native town for the town's fiesta. Don
Roberto, Roberto's father, is the town's fireworks expert and also
serves the surrounding communities.

The extreme formalism between Arturo and Manilla, expressed
by their use of the second-person formal *usted* ("thou"), is a consequence of Manilla having served as Arturo's marriage broker to

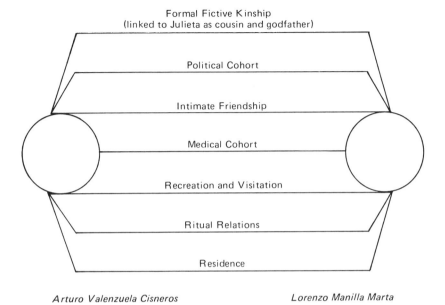

Arturo Valenzuela Cisneros   *Lorenzo Manilla Marta*

Fig. 29. Multiple ties between Arturo Valenzuela Cisneros
and Lorenzo Manilla Marta.

Julieta's politician-father in their home state, and of having served
as their *padrino de matrimonio* ("marriage godfather"). The formalism breaks down during the nocturnal sessions or during ritual
occasions at either of their homes, when men are relaxed and not
posing. Although Manilla knows of Arturo's peccadillos with
other women, this does not seem to strain their relationship.
Furthermore, during periods of relaxation when the men are in the
midst of bawdy stories, Manilla refers to Arturo as *"macana de
acero"* ("cudgel of steel") for his amorous relationships. Figure 29
illustrates their relationship.

Jorge López Cobos, Roberto's younger brother, although formerly a CRC participant and supporter of Arturo, no longer participates in political activities. As a tailor, Jorge has access to low-
cost clothing materials and supplies Arturo and wife with uncut
material. This support is extremely important, given Arturo's

intermittent income. Although Jorge had not participated in the political activities that led to Arturo's arrest, it was Jorge and his brother who managed to raise bail money to obtain Arturo's release from jail. This money, in combination with an arrangement made by the former head of the CRC with the city mayor (see chapter 5), expedited Arturo's release and allowed him to go into hiding in Ecatepec long enough for things to cool down sufficiently to have his "inciting to riot" charges dropped.

Jorge's invaluable assistance at a time when even Arturo's parents and brothers had abandoned him to the authorities is recalled by Arturo with some frequency during conversations with Roberto and also in situations where Jorge is present. In addition, Arturo and Jorge participate in the same *tanda*, and the two have borrowed money from each other.

Because Jorge is a frequent nightly visitor to Roberto's home, and since Arturo is often present as well, an intimate friendship has developed. Arturo has often performed the unwanted role of broker for Jorge. Jorge suffers from acute alcoholism and lives much of his life in a dream world of fantasy and frustration in which he sees himself as a successful entrepreneur making suits for wealthy patrons. In reality, he is a jobber to whom occasional orders are given by some of the better men's clothing stores in Mexico City. The disparity between fantasy and reality is expressed by Jorge in frequent drinking bouts, conflict with his spouse and her immediate family, and not infrequently with Roberto, his brother. Arturo sometimes intercedes with Jorge's mother-in-law, who has twice had Jorge arrested, and with Roberto, whom Jorge alienates during his binges.

Nevertheless, the relationship between Arturo and Jorge is basically egalitarian, with Arturo referring to Jorge jokingly as *cuñado* ("brother-in-law"), in reference to his romantic relationship with Jorge and Roberto's sister, Gloria. Sometimes even Arturo cannot cope with Jorge's rather heavy hand (a chronic back-slapper seemingly disguising some sort of pent-up rage) and has threatened to have him castrated by some of the *"viejas chingonas"* of the CRC or spanked by "Bigotes." But conflict between them is usually settled rather quickly, and Arturo provides herbal

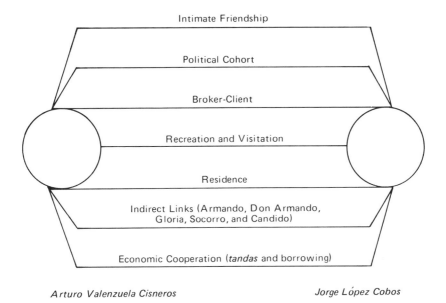

Fig. 30. Multiple ties between Arturo Valenzuela Cisneros
and Jorge López Cobos.

prescriptions for Jorge's hangovers. Figure 30 illustrates their relationship.

Petrolino Valparaíso Sánchez, like *compadre* Juan Limón, is
ritually tied to Arturo and his wife, Julieta. Arturo is confirmation
godfather and Julieta is considered godmother, although only
Arturo actually sponsored Petrolino's eldest child. Doña Carmen,
Petrolino's spouse, frequently exchanges visits with Julieta and
often discusses with her the subject of Arturo's unfaithfulness.
Both of them agree that "even the best of men should be burnt in
green wood,"[5] but Doña Carmen, with Doña Margarita—Arturo's
mother—has been instrumental in convincing Julieta to remain
with Arturo.

Through Petrolino, Arturo has learned of Doña Carmen's intercession and very much appreciates her friendship as well as Petrolino's. In addition, Doña Carmen assisted Julieta during a time

when Julieta, Arturo, and three of the children contracted typhoid. It was Petrolino and Carmen who cared for them all, feeding, washing, and doctoring the Valenzuela family. With the help, too, of Arturo's consanguine family, all members of the Valenzuela family survived.

Petrolino and Doña Carmen were also ardent political supporters of Arturo between 1970 and 1973. Petrolino, as former minister of vigilance for Arturo's local subcommittee, was responsible for getting the subcommittee's members to meetings, overseeing their behavior, assisting in the collection of dues, and making sure that members carried their membership credentials. Doña Carmen, one of the *"viejas chingonas,"* is among the toughest of the women and was instrumental in some of the violent confrontations with police.

In addition, Petrolino has a share in the building cooperative and participates in the monthly meetings of its members to discuss finances and the constant problem of delivery of materials because of the ancient trucks the cooperative owns. Petrolino, too, received a taxi certificate from Arturo and drives his own automobile, which he purchased with money borrowed from a local agency through Arturo's intercession. Petrolino also participates in *tandas* with Arturo, Juan Limón Quiñones, Roberto, and "Bigotes." Figure 31 illustrates their relationship.

Librado Garcilazo Salas is an itinerant photographer who was an agent with the state judicial police in 1970. His duty, among others, was to spy on the CRC for the governor's office. Yet between 1970 and 1971, Librado complicated the spy business and became a sort of double agent for the CRC. He supplied the CRC with secret police-reports and notified the executive committee when arrests or raids were to be made. The reasons for the switch in allegiance are quite complicated and beyond the scope of this description, but they included financial support from the CRC; an assault on his wife by state police during a demonstration, while she was going to market; and the creation of an intimate friendship with Arturo through Jaime Valenzuela Cisneros, Arturo's eldest brother, before Arturo's rise within the CRC. In this case, "entanglement" with Arturo, as an intimate friend, eventually resulted in Librado's dismissal from the state police.

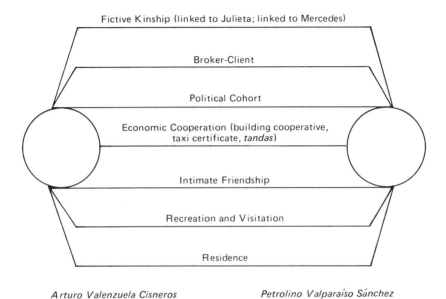

Fictive Kinship (linked to Julieta; linked to Mercedes)

Broker-Client

Political Cohort

Economic Cooperation (building cooperative, taxi certificate, *tandas*)

Intimate Friendship

Recreation and Visitation

Residence

Arturo Valenzuela Cisneros   *Petrolino Valparaíso Sánchez*

Fig. 31. Multiple ties between Arturo Valenzuela Cisneros
and Petrolino Valparaíso Sánchez.

Librado is a comic person and a master of the double and triple entendre, which in the stressful ambience of Arturo's activities is a very welcome relief. In this role, Librado is seldom listened to and does not command respect from the others or from Arturo. Arturo supplies him with leads on photography jobs, employs him occasionally as a bodyguard (Librado is a large bear of a man), and once in a while loans him money.

Of all the intimates around Arturo, the relationship with Librado is the most asymmetrical, with Arturo fulfilling more the role of traditional patron and Librado that of client. From my observation, there has been a constant irritation present in their relationship, as evidenced by the exchange of cutting remarks in which Librado calls Arturo "El Amo" ("the master") and Arturo calls Librado "El Sapo" ("the frog"). There have been occasions in which this irritability has almost resulted in physical violence. Yet Arturo and Librado do participate in the same *tandas*, Librado has

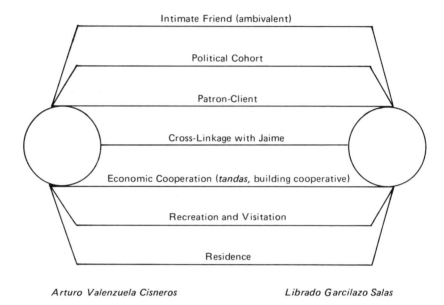

Arturo Valenzuela Cisneros   Librado Garcilazo Salas

Fig. 32. Multiple ties between Arturo Valenzuela Cisneros
and Librado Garcilazo Salas.

a share in the building cooperative, and both frequent the nocturnal sessions at Roberto's place. Of all of Arturo's relations, this
one is strikingly ambivalent. Figure 32 illustrates the relationship.

During the day or during part of the evening, one or more of
these relationships will emerge, directly or indirectly, at Roberto's
home, at Arturo's, in the street, where men occasionally meet to
talk, or simply in conversation with others. These relationships—
the second-order relationships—make up an important facet of
Arturo's locality. These, like the familial relationships, serve to
"locate" him in time, in space, and in social activities. These, like
the others, help define Arturo's sense of public self, but also his
sense of private self. They give him the ability to mirror socially
and to create the reflections important in maintaining networks of
relationships. Without the ability to mirror and to create reflections in social relations, Arturo would become "delocalized"—i.e,

deprived of context. These relations were the basis of Arturo's former political support. By 1974 he had become too entangled in the domains of elites to rely on local support of the kind he once had. His "mirrors" became located among elites, and in time he was unable to create reflections in this new context, for it was merely "political" and not at all social.

Arturo's networks had provided him with a sense of self-reference and social identity. He became caught, however, in relations that eventually led to his being stripped of these referents. The remaining sections of this book explain this process of "delocalization."

PART III

The Structure of Marginality Politics

This section of the book advances the argument that national "integration" is the broadest and highest-level myth of marginality, a myth that makes possible the utilization of politically and economically marginalized populations as further resources for private and public elites. This argument is confirmed by showing the manner in which the CRC was "institutionalized," and the population of Netzahualcoyotl used by elites as a resource. Arturo Valenzuela Cisneros, it will be seen, played an important part in this process but was ultimately unwilling to join with others in the institutionalization of illegitimacy. Nevertheless, he lost his most important sources of legitimate support—the primary and secondary orders of his locality. Without them he became enmeshed in the processes of political brokerage and swallowed up in the rituals of marginality. In the wake of this, it was Valenzuela's opponents who became "integrated." Finally, this section will illustrate that the rituals of marginality at the local level—those involving activities of everyday life and death—are in opposition to those rituals of marginality of the nation, state, and municipality. When the two complexes of rituals enter the same social field, some sort of resolution must occur. For the networks of *compadres* and *comadres*, this resolution entailed withdrawal from politics and acquired insight into the myths of nation, state, and elites. For elites, political ascendancy is made possible at the expense of the locality. For Valenzuela, the retention of an archaic ideology and physical deterioration was the outcome.

8

The Myth of Political
Integration: The CRC

THE ENTANGLEMENT OF LOCAL leaders like Valenzuela in elite
domains is inevitable. But the eventual "integration" of the CRC
leadership into the public-sector domain was, in part, the result of
characteristics that developed at the local level. The supporters of
the CRC were quite heterogeneous, reflecting a variety of goals
and a variety of problems, from land tenure to the protection of
property from land invasions. Supporters included land invaders
as well as property owners. Supporters came from the various geographical areas of the city, and each context defined the types of
goals supporters advocated. Some wanted land developers to provide services, others wanted schools, others wanted protection
from the police, and still others wanted land. It is this heterogeneity that was responsible, in part, for the eventual "integration" of
the CRC leadership. With so many goals, needs, and agendas, and
with the existence of resources that could solve these needs outside
the locality in the domains of the elites, pressures toward entanglement extended from the local level.

Entanglement is inevitable for social-structural reasons, but it is
also an artifact of heterogeneity and widespread need at the local
level, as was true for the population in Netzahualcoyotl. Since
only the "formal" public sector can address these issues, entanglement within these domains is inevitable. The central unintended
consequence of this entanglement was exactly opposite of what

was sought by the local population. As will be demonstrated, *the formal public sector is the most important mechanism through which economically and politically marginalized populations become further exploited by the private sector in Mexico, and contribute further to the political ascendancy of public-sector elites.* Integration, in fact, involves the "assimilation" of certain *individuals* at the outer edge of the elite sector, while the rest of the population becomes further pauperized. The myth of "national integration" of such marginalized populations includes the ideology that the national public sector is somehow a neutral body, "universally" representing the interests of all sectors. As will be demonstrated, such was not the case in Netzahualcoyotl, where the population became further pauperized, to the benefit of the private sector, and was used as a political stepping-stone for members of the public sector. For those at the local level, like Arturo Valenzuela Cisneros, who do not quite fit *individually* within the elite's scheme of strategies, political and behavioral consequences are extreme.

INSTITUTIONALIZATION OF ILLEGITIMACY

Between 1972 and 1973, the CRC continued to provide protection against land developers for persons boycotting mortgage payments. It had provided protection in various forms since 1970, as will be recalled, such as the women surrounding and protecting lots. The CRC offered protection against local, state, and federal institutions to those refusing to pay various fees, licenses, permits, utilities, and so on. In addition, the CRC provided protection against eviction by local and state authorities to persons who had "squatted" on privately held land. It must be recalled that the general strategy employed by the leadership of the CRC was to boycott all payments to all authorities, private or public, until the basic goals were accomplished. In time, such a strategy resulted in a quite heterogeneous mix of supporters with different ideas about the type of leader they would support. Hence, divisions and conflicts surfaced within the organization. The CRC's collective-protection strategy varied according to the specific needs in different geographical areas; this, in part, defined the manner in which divisions hardened within the CRC, and it ultimately defined the way in which these divisions were expertly exploited by public-sector elites for their own purposes.

The heterogeneity of support and the attendant contradictions in objective within the same social field, the exploitation of this situation by the public sector, and the misguided tactics of Arturo Valenzuela Cisneros eventually led to the cooptation of the CRC. The processes that led to this result emerged in part because of the protection provided by the CRC against eviction by local and state authorities in those areas most in conflict. This protection resulted in subcommittee presidents accumulating segmented power domains that were controlled through the various informal networks that Mondragón had established. It was not long before subcommittee presidents, who were also executive-committee members of the CRC, became engaged in the sale of lots illegally, the negation of public services, and the creation of coercive relations with supporters. These were the very activities against which the CRC had been formed. It was from this segment of the CRC that individuals were "integrated," and from which Valenzuela was excluded.

THE PROCESS

By merely paying a 50-peso fee, an individual could join with many others and receive the protective sanction of a CRC *credencial* ("credential"). But within some subcommittees, presidents in fact charged not only for the *credencial* but also for costs supposedly incurred in the resolution of specific problems. Such fees were not standardized but were individually determined by the subcommittee presidents. Those seeking protection were the land squatters, who were charged as much as 200 pesos by some subcommittee presidents. Of the seventeen members of the executive committee, twelve became involved in such practices.

Furthermore, it was not long before four of these persons also became involved in the sale of lots under the banner of the CRC.

Of the fifty-eight subcommittees, at least fourteen presidents became involved in such lot sales. By 1973 a total of eighteen subcommittees were illegally selling lots. Such activities, however, were known only among the core of the executive committee and those closest to the secretary-general. The core of the executive committee consisted of six men, four of whom were bound to Mondragón by bonds of kinship, friendship, and political support. In turn, however, these four had a core of followers similarly bound to them.

Valenzuela and the head of propaganda, Carlos Serrano, also had networks of supporters within the executive committee who were bound to them in the same manner, but neither of these men was involved in the sale of lots or in the sale of 200-peso "protections." Thus, the cleavages that later developed in the CRC had roots in legitimate or coercive support; it was these roots that became the source of the schisms that developed in 1973.

Furthermore, each subcommittee also had its core of followers who were tied to the president of the subcommittee. The nature of these ties was similar to the ties between Mondragón and his core support within the executive committee, and to Valenzuela and his core of support. But the subcommittees themselves were rent by divisions according to the interests of supporters. Such divisions reflected the manner in which supporters gained control of their lands.

In subcommittees located in areas where the concentration of land squatters was high (sections 32-35, 63, 64, 66), few divisions occurred among supporters over the definition of goals. Such persons had joined the CRC with "protection" as their primary goal, and they aligned themselves unequivocally on this basis. In addition, they ultimately formed double and triple ties to the presidents of their subcommittees.

In those areas where both land squatters and legal lot owners were concentrated (sections 37, 51-55, 60, 67-78), divisions among supporters crosscut horizontal ties of fictive kin and friendship relations: coercive and legitimate support of the CRC's public goals divided followers, but relations based on friendship and fictive kinship crosscut such cleavages. But these horizontal ties, when broken, snapped with violence. When schisms surfaced in 1973, no quarter was given or taken.

Divisions within subcommittees in those areas (sections 48, 49, 53, 55-60) where supporters were primarily land or lot owners were highly personalistic—that is, they reflected old conflicts between *comadres*, fights between friends, rivalries between males for the attention of the local subcommittee president, or the pursuit of favors at the expense of other supporters. Nevertheless, the nature of the relationship between subcommittee presidents in these areas and their followers was much like those in other subcommittees. The main difference was that divisions within subcommittees in these areas were not based on lot ownership but rather on the reciprocation of favors for their support. Such favors as getting someone released from jail, waiving a fee for a license, intervening in the public-works department in support of construction on a lot whose owners could not show an up-to-date mortgage-payment booklet—these were all competed for by followers.

Thus a woman entering one of the subcommittee offices to seek intervention on a matter was referred to by another woman in the following manner: *"Ahí viene otra vez la pediche para quitarle el tiempo al jefe y a mí"* ("Here she comes again, the beggar, to take time from the chief and from me"). Such comments expressed not impatience for time lost but rather resentment of attention given to another person. Where attention is scarce, attention given to one is taken from someone else. Thus rivalries developed for the attention of the newly developing *caciquitos*.

These divisions among supporters in the various sections of the city also reflected divisions within the CRC core, and although bonds of friendship, fictive kinship, and sometimes consanguine kinship existed, these bonds were broken when the divisive forces became too strong.

Table 16 illustrates that the CRC was divided among three central figures—Mondragón, Valenzuela, and Serrano[1]—with subcommittee presidents coalescing under each major figure. This process was rather complicated in that these three central figures were also presidents of the largest subcommittees in Netzahualcoyotl: Mondragón, subcommittee 19; Valenzuela, subcommittee 22; Serrano, subcommittee "L. Cárdenas." Thus, each man had an independent source of support within the CRC, with Mondragón's based on the selling of lots by subcommittees. These power spheres that developed changed the composition of the political field by 1972 into a tripartite coalition under the same CRC banner. Although this division among the three leaders was largely a balanced one, the coalescing of the three groups was unstable, as was demonstrated when the political facade of the field changed again in September 1972.

In the meantime, there were some indications of stress between Mondragón and Valenzuela in the summer of 1972 (Serrano, through February 1973, was largely not yet in the game and supported Valenzuela until that date). Valenzuela often accused Mondragón of "being lazy," which was a euphemism to describe the conflict over the sale of lots, and also expressed his irritation with Mondragón for not assisting him with the Agrario (the Agrarian Department). By the end of the summer of 1972, the Agrario had agreed to discuss substantive issues concerning the CRC's public goals and the communal landholders of Chimalhuacán.

This agreement to discuss substantive issues was related to complicated strategies of elites, because around this time an offer was made by the Confederación Nacional Campesina to help the CRC resolve the basic problems in Netzahualcoyotl.[2] The agreement by the Agrario and the offer by the Confederación Nacional Campesina (CNC) needed only a tactical decision by the CRC leadership to merge with the CNC before the final supralocal scenario could unfold and the structural marginalization could become complete. Such strategies, coupled with the illegal sale of lots and the selling of "protection" by subcommittee presidents with the sanction of Mondragón, could only lead to the eventual structural marginalization of the CRC and to the "integration" of those most involved in illegal activities. This combination of events needed only Valenzuela's misguided tactics to seal the fate of the CRC and its supporters.

TABLE 16
POLITICAL ALIGNMENTS WITHIN THE CRC

Mondragón		Valenzuela		Serrano	
Section	Subcommittee Number	Section	Subcommittee Number	Section	Subcommittee Number
32-35	15,16,17	48	9,11	60	E. Zapata
37	18	49	12	74	L. Cárdenas
54	19	51	13	75,78	F. Villa
63	—	52	14		
64		53	—		
66	Villada, Revolución	55			
67	1910	56	22, Benito Juárez		
68	—	57	20		
69-73	23,24,25,26,27	58	16th of Sept.		
76-77	28,29,30	59,61-62	5 de Mayo		

NOTE: Thirty other subcommittees were scattered throughout the city, but I could not locate them. These, like subcommittee 8, consisted of very small memberships of twenty or less.

VALENZUELA'S TACTICAL DECISION AND MONDRAGÓN'S ABSENCE

When the CNC's invitation was extended to the CRC in September 1972, Valenzuela considered this to be an indication of the CRC's strength. He assumed that, with acceptance, the Agrarian Department could then be pressured to negotiate. Furthermore, with the power of the CNC behind the CRC, Valenzuela thought, first, that the Agrarian Department would be forced to listen carefully, since demonstrations as a tactic were time- and energy-consuming for both sides. Second, the CRC's influence with the CNC could be utilized against the local and state authorities in any future negotiations concerning land-tenure problems or in providing "favors" for supporters. Third, the incorporation of the CRC into the CNC could provide its membership a modicum of protection against local and state authorities—exactly the kind of protection demanded by CRC supporters. By September 1972, Valenzuela had announced to the CRC executive committee that such an invitation had been extended, and, after brief debate, the invitation was accepted. Mondragón was conspicuously absent during the debate.

Yet the three reasons cited here were not quite sufficient, in themselves, to enable Valenzuela to push for the incorporation of the CRC into the CNC. It was during negotiations with supralocal officials concerning the major public goals of the CRC that a Fidecomiso[3] was proposed by the Agrarian Department as a viable organizational solution: it would settle the land-tenure and urbanization problems in Netzahualcoyotl as well as the land-tenure problems of the Comuneros de Chimalhuacán. Such a Fidecomiso would consist of Felipe Carranza,[4] serving as the president and representing President Echeverria, a land developer, a representative from Chimalhuacán, a representative from the Agrario, a representative from the CRC, a representative from the *municipio* of Netzahualcoyotl, a representative of the state of Mexico, and a representative from the technical section of the Nacional Financiera (the national banking system)—all of whom would form the technical negotiating body of the Fidecomiso and would work to resolve land-tenure problems.

Mr. X advised Valenzuela that in joining the CRC with the CNC, an extra vote could be counted on within the Fidecomiso, and that he, Valenzuela, could be assured of his own selection as the CNC's representative, with one of his friends representing the CRC.[5] Together with the *comuneros*, the representative from the Agrario, and Carranza, the ability of the Fidecomiso to formulate the final solution for Netzahualcoyotl and the *comuneros* could be assured. This was the strategy and hope for the incorporation of the CRC into the CNC. It appeared that with such backing, the Fidecomiso would function to fulfill the CRC's goals.

It was at this juncture that the elite strategy began to emerge in the form of an added offer by the state of Mexico. Furthermore, Mondragón's absence at the time the decision was made to incorporate the CRC into the CNC becomes clear.

GENERAL STRATEGIES OF FEDERAL AND STATE OFFICIALS

The first element of the general strategy included the incorporation of the CRC into the CNC; the second was the acceptance of the Fidecomiso as the mechanism for conflict resolution. The third element, and the most interesting, was the state authorities' attempt to split the leadership troika of the CRC along manageable lines. This would be accomplished by offering Mondragón, the secretary-general of the CRC, a councilman's position within Ciudad Netzahualcoyotl. In exchange, Mondragón would support the mayoral candidate (in July 1973).[6] Mondragón would then select from his cohorts suitable candidates for the offices of federal deputy and third councilman's alternate; in addition, he would select officials for jobs ranging from judgeship to license inspector —all part of the patronage spoils. Valenzuela would be offered the office of third councilman's alternate.

This offer to Mondragón was accompanied by the appointment of the state secretary of governance as state representative to the

Fidecomiso, and by a parallel appointment of Mondragón, after accepting the state's offer, as representative of the CRC before the Fidecomiso.

What then occurred was as follows. First, Mondragón accepted the state's offer and did become a councilman for the city and the CRC's representative to the Fidecomiso. Second, Valenzuela was offered a councilman's alternate position, but he refused. In his refusal, he cited the sale of lots by subcommittee presidents who were also members of the CRC executive committee. These particular subcommittees formed the basis of Mondragón's power. Unless Mondragón was willing to eliminate these individuals from the CRC, Valenzuela vowed he could not agree to any relationship between the CRC and the city and state authorities. Valenzuela was then expelled from the CRC executive committee and from the organization. Serrano, the third member of the troika, quit the CRC, created his own organization, and vowed to continue the mortgage boycott and to fight the Fidecomiso.

The last part of the strategy, however, became even more interesting: Felipe Carranza, president of the Fidecomiso, chief of the judicial branch of the Agrarian Department, former justice of the Supreme Court, personal counselor to President Echeverria, former director of the Agrario (the present director of Agrario was the intimate link to Mr. X, Valenzuela's leftist *asesor*), and personal choice of President Echeverria to resolve conflict in Ciudad Netzahualcoyotl, resigned in March 1973. The secretary of governance thus became the president of the Fidecomiso.

The total supralocal strategy included the following elements: (1) neutralizing Valenzuela by inducing him to be the representative of the CNC to the Fidecomiso; (2) splitting the troika, suborning Mondragón, and guaranteeing his vote on the Fidecomiso; (3) replacing Carranza with the secretary of governance, who would represent the interests of the state and control the agendas of the Fidecomiso; and (4) ensuring that the Fidecomiso would be made up of persons largely reflecting the position of the state, the municipality, and the land developers. The secretary of governance, as president of the Fidecomiso, represented the state of Mexico. Mondragón, as a representative of the CRC and as a councilman, would be voting in the state's interests. The newly elected mayor of Netzahualcoyotl was the municipality's representative. The land-developer representative would obviously be voting in favor of the state, and in the interests of the land developers. The representative of the Agrario, linked to Carranza and to the director of the Agrario, would vote with the elite domains. The representative from the technical section of the Nacional Financiera was largely concerned with presenting data and systems of information. The only partially "independent" person was Valenzuela, who was now a representative of the CNC rather than the CRC, and therefore functioned as part of the *arreglos* of a peasant organization, not of the urban CRC. The representative from Chimalhuacán was solely concerned with the interests of that community.

The need remains, then, to explain the reasons behind these rather elaborate elite strategies. In part, the reasons can be extrapolated from the resulting solution devised by the Fidecomiso of Netzahualcoyotl for the entire population. First, for those who had joined the boycott, and for those who were land squatters whose lots had been regularized and whose land tenure recognized by the Fidecomiso, a 25 percent discount from the market purchase price was given to them. Such persons, however, eventually paid more for such land through payments to the Fidecomiso, which in turn reimbursed the land developers holding the contested land. Legal lot owners also received a 25 percent discount on payments not made, but they had to pay all interest owed since 1969. Second, the land developers were not brought to trial for failing to supply urban services or for selling lots to multiple persons; neither were those selling lots under the CRC banner ever prosecuted or their actions circumvented by the Fidecomiso. Third, even more central to the reasons for the elaborate supralocal strategies was that after payments were resumed, land developers received 40 percent of the amount of payments not paid to them over the five-year period of the CRC boycott, as well as the remaining balance on mortgages. Developers were not required to provide the urban services that initial contracts had stipulated. Fourth, the state of Mexico agreed to provide these services through a special fund made up of a further 40 percent of payments received. The elite's strategies now seem quite clear. Both the state of Mexico and the private land-developers were in a position to lose most if the CRC had continued to operate its boycott and had achieved its public goals.

The state, through the Fidecomiso, was guaranteed the repayment of its 600-million-peso loan from the Chase Manhattan Bank for urban services by receiving the remaining 20 percent from resumed payments. The state also "integrated" the squatters and the questionably tenured owners into the state taxation and fee system. In addition, the state was able to provide further "urban infrastructures," such as new roadways, sewer lines, schools, and even courses on public administration for municipal officials from a private university in Los Angeles. All funds, however, were extracted from the population of Netzahualcoyotl when they should have been generated from the private-sector groups responsible for the development of the city in the first place.

COOPTATION AND ENTANGLEMENT

These events illustrate the process of "entanglement"; for a population to become entangled in a national system of political and economic relations, as was true in Netzahualcoyotl, requires that population ultimately to pay a cost. The population of Netzahualcoyotl did not become "demarginalized," but instead, following the national ritual of marginality, became entangled structurally. Their leaders were "integrated" and individually rewarded; the population became part of the institutionalized system of taxation and fees that provides public funds for infrastructures in spite of private-sector obligations; and the gaps between the formal and informal sectors became institutionalized in the form of political offices and representatives. The mass of the population not only remained excluded from the benefits of "integration" but in fact became further exploited by the public and private sectors. Already economically and politically marginalized, they became further marginalized by means of the state's legal apparatus, which more aggressively extracted the few resources in their possession in the form of fees and taxation, further diminishing their already economically precarious ability to live in this environment. While many persons had achieved an edge on survival by boycotting mortgage payments, utilities, and other payments, this margin was erased through "integration." The mass of the marginalized informal sectors of Ciudad Netzahualcoyotl remain excluded and exploited.

These events and their consequences demonstrate that the myth of "national integration"—that the public sector is somehow neutral and "universally" represents all sectors of Mexican society—is hollow indeed. It would be more accurate to argue that the formal public sector is a very important mechanism through which economically and politically marginalized populations become further exploited by the private sector in Mexico. The myth of universal access and the denial of inequality and scarcity mask events like those that took place in Netzahualcoyotl by couching resolutions in terms of "someone has to pay for services" or "the state has a right to collect taxes." Such platitudes mask the reality of the public sector's functioning as an important mechanism for private-sector interests in prospering at the expense of already marginalized populations. Such myths are part of the cult of elites of the public and private sectors.

For those who "fit" the strategies and myths of the elites, rewards in the form of offices, salaries, and graft are certain. In addition, however, such schemes ensure the political ascendancy of elites who manipulate such strategies, as will be shown in the last chapter. Here we find that the governor of the state became the mayor of Mexico City, the secretary of governance became the head of research for the governmental party (PRI), the mayor of Netzahualcoyotl became a federal senator, and all others who became "integrated" did well for themselves. The cost of their "integration" was the further marginalization of a large part of the population of Netzahualcoyotl as well as their paying the cost for persons ascending the political ladder. We have seen that the public sector acts as an important mechanism to ensure that private sectors can utilize marginalized populations as resources, and that such utilization, when institutionalized, has been described by elites as "national integration." From the point of view of these populations, the effect is further marginalization.

POLITICAL CONSEQUENCES FOR THE UNFIT

The political consequences for individuals not fitting the strategies of elites, as was true for Arturo Valenzuela Cisneros, are manifested in the shift of the nature of support from legitimacy to coercion, and with this shift, the role that leaders fulfill changes from political leadership to brokerage. For Arturo Valenzuela Cisneros, this is exactly what occurred between 1973 and 1974, combined with increasing episodes of paralytic hysteria. Valenzuela was "delocalized" of much of the primary and second-order local support of his *comadres* and *compadres*, and with it went his sense of social esteem. He became entangled in networks of "political friendships," and in so doing he became submerged in the "rituals of marginality" of political brokerage, instrumental friendships, and exchanges of favors based on short-term considerations. These became single-interest and coercive relationships, largely unequal and utilitarian. The irony is that he never really "fit" because he had refused to condone the illegal sale of lots.

By the summer of 1973, Valenzuela's status was largely confined to that of a broker within the network of relations he still maintained in the city of Netzahualcoyotl—the Transit Department of the state of Mexico, the Agrarian Department, and the Fidecomiso, in which he continued his membership through 1975. His nemesis, Mondragón, had dispensed the spoils of patronage to his core following, and by the summer of 1973, he was firmly entrenched in his new status as third councilman. He also retained his secretary-generalship of the CRC and his subcommittee presidency. For the most part, Mondragón's followers consisted of persons in the land-invaded sections of the city, which he controlled through his "core" of four men. These men, in turn, controlled their own subcommittees, which were also largely located in the land-invaded sections of the city. Mondragón also continued as the CRC representative to the Fidecomiso, of which the state secretary of governance was president.

With the ascendancy of Mondragón, Valenzuela's status plummeted. He had played the "game" in domains where power was the exclusive right of those whose access was assured by either influence or *conección*; but the *arreglos* were much too powerful for the likes of Arturo Valenzuela Cisneros. What was left of him at the end of this sequence of political activities was the devastation that accompanies political fratricide in Mexico.

Between January and May 1973, Valenzuela's household was attacked three different times by Mondragón's supporters; Valenzuela's supporters, in turn, defended but did not initiate attacks. In fact, whereas Valenzuela's support had centered among lot owners, these supporters fell away as soon as the Fidecomiso announced in February that urban services would be guaranteed and that a small discount from the original purchase price of the lot would be made. For these supporters, the public goals had been accomplished.

Although he still maintained a core of *"viejas chingonas"* ("fucking strong women") and a core of friends within four subcommittees, Valenzuela's support had shifted primarily to the market group, taxi drivers, and, to some extent, the *comuneros*, who still maintained the multiple relations established with Valenzuela even though they were promised an indemnification by the Fidecomiso of 50 million pesos for their illegally developed land. The final aspect of Valenzuela's political demise occurred in May 1973, in his own front yard, when Mondragón's supporters tried to shoot him. They missed, but did manage to capture his subcommittee standard. As one former supporter stated, *"A mi pobre compadre le dieron de la madre"* ("They really screwed over my poor compadre").

Valenzuela, nevertheless, continued to try to recoup his losses, from the time of his ouster in March 1973 through the end of my fieldwork in late 1974. However hard he tried, no matter how many demonstrations he organized, no matter the number of impassioned speeches he gave on weekends before small numbers of persons in the various *colonias*, inevitably groups of Mondragón's supporters would disperse the listeners, chasing them through the mud-covered streets of Netzahualcoyotl. His political power and control by this time, compared to Mondragón's, was practically nil.

As long as Valenzuela advanced the argument that Mondragón and his supporters were "coyotes," and that he was fighting against the selfish interests of the municipality and the land developers (whom he regarded as Mondragón's allies), while simultaneously belonging to the Fidecomiso, Valenzuela was regarded suspiciously as having "clay feet." This explanation of a former supporter was repeated numerous times in various forms, both to Valenzuela and to me: "They [the elites] entrapped him, and he does not have a solution. Because now the people will not believe him again if he leaves the Fidecomiso, once having said that the Fidecomiso would resolve everything. It resolved everything for the ones on top—for us, *atole con el dedo* ('a sip of the soup')." Even Valenzuela conceded his untenable position, one that he still held in 1975. In October 1973, he said: "How do I get out? I promised and lost. No choice. I have to keep struggling."

But the political field had changed drastically for both supporters and leaders within the CRC, and certainly for Valenzuela. Deprived of his legitimate political status, by the summer of 1973 Valenzuela had become a broker for supporters whose requests for *favores* and immediate payoffs characterized the essential nature of the political field that, by 1979, even he gave in to. In chapter 9 I will show that there were those from the old political field who remained loyal to Valenzuela in other arenas of action; this, at one point in 1974, seemed to give strength and legitimacy once more to Valenzuela's attempts to regain power.

For the most part, by 1973 Valenzuela's primary support came from those who wanted something resolved immediately. Even though he had invested himself with a new organizational name—the Coalición Renovadora de Ciudad Netzahualcoyotl—his functions were primarily those of a middleman and organizer of support for CNC-directed activities.[7] Thus, when President Echeverria needed "instantaneous" demonstrations of support, Valenzuela would be contacted by the CNC, and he would round up as many persons as he could, arrange for buses, and then lead an "admiring" delegation to the Zocalo.

It was Valenzuela's daily activities as a political broker that made clear his degeneration into an object of coercive support. Such daily activities have been described generally, but the following detailed accounts of specific cases illustrate the only type of support Valenzuela commanded during the period from late 1973 and early 1974 through 1975.

Case 1

A niece of Valenzuela—a young woman of twenty—and her husband asked for his intervention with the local municipal authorities on behalf of a male cousin of hers (unrelated to Valenzuela). This cousin had been living with a woman for a number of years and had sired two children. Recently, this man had become enamored of a sixteen-year-old girl whose mother did not object to the relation. In fact, the girl's mother invited the man into their home, bedded him down with the girl, fed him, and the two established a common-law relationship.

The first wife, meanwhile, learned of the situation, took her husband's belongings, and retreated to her rural family home. On hearing this, the man then took the sixteen-year-old out of her mother's home, where they had been living, and settled in his former house.

The mother reported the man to the police for carnal violation of a minor, and had him arrested together with a sixteen-year-old male cousin of the young woman and his girlfriend. A 3,000-peso bribe was demanded of each one for their release. Valenzuela intervened, and the four persons were set free after paying a bribe of 500 pesos.

Case 2

On November 7, 1973, three children were burned to death in their mother's home. She could afford to pay for caskets for only two of the children; so only two children were released from the morgue for burial. Valenzuela appealed to Mayor Loya, and municipal funds were provided to pay for the third casket and the burial.

Case 3

Before Valenzuela's political demise, he had been provided with ten taxi certificates by the governor of the state. Seven were sold at a nominal price to former CRC pals, two were kept for himself, and one was given to his brother. The seven who bought the licenses formed a taxi cooperative, and because of Valenzuela's relationship with the transit authorities, were protected from the transit policemen, who are notorious bribe seekers. A taxi union then tried to pressure the seven into joining, but their advances were rebuffed by Valenzuela and his pals, who were also his clients. The head of the union reacted by convincing one of the transit police captains to issue moving violations to Valenzuela's pals.

Ardilla ("Squirrel"), one of the taxi drivers, was arrested for speeding, and his car was impounded by the police captain. When notified of this action, Valenzuela contacted the municipal delegate in charge of the transit district in which the violation occurred, a man with whom he had a relationship, and Ardilla was set free, his driver's license returned (licenses are confiscated when tickets are issued), fines rescinded, and his car released.

Case 4

A lot owner who had been absent from his lot found, when he returned, a newly constructed *jacal*. His complaint to state and municipal authorities was not responded to by either.

Valenzuela then intervened on his behalf with the secretary of governance, who referred him to a state judge. The judge, in turn, issued a court order directing the municipal police to assist the man in breaking the lock on the door of the new construction on his lot.

Since the building was owned by a supporter of Mondragón who had been given permission to build the house illegally, the police hesitated to help. Valenzuela then visited the police chief, who accompanied the lot owner to the *jacal*. The lot owner then removed the furniture belonging to the builder from the site.

The owner of the *jacal* then called upon Mondragón, who, in turn, sent some of his supporters to the lot, where the owner was beginning to tear down the illegally constructed *jacal*. The lot owner was pistol whipped, 3,000 pesos were stolen from him, and the laborers who were tearing down the *jacal* were chased away. After expressing his displeasure to Valenzuela, the lot owner paid a substantial amount of money to join Mondragón's subcommittee, in return for permission to tear down the *jacal*. He then paid indemnification to the *jacal's* builder and built his own house. This expenditure is a kind of fee expected of most persons seeking to build in areas controlled by Mondragón.[8]

Case 5
A thirty-seven-year-old widow and mother of three children living
in Netzahualcoyotl sought Valenzuela's intervention with judicial
authorities. Her husband's paramour claimed inheritance rights to
the home in which the widow lived, offering the last will and testa-
ment of the dead male as proof. Valenzuela double-talked the widow
and referred her to a friend and lawyer who took the case and later
lost it.

Such cases are quite typical, and an average of twenty-five persons per day contacted Valenzuela's household during 1973-1974
with similar problems. From resolving family squabbles to providing a kind of information-and-referral service, Valenzuela's office-
without-portfolio combined the roles of counselor, mediator, taxi-
cooperative head, and broker. Table 17 illustrates the patterns of
assistance and support given those who contacted the Valenzuela
household between November 1, 1973, and February 1, 1974.

Table 17 shows that of the 434 persons seeking assistance, 356
were male and 78 were female. Of the total males, 203 sought legal
assistance concerning housing, lots, or litigation with the municipality, state, or federal authorities. Thus, the majority of the
males entering the Valenzuela household sought assistance with
nondomestic problems. In contrast, 50 of the 78 females seeking
Valenzuela's assistance sought intervention in domestic problems
—marital disputes or difficulties with recalcitrant children. Thus,
the majority of the females required nonlegal assistance. Those
males in categories A and C who were in the twenty-to-twenty-
eight age group required help for parents who were unemployed,
sick, or infirm. Males in the forty-two-to-forty-four age range
who were in the C category sought assistance in employment and
connections with employers. The oldest age groups of males in the
C category, including ages fifty-two through seventy-five, sought
basically financial assistance in the form of personal loans or information about local loan sharks with whom Valenzuela had
arreglos.

Regardless of the problems that these persons sought to resolve,
most of the support that persons extended *to* Valenzuela was based
on his ability to resolve issues. As in case 4, persons sometimes

turned to Mondragón for assistance as a last resort, when few other alternatives were available. This support for Mondragón, however, was based not on any "legitimate" exchange but on a rather pragmatic, realistic assessment of Mondragón's power compared to Valenzuela's lack of it. If Mondragón was unable to provide favors, such supporters would switch their allegiance to someone else, just as they had switched from Valenzuela to Mondragón. It is obvious that Valenzuela's source of support was based on a sort of pragmatism in which short-range expectations are satisfied. Mondragón's support also was based on such expectations, with the crucial difference that he maintained an independent source of power: the land squatters. But when this group no longer needs his services, they too will desert him. By that time, however, Mondragón will have become part of high-power domains, where support is based not on the intimacy of horizontal relations but on the type of strategies employed by the elites toward the population of Ciudad Netzahualcoyotl.

Such was the field of political activity in which Valenzuela and Mondragón vied in 1973-1974 and probably, to some degree, in 1975. Meanwhile, Valenzuela's power and support waned radically within that period. His taxi-cooperative supporters were harassed by the police and received little "protection" from Arturo's connections; the market people grumbled for the same reason. Even with his close pals like Roberto and Juan, disagreements almost became violent, and Valenzuela seemed to be on the verge of psychological collapse.

His first collapse did in fact occur in December 1973. It was then that his eyesight blurred, his speech slurred, his temperature fluctuated, his gait became uneven, and he experienced chest pains. This was diagnosed as paralytic hysteria.[9] Between the middle of December 1973 and December 1974, Valenzuela experienced nine such hysterical episodes during which he could not move his legs or arms. The stressful consequences stemming from his changing role, his loss of intimate support, and the inevitable erosion of his sense of self-worth contributed to such episodes, and were assuaged only by volumes of alcohol. He received temporary respite only when the old bases of his support and self-worth returned to

TABLE 17

PERSONS SEEKING ASSISTANCE FROM ARTURO CISNEROS VALENZUELA (NOVEMBER 1, 1973-FEBRUARY 1, 1974)

Age Range	Problem Category* A	B	C	D	Male Total	Problem Category* A	B	C	D	Female Total	Total
15-19	4	3	1	1	9	—	—	—	—	—	9
20-24	10	10	5	3	28	5	1	—	—	6	34
25-28	7	31	3	1	42	3	1	—	—	4	46
29-32	7	36	9	7	59	4	1	—	—	5	64
33-36	3	21	2	5	31	12	3	2	—	17	48
37-40	3	41	7	5	56	9	4	1	1	15	71
41-44	—	19	9	5	33	6	1	1	—	8	41
45-48	7	21	12	—	40	5	6	1	—	12	52
49-52	2	18	1	1	22	2	2	—	1	5	27
53-55	1	6	1	1	9	—	2	—	—	2	11
56-59	3	4	3	—	10	—	—	—	—	—	10
60-63	7	2	2	—	11	1	—	—	—	1	12
64-67	2	1	1	—	4	—	—	—	—	—	4
68-71	—	—	—	—	—	3	—	—	—	3	3
72-75	—	—	2	—	2	—	—	—	—	—	2
76-79	—	—	—	—	—	—	—	—	—	—	—
Total	56	213	58	29	356	50	21	5	2	78	434

*Problem category refers to the nature of the request for assistance, according to the following categories: A = domestic, as in case 1; B = legal, as in cases 4, 5; C = personal, as in case 2; D = other, as in case 3.

the political field. Unfortunately, he was able to maintain neither his support nor his sense of self-worth, as the next chapter describes. He had become effectively "delocalized" of many of his primary and secondary orders of social support. Yet he had refused to "fit" within the framework of corruption and graft promoted by those in political ascendancy. He became a man alone, but bound to the "rituals of marginality" of political friendships.

9
Local-Level Rituals and Rituals of Marginality: Power, Symbol, and Culture Change

WITH NETZAHUALCOYOTL'S POLITICAL leaders properly "entangled," Valenzuela ill and involved only in standard political-brokerage roles and relationships, and Mondragón and his pals reaching the pinnacles of "integration," the national rituals of marginalization continued to operate with efficiency. The repercussions of this were manifested daily in Ciudad Netzahualcoyotl by the troops of persons seeking help from Valenzuela, as was detailed in the last chapter, but also by Mondragón and his cohorts protecting the illegal sales of lots through Mondragón's councilman status in the city. Mondragón and his core supporters were now "integrated" at the edges of the public-sector elites. The rituals of marginality, jeopardized by the former activities of the CRC, were now secure.

Such rituals of marginality are part of a cycle of state and national rituals, the most important of which, as has been argued, is the ritual of "integration." Between the narrowest rituals of marginality and the broader, more inclusive rituals are intermediate ones that also find expression. National holidays, in part, define the national rituals of marginality; at the intermediate level, the "state of the state" addresses, occurring in the different states throughout Mexico at the beginning of the new year, provide such definition.

These state of the state addresses, given by the governors of the various states, symbolically express the "proper" relations of political dominance and subservience. These intermediate-level rituals express as "statements in action" (Leach 1979:13) the underlying myths of what constitute socially approved "proper" relations between individuals and groups. The difference between the state of the state addresses and other rituals is that these addresses take place at the state level, not at the local level or at the national level. Thus, they are intermediate rituals.

These various levels of rituals of marginality function to subordinate, exploit, and marginalize local populations, such as that in Ciudad Netzahualcoyotl. But these populations also operate *within* local ritual contexts, which express not only power relations but also the "proper" relations between networks, with multiple relations of social exchange based on equality, affect, and *confianza*. These rituals involve the reality of daily life and serve not the exploitation of others but the moderation of uncertainty of daily life in Ciudad Netzahualcoyotl. These rituals have little to do with the myths of the state but involve, rather, local myths of intimate fellowship, mutuality, and trust.

Such rituals at the local level, in primary and in secondary spheres, consist not only of religious acts such as baptism, confirmation, communion, marriage, blessing the home, and saints' days but also of everyday rituals of social exchange. For example, *tandas* ("rotating credit associations"), care of children, and information exchange between women and between men, all reflect rituals of mutual social exchange. Other everyday rituals involve men and women bantering and joking during massage sessions, such as those with "La Negra," or simple chatter with *comadres*, *compadres*, and family friends before the night closes. These are among the hundreds of daily rituals in which persons participate and express "proper" relations.

These rituals, and the relations expressed, are quite different from and in contradiction to those utilized by national, state, and local officials and politicians. For persons like Arturo Valenzuela Cisneros, local rituals and the "proper" relations comprising them provided the basis for his social identity and the source of his political support. For the most part, Valenzuela lost this support and came to depend on the largesse of elites through "political friendships." He is, nevertheless, *of* the locality, and when local rituals converge in the same social field with those of the state, then Arturo must accommodate the conflicts that emerge from the contradictions between rituals. The rituals of the locality and the rituals of marginality are based on opposing social principles: the former on mutuality, the latter on subordination.

The two varieties of rituals did converge within the same social field, and, as will be seen, the unintended consequences included cultural change of the most basic sort among the networks of men and women who had been Arturo's source of support; for Arturo, the consequences included his final political demise within the locality and his eventual "integration" on the edges of the formal sectors.

THE INTERMEDIATE RITUAL OF MARGINALITY

On January 10, 1974, the governor of the state of Mexico gave his "state of the state" speech. As in most addresses of this sort, it was expected that he would outline the accomplishments of his administration—its expenditures, educational advances, social-service improvements, and so on. This speech followed the accepted pattern and was received with great fanfare in the local, state, and national press. Advertisements purchased by labor-union heads, chamber of commerce presidents, and clients of the governor applauded the efforts of the governor in an exaggerated manner. In addition, rural and urban *caciquitos*, with and without portfolios, paraded their networks of supporters before the governor. These acts of obeisance provided the governor with manifestations of loyalty, affection, warmth, and friendship. Such manifestations also have more pragmatic functions. Indeed, they reveal the content of the relationship between the governor and his clients—the "proper" relations of dominance (Leach 1954:15).

It is on such occasions that "heads can be counted"—those who have won and lost the local battles of opposition; those in the process of losing or winning at their level of activity. Moreover, these are times when realignments, promises, and new relations are made between the governor and successful and unsuccessful clients. This is the view held by those who consider themselves in control—persons who consider themselves to have the power but who, in a very real way, are prisoners of their own domains.

The expectations of those in power can be offset, however, by processes completely unknown to power holders such as the governor. This occurred when Valenzuela's supporters came to pay "obeisance" at the governor's palace on March 3, 1974, in opposition to the governor's expectations and to those of Valenzuela himself.

It was customary that during the three-month period between January and March, political-party organizations of the state of Mexico, such as the INJUVEN, the CNC, the CNOP, and the CTM, appeared before the governor's palace at the state capital in Toluca.[1] In Netzahualcoyotl, the various power spheres sent as many of their supporters as were available in buses supplied by the governor through the local PRI organization. For example, Sergio Maldonado López, the original founder of the CRC, sent only one filled bus with his immediate clients to Toluca. In contrast, Antonio Mondragón, who had directed the expulsion of Arturo Valenzuela Cisneros from the CRC, who had taken the third councilman's seat, and who was at the apex of his political authority and prestige, filled fifty-one buses with his supporters and provided a band of musicians from the state of Veracruz, folk dancers, and decorations, banners, and flags.

There was great fanfare in Toluca when Mondragón and his cortege arrived. The governor personally greeted Mondragón and his underlings with expressions of friendship (*amistad*), *abrazos* ("embraces"), and smiles. After Mondragón's speech to the governor, and after the dancing and eating among his supporters had terminated, the governor invited Mondragón and his core of four men to dinner at his private estate. There, in the governor's dining room, at the exquisitely carved 200-year-old table, *canard à l'orange* was served. In contrast, a few months earlier, Salomón, Mondragón's newly appointed municipal judge and one of his core of four, had eaten tortillas and a thick gruel of *atole* with his fingers. These same fingers also parted and cut lice-infested hair in a makeshift barbershop behind the lot of his *jacal*. For Mondragón and company, this was their victory celebration—the joining of political fates—a time in which the payoff included even eating *canard à l'orange*.

At the same time, Valenzuela's sphere of influence and power was waning. The nature of his political downfall has been described. Outside of the field of political competition stood those with whom Valenzuela maintained ritual relationships: persons whom he had treated for pulled muscles, children for whom he was *padrino* ("godfather"), those who had hidden him occasionally over the past years (1969-1974) when the judicial police had searched for him, those with whom he had argued, joked, fought, cried, and loved. These were the relationships that bound others to him, and it was the death of one of his friends that set off processes that neither the governor nor Valenzuela could control.

These processes were rooted in the face-to-face encounters of the moral realm, where equality, both political and social, prevail. In this realm, obeisance, kowtowing, and subordination are antithetical to deeply held values. Ironically, such processes inadvertently contribute to the reinforcement of power relations that ultimately involve deference to authority and power and the maintenance of inequality. Such processes would be set off in the midst of Valenzuela's arrangement to pay an act of obeisance to the governor in Toluca.

RITUAL PROCESSES OF THE LOCAL LEVEL

On January 27, 1974, Emilio García López died of intestinal parasites, diagnosed as duodenal ulcers prior to his death. Although he had not participated in Valenzuela's political activities since November 1972, he had maintained a close, intimate friendship with Valenzuela. This relationship was part of a larger sphere of mutual friendships that has already been described (see chapter 7). Upon his death, Emilio's many relationships were recalled in ritual, and obligations that had previously gone unpaid were now fulfilled.

On February 17, 1974, a *novena* was held for Emilio. This ritual involves the dedication of a cross to the deceased, usually accomplished nine days after his death. In this case, the *novena* was delayed because "Bigotes," Emilio's brother, had not sold his lot and home to pay for the rituals attached to the *novena*. By February 16 he had done so and had arranged for the first ritual, which preceded the dedication of the cross and the mass celebrated at the cemetery.

On February 16, 1974, between 5 and 8 P.M., on a cloudy, acrid evening, sixty-five persons crowded into Emilio's home. Among those present were Julieta Valenzuela, Doña Carmen, Doña Mariana, and Doña Beatriz—the latter three *"viejas chingonas"* who had formerly been among the toughest of the CRC supporters but who had dropped their support of the organization. Nevertheless, they maintained *comadre* relations with Valenzuela's mother and his wife, Julieta, and they attended because Julieta had called upon them to contact the rest of the *comadres* for the two days of ritual. Their only relations with Emilio and his family were single-stranded political ones.

In addition to these three women, eleven others accompanied them who also did not know Emilio's family but were part of the fourteen-woman network of *comadres* surrounding Julieta Valenzuela and her mother-in-law, Doña Margarita. Of the males present, twelve were Emilio and "Bigotes's" pals from CRC days, including Arturo Valenzuela and Roberto López. The other participants included both close and distant relations: two brothers and their families; cousins on both sides of Emilio's and his wife's family; and the assorted children from all of these families. Such was the social composition of those present, who awaited the arrival of Padre José, "El Sacerdote Subversivo" ("the subversive priest").

Crowded onto the patio of the three-room *jacal* and into the adjoining goat shelter, sixty-five persons waited. Some were seated on two long benches on each side of the patio, others occupied wooden chairs, and some sat on their haunches. Still others stood in small groups, chatting and commenting on the cause of Emilio's death, the length of his illness (two years), his participation in political activities, and the tragedy of a poor *"busca-chamba"* ("seeker of work") leaving his wife and seven children without support. All of these persons waited on the patio next to a table covered by a white tablecloth, on which sat two bunches of tulips in empty preserve jars, a glass of water, and an unlighted red candle.

In the living room of the *jacal*, the widow, her eldest children, her mother and father, her sister and brothers, and Emilio's father, eldest brother, and two sisters sat on three aging sofas. This was the "private" place for close relatives; the patio was the "public" place for less intimate relations. Nevertheless, it was expected that each person, upon arriving at the *jacal*, would convey his sorrow to those in the "private" quarters and then exit to the "public" area. Padre José, however, remained with the immediate family after his arrival and continued to stay with them until the beginning of the ritual of the *novena*.

In the meantime, Padre José prepared for the ritual with the assistance of his acolyte. He removed his shabby, soiled, polyester jacket and ripped denim shirt and carefully and slowly replaced them with his vestments. As each piece was donned—from the white linen alb to the final purple silk-brocade chasuble—those waiting began to filter toward the front of the altar, their conversations waning, their faces becoming serious. Men moved their arms to the front of their bodies and clasped their hands; women took out black rosaries, shifting their black shawls over their heads to almost cover their faces; the widow, carrying a nine-month-old infant wrapped in her black *rebozo* ("shawl"), walked onto the patio escorted by "Bigotes," who held her by the right elbow.

A moment of absolute quiet ensued before Padre José folded his hands across his waist and addressed the gathering:

> My friends, comrades, and family of Emilio: we are all here in Emilio's home to pay homage to Emilio García, father of children, husband who is loved [not loving husband], friend and companion of many of you who are here. We do not pay homage with sadness, because that, we are sure, Emilio would not like; and more important, because we know that the Great Lord, in His great wisdom, has

provided a place for Emilio next to His hand. We are all united here
to celebrate—all of his friends, all of his acquaintances; all who lived
with Emilio; all those who drank of life with Emilio; all those who
suffered and struggled with Emilio—all celebrating this day with him
and for him. Clearly he is much missed by his children and wife, and
without doubt, life here is sufficiently difficult without more tragedy. But my dear brothers, all of us now have the opportunity to
help, to give counsel to his children and protect the widow. Clearly
the relatives, the sisters, the brothers, the *compadres* will do that.
Beyond that, all of the comrades (female and male) who struggled
with him have the responsibility to help, to counsel, equally with the
rest. We know that here, the one who does not help the other cannot
survive these conditions. We have all struggled—all. Emilio struggled as a father and as a husband to give food to his family, but he
also struggled for many of us. Let us, then, celebrate this mass in his
honor, but before we do, it is necessary that not only I speak but
that all members of his family, his *compadres*, his friends, his comrades say how they feel about their friend Emilio.[2]

This particular request was met by silence and confusion. The
majority of those present were not accustomed to participating in
nontraditional Catholic rituals. Persons looked at one another for
keys to the situation until one male said in a loud voice: "Let it be
Anastasio ["Bigotes"] who speaks." Anastasio, who had been
standing next to his sister-in-law and nephew, looked around,
with his lips quivering, and said: "It is difficult . . . it is difficult . . .
it is . . . it is . . . difficult to speak of my . . . brother." At this time,
the widow began to cry audibly, other women began to sob, and
three of the men wiped tears from their eyes, turning away so as
not to be seen. An almost embarrassing silence followed as he
struggled to speak: "He, besides . . . being my brother, was father
to his children. He always wanted to do the best . . . for his children and his woman. I do not know why . . . this happened . . . and
even more when his children . . . need him so much. . . . I do not
know how or why. . . ." He broke down and began sobbing, one
hand covering his face; Roberto stepped over to Anastasio and
placed an arm around his shoulder.

The widow then moved toward the altar, clutching her child,
tears rolling down her cheeks, and spoke haltingly: *"Padre, él era*

un hombre... como todos los hombres... pero era bueno con-migo y con sus hijos" ("Father, he was a man...like all men... but he was good to me and to his children").

The priest then looked at them and spoke: "We have heard from the members of the family. What they have said—they have said that the family respected Emilio—they have thus said, and what is it that you say?"

Roberto, with arms crossed over his chest, head slightly down, leaning on one leg, spoke: "We all agree that Emilio was a family man, and that is the best thing that can be said for any of us. But besides that, for me he was a friend—my friend. When I needed him, he was always there. I would say: 'Hey brother, I am in bad shape, and I need your help.' And he would always respond to me. That is the way Emilio was with all of us."

Roberto then lowered his head. Scattered *si*'s were murmured throughout the gathering. Padre José then thanked Roberto and said: "That is the way he was, my friends. We have heard the words of his wife, his brother, and his friend. Then, my brothers, let us celebrate this man and say this holy mass in his name. May God bless you." He then began the mass.

The mass itself was the "short version," with twelve persons receiving communion. The priest stopped the mass before the actual communion service and announced that it was no longer necessary for them to attend confession if they instead said the act of contrition and were truly sorry. Many of the women looked around; some nodded to each other, asking if they were going to receive communion. Many shook their heads negatively; some smiled, their foreheads wrinkled in embarrassment. The result was that twelve persons accepted communion: nine were women, and three were children, one a young male of twelve and two girls under nine years of age. Of those nine women, all but two were part of Emilio's immediate consanguine or affinal relatives. These two were members of the new support and were not part of the original network of *"viejas chingonas."* Nevertheless, as the ritual progressed, a few commentaries were visible in the form of facial expressions and giggling between Doña Carmen and Doña Mariana. They covered their mouths with their shawls and then nodded their heads toward the two women who had received communion. They then began to giggle, turning their eyes toward the sky in a pseudopious manner. This behavior, however, ceased when the priest terminated the ritual and again addressed those present. Padre José said:

> After this holy mass, we are all in agreement that each one of us will contribute morally or economically to benefit Emilio's family. All know that life is very difficult here, but, my brothers, we have the responsibility—and this I cannot repeat too much—of helping this woman and Emilio's seven children. I am sure that God will, in one way or another, assist us all.[3]

Immediately following this last speech, the priest turned and began to remove his vestments. The chalice and altar cloth were removed by the acolyte, and the women began bringing out *pan de huevo* ("round bread," approximately four inches in diameter), chocolate, and coffee for those who wanted it. The table, which had been used as an altar, was now used to serve the bread. The benches were once again used as seating for social intercourse, and the group settled down to conversation.

Perpendicular to the altar (table), another table was set up. Here Padre José, the acolyte, a well-dressed couple who lived two hours away in a medium-sized town, Emilio's uncle, Arturo, Roberto, and at times "Bigotes" sat and talked. The rest of the guests sat along the walls on the backless benches or stood in small circles. Meanwhile, the widow and her immediate female relatives served the chocolate, bread, and coffee. It was as if the men's expectations of the women had been reinstituted at this particular time, that the tragedy of Emilio's death had been diminished, and that normalcy had returned. There was no crying, no hushed tones; instead, there were frank discussions of Emilio's death, comments that distance prevented more visitations between relatives, recognition that certain members of other families were not present because of difficulties in getting to work, and joking between two men and a twelve-year-old girl about her attractive sister, whom neither man had seen for some time.

While shortly before and during the ritual a pervading emotional gloominess was felt by many, that gloominess now lifted, and although a few persons expressed anxiety for the future of Emilio's children, most of those present smiled, joked, and in general seemed engaged in nonaggressive discussions and conversations. It was as if the ritual had provided a means of emotional release—an activity in which values concerning the worth of the home, the obligations concerning the widow and child, and the efficacy of living were reconstituted within this alien environment.

This ritual also provided a means through which old ties, friendships, and acquaintances could be renewed. In the moments after the mass, these persons were part of a community of members. The anxieties that face-to-face relations inevitably engender had been muted; the ritual successfully brought together old comrades, and old relationships nurtured in other contexts again flourished. All these relationships were further reinforced the following day when the ritual of placing the cross for Emilio took place.

After the mass, fellowship seemed to be the pervading emotion. This fellowship was apparently based less on the community of love than on the community of relief—relief that this mass was not being said for them, that they had a chance, even in these miserable circumstances, at the good things in life. In addition, the ritual provided a demonstration that if they died in this misery, there would be others who would eat *pan de huevo*, drink chocolate, and perhaps have a chance to be successful.

At this level of human activity, few had much faith in the inevitability of a just reward, especially the nonchurchgoing network of *comadres* who had been in the struggle only to see their dreams frustrated in one way or another. Doña Carmen, Doña Mariana, Doña Beatriz, and their networks had been cronies of Arturo for many years; they had fought the good fight; they had prayed as women are expected to; they had given birth to children; they had suffered all those things that women expect to suffer. But they had acted together politically; they had been momentarily successful against men and their pretentious politics. The women had acted in concert and knew one another intimately. Furthermore, they all had little use for the pious or for piety; they were extreme pragmatists and believed in little but power and strength of effort. Yet,

paradoxically, the ritual still touched them, not so much in its content, and not in the priestly pronouncements about reward, but
rather in the affective sorrow, the feelings of tragedy, and the reminders of dependency that reinforced the emotional content of
the ethos shared among the *comadres*, shared with those whom
they trusted, and shared with the leaders, of whom they were the
gente ("people"). It was on the next day that additional ritual
activity accentuated this affect, and was inevitably incorporated
into the political field.

Novena

On February 17, 1974, sixty persons gathered at Arturo Valenzuela's home to travel together to the cemetery of Chimalhuacán
to conclude the *novena* for Emilio García. Valenzuela had arranged with one of the bus lines to supply transportation to San
Juan Chimalhuacán since Netzahualcoyotl had no cemetery of its
own.[4] He also purchased and had delivered by one of the taxi con-
cessionaires a large wreath, on behalf of his new political organization (Coalición de Obreros y Colonos del Valle de México). The
women were mostly inside of Valenzuela's enclosed yard, seated
on long wooden benches; the men stood outside of the yard, in
small two- and three-person groups. Within the yard, the *comadres* of the old network sat next to one another. The two
women who had received communion the previous day and four
others, who had not been present at the first ritual but who had
been in the new organization for about four months, stood against
the wall of Valenzuela's home, about three feet from the seated
"*comadres*," most with their backs turned away from those seated.
Only one of the two who had received communion the day before
faced those seated.

Outside the yard, twenty-three men, most with arms crossed,
kicked the dust with the toes of their shoes, awaiting the arrival of
Arturo and the bus. The men stood in small semicircles facing the
yard and together formed an arc, with "Bigotes," Emilio's brother,
at the center. Of the males present, ten had been participants in the

CRC prior to the schism of 1973, and five of these were related to Emilio by fictive kinship. The other five were considered pals. Of the other eight men (eighteen total), three were recent participants (within the last six months) and five were consanguine relatives (i.e., Refugio and "Bigotes," brothers of Emilio; Tino, first cousin to Refugio and "Bigotes"; and two paternal uncles). In addition, Emilio's widow and sisters were inside of the home with Julieta, Julieta's mother-in-law, and one of Julieta's close *comadres*. Finally, the children of Emilio, those of the *comadres*, and those of the other women were also present, making a total of eighty persons.

Between 9 and 10:30 A.M., most of the conversation centered on topics that had nothing to do with the ritual at hand; in fact, most pertained to local events, the weather, the price of beans and tortillas—in short, daily problems.

At 10:30 or so, Doña Beatriz exclaimed to the woman who had been standing facing those seated: *"Tu te crees muy chingona, ¿no?"* ("You really think you're something, don't you?"). The following exchange ensued:

Woman Standing (WS): What did you say? What?
Beatriz: Why do you think you are so great, saying that Arturo should hurry?
WS: I do not think I'm great. I just am tired of waiting for him. That is all.
Beatriz: Tired of waiting—what? What do you know of waiting for Arturo? What do you know of waiting? You really think you are so fucking good.
WS: I do not think I am so fucking good. I just do not like to wait when I do not have to do so.
Beatriz: Why do you not leave, then, bitch (literally, "she-goat")?

Meanwhile, the women standing and those sitting began to murmur, and a few of those seated asked the two to be quiet. This was not the time for them to be using such language. The men, meanwhile, looked at one another, shook their heads, and smiled. Beatriz then looked around at the other women and said: *"Es que ésta se cree muy chingona—ayer en la casa de Emilio y ahora aquí, haciéndose la simple"* ("It is just that this one thinks she is really great—yesterday in Emilio's home and now here—acting in a simpleminded manner"). At this point, the voices of the two rose in volume, and they began to square off, moving slowly toward each other.

> WS: And why simpleminded in the home of Emilio? What did I do that you say I am simpleminded? What the fuck do you want with me?
> Beatriz: You think you are a saint, you bitch. You think you are saintly, and you know what I have for you.

As they began to yell at each other, Julieta (Valenzuela's wife) peeked out of her doorway. The men drew closer to one another, most of them smirking.

> WS: Whenever you want, bitch, whenever you want. I do not fear you. What the fuck do you think?
> Beatriz: Look, bitch, don't be fucking around or I'll beat you to a pulp (literally, I'll beat you so badly that it will look like a gang beat you). You daughter of a whore, fucking whore. You must have just come from whoring with Mondragón, and then you come around here saying what you want, and saintly too. Fucking whore![5]

After the last comment, Julieta walked out into the yard, said nothing, but glanced at Doña Beatriz and Doña Carmen. Doña Carmen then took Beatriz by the arm and told her to be quiet. Beatriz responded by saying: "Bueno, pero qué chingado—esa puta—qué se cree? Aquí anda con nosotros como si fuera tan luchadora. Siempre ha andado con el chaparro—lamiéndole las nalgas—eso no se olvida" ("All right, but what the fuck. That whore—who does she think she is? Here she is with us as if she were such a fighter. Always she had been with the short one, licking his ass. That is not forgotten").

At this point, WS (Graciela) began to walk from the yard and immediately was followed by three of the other women who had been standing. Those who had been seated began to laugh at Graciela; however, Graciela said nothing and walked out to the edge of the yard, where she looked back, paused, and extended the middle finger of her hand in an obscene gesture. Then she quickly walked away. The seated women began to hoot at her by raising their voices to high pitches and maintaining it for three or four seconds. The sound was much like that of the wailing occasionally heard at funerals. It soon quieted down, however, and the *comadres* returned to conversation about daily problems. Meanwhile, Graciela stood outside with one of the women of the original group of six (the other woman who had received communion with her).

At 10:30, Valenzuela arrived in one of the taxis with another wreath on top of this car, and he asked a few of the men to place it inside of the yard. In the car was Padre José and Machito, the acolyte. Valenzuela, Padre José, and Machito then walked into the yard, stopping briefly to exchange greetings with those present. They all then entered the *jacal*, and Arturo and his wife, Julieta, began to converse:

Julieta: You came too late. You don't know what you missed.
Arturo: What?
Julieta: Well, they got into a quarrel—Beatriz and the others [*comadres*]. What's her name—the one who was with Mondragón before?
Arturo: Which one?
Julieta: The one who was sold a lot by Mondragón.
Arturo: Who knows. There are many. No matter—these women are so scandalous. They are always with gossip—busybodies.

The bus came shortly after the arrival of Valenzuela, and all persons, except Graciela and the woman with whom she had received communion, boarded it. The priest, acolyte, the widow and her smallest child, and Valenzuela went in the taxi; Julieta, her two youngest children, and Armando traveled by private auto. Twenty minutes later, all had arrived at the cemetery of Chimalhuacán.

Although the cemetery is situated in the same valley as the city, it is not part of the city but rather a part of San Juan Chimalhuacán, as it has been for at least 200 years. It faces a small range of

sloping hills (to the west, since the cemetery faces east); to the
south are clumps of poplar trees, and to the north are more sloping
hills. The vegetation surrounding the cemetery contrasts sharply
with the barren saltpeter soil of Netzahualcoyotl a few hundred
meters away. To reach the cemetery most directly, one crosses a
barren field of dusty, rutted soil that adjoins the new Netzahualcoyotl industrial park, passing across a contaminated concrete-
lined canal bordering the barrio of San Lorenzo, and thence into
Chimalhuacán and to the cemetery. The canal marks the limit of
Netzahualcoyotl and the beginning of San Juan Chimalhuacán in a
very striking manner.

For these former rural people, San Juan Chimalhuacán is the
closest thing to "down home" that they have—the air is cleaner,
there is pasture a few hundred meters away, corn fields surround
the sloping hills, and some terrace farming is still carried on. The
town is set out in the usual grid pattern, extending as far as it can
go into the surrounding hills. In fact, Chimalhuacán surrounds
one major hill—the Cerro Chimalhuaque—that adjoins Mammoth
findings.

San Juan Chimalhuacán is also where Netzahualcoyotlians go to
drink pulque (an alcoholic beverage made from the century plant)
on Sunday picnics, and to "get away from it all." Levels of meaning attached to the area of which the cemetery is part contrast
sharply to the levels of meaning attached to Netzahualcoyotl. As a
result, going to this cemetery shifts the affect content of the ritual,
in addition to adding different meaning to the ritual. Thus, the
previous day's ritual was preparation for this day's ritual, and the
environment, the meanings, and the participation of the comadres
in the ritual are all extremely crucial to the understanding of the
effect of political statements made at this time.

This ritual, unlike that of the previous day, was the final, formal homage. The erection of the cross at the foot of García's grave
marks the end of all his previous roles and his unequivocal demise.
The previous day's ritual was a preparation for this. Behavior during the ritual of February 16 seemed "normal"—little wailing, little
crying, little sorrow, except during the reminiscences. But the
drinking of chocolate and the eating of bread healed these open
wounds. This day's ritual was different. Although the mass was

again the central focus, the layers of meaning that unfolded were different, and the affect attached to political statuses influenced future events. The ritual itself took place among the gravestones. Three feet from the top of García's grave site were two old chairs, over which lay a door that was to serve as an altar for the service. Immediately to the rear of the altar was the wreath purchased by contributions from those in the Coalición. It was basically a wooden structure in the shape of a cross, covered by purple paper, green ferns, and red and white carnations. Behind this wreath was a family wreath shaped like a horseshoe and placed there on the day of the burial. Between the new wreath and the altar stood the cross, approximately three feet high, made of wrought iron and painted black. On the cross was welded a black plate inscribed with Emilio's name, date of birth, date of death, and a gold-lettered epitaph that read:

> Emilio García López, father and beloved husband. He struggled against the powerful and won the everlasting respect of his comrades. Valiant, honest, and at the forefront of the movement, Emilio will always be accorded a place of honor in our struggle.
>   On behalf of his comrades of the Coalition of Workers and Settlers of the Valley of Mexico.[6]

Those present were divided into two groups facing the altar. On the right side were members of the family, including the widow and her immediate kin—"Bigotes," all of Emilio's children, sisters, brothers, and, as far as I could ascertain, twelve persons who had not been in Arturo's yard and who were consanguine relatives of the widow. The left side of the audience consisted of the comadres, the men previously mentioned, a newspaper reporter, with camera in hand, and a few others who could not be identified.

Padre José stood at the middle of the altar and put on the vestments for the mass, assisted by Machito in the same manner as before. The main difference was that the chasuble was green rather than purple—a significant difference in that the purple of the previous day's ritual is worn only in mourning services. Green is worn at resurrection services, such as Easter.

Before the service began, Arturo Valenzuela Cisneros stood

erect at the priest's left, approximately three feet away. He stood before, during, and after the service in exactly the same place—away from the rest of those present and, aside from the acolyte, the closest person to the priest, unseparated even by the altar. He was, in a symbolic sense, sharing the prestige of priesthood with Padre José. Of all those present, no one else stood as near to the priest and altar; nor was any person's status so obviously distinguished. As perceived by those present, Valenzuela was figuratively on an equal footing with the priest, which not only lent him prestige but also reminded everyone that he was responsible for organizing this ritual. This state of affairs emotionally obligated those present to Valenzuela. Therefore, the cathected feelings that unfolded during the ritual could be used as an affective reservoir for political purposes by Valenzuela sometime after the ritual. This cathexis could have its drawbacks, however, if the emotional content of these relations were frustrated by a failure to carry out the expectations stimulated by these feelings.

The physical environment and the meanings attached to it, the role mixture between Valenzuela and Padre José, the expectations of the comadres and their inherent contradictions, the finality the ritual signaled, and the emotions of one family member stimulated by that finality, in their totality (and together with previous expectations and meanings), had profound effects on the nature of future political relations between Valenzuela and his followers. Such conditions also affected the level of psychological anxiety experienced by Valenzuela.

Meanwhile, Padre José, looking over the gathering before beginning the mass, said: "All present know that today we come to dedicate Emilio's cross, but beyond this to also recall that Emilio was part of the struggle against the exploitation of his children—of all our children here. For these reasons, we are united here, my good friends." He then dipped his hand into a glass of water and sprinkled drops behind him onto the cross, saying: "In the name of the Father and of the Son and of the Holy Ghost, we dedicate this cross from his comrades." Padre José then looked briefly at Arturo, and at those present, before bowing his head to begin the "short version" of the mass once again.

The mass itself was not significantly different from the previous days, and it was carried out with the usual decorum. At the time of communion, however, one significant act occurred: Doña Mariana, one of the three *comadres*, participated in the communion. Doña Carmen and Doña Beatriz did not, but no immediate result seemed apparent.

After the service terminated with the final blessing, Padre José moved slightly to his left, almost touching Valenzuela's shoulder, and began to speak:

The mass is finished, but Emilio's fight, and the fight of men and women like him, is not. It is necessary that all of us here are united only to win the patrimony of our children, and to improve the living conditions of our families. We have to stop the exploitation of the people of Netzahualcoyotl, and the only way to fight the land developers is to fight together as a community should. All of us know that the struggle cannot be fought alone. One cannot win alone. Alone one is eaten in one way or another. They will eat one up by buying him dishonestly or with force or threats. Alone one does not have power. Alone one is nothing. But together, helping each other, the struggle can be won.[7]

Padre José then turned to his immediate left, took a half step in that direction, and said: *"Y ahora unas palabras de Arturo. Un amigo y compañero de lucha"* ("And now a few words from Arturo, a friend and comrade in the struggle"). Arturo turned to the priest, nodding affirmatively and breathing deeply. He then looked at those present, and with quivering lips, which he licked frequently, he began to speak:

My comrades—all of us, all!—there is not one person here who has not struggled in one way or another against the forces of the state, against the forces of the land developers. We remember when we were all together—the beatings the authorities of the *municipio* gave us. But all of us here struggled at times against naked force, with flesh against arms, with rocks against rifles, with slingshots against carbines. That courage, that strength, was established by the work of men and women like the brave Emilio. We all have the obligation not to forget those sacrifices, so great and so painful, that Emilio shared with us. The struggle continues against the land developers

and against the governor—not with him! [now speaking with greater
passion] Yes, I am going to ask, What are we going to gossip about
with him? with the governor of the state? What are we fooling our-
selves for? That gentleman and the land-developer coyotes are to
blame for all of this. [here with a sweep of the right hand, implying
Emilio's death] But, my comrades, that crime cannot be paid for unless we help and support each other. And with this strength, the
Constitution will be fulfilled. All Mexicans of the country have the
right to live tranquilly, educating our children, living in clean
homes, with food that will give us strength, with judicial protection,
without fear, with work that pays us what we deserve. But what has
happened? The coyotes, the politicians—great and small—have us
like slaves, as if we were their peons. No sir, no, that is not just, It
will never be just. And for that justice, Emilio always fought, and
that is how he died. We have to continue the struggle—all of us, men
and women alike. We have to do this. There is no choice.

And now, on behalf of the Coalition of Workers and Settlers of
the Valley of Mexico, we thank you for coming to dedicate this day
to our comrade Emilio. Thank you.[8]

Immediately after Arturo's speech, one of the *comadres* began
to pass out religious pamphlets that Machito had placed on the
altar after the end of the mass. As she went from person to person,
each one accepted the pamphlet without a murmur of dissent. This
was significant, and was influenced largely by the emotional
underpinnings and the "sacred" quality of Arturo's speech. It was
not that the *comadres* had been "converted" or that they accepted
the ideology implied in the formalism of the ritual; but not only
did the priest's prestige merge with Arturo's but also their statuses
and expectations blended at this time. This is not to suggest that
the ritual and the priest's presentation became interchanged or
syncretized with Arturo's political activities and his presentation,
but rather that Arturo gained legitimacy through symbolic inter-
actions with the priest at a time when his support was based on
pragmatism and its attendant short-range goals. It was at this time
that the *comadres* and their networks of relations returned to the
political field and thereby influenced the nature of support between Arturo and his followers.

The passing out of the religious pamphlet signaled not only a favor done for a priest but also that the gathering was not one of just passive observers; nor were they simply paying back an "obligation" to a friend (Arturo and/or Emilio). Instead, by accepting the comadre's pamphlet, the other comadres symbolically conceded the ritual's relation to political activities, for the comadre who passed out the pamphlets was Doña Mariana, one of the threesome of "chingonas." This action by Doña Mariana, and the acceptance of it by the other comadres, including high-prestige individuals like Donãs Carmen and Beatriz, set off earlier expectations based on previous political activities with Arturo. These resurfaced expectations included reenvisioning Arturo as legitimate protest leader, man of integrity, and paragon of noble values— values concerned with justice, equality, and the "good" life, as opposed to the values of compromise, acquiescence, cowardice, and deference to power figures. It was these expectations, combined with the cathexis of ritual affect in the face of these expectations and the other multiple expectations rooted in contexts of the past, that ultimately proved crucial to the events that transpired prior to the annual visit to the governor's palace.

THE AUTONOMY OF SOCIAL POWER: THE LOCALITY AS MEDIUM

Between February 18 and March 1, Arturo's political activity was humdrum. The daily tasks of pressuring local authorities to get cousins of compadres released from jail, to get a taxi driver to take a sick old woman to a hospital in Mexico City, to assist a compadre of a compadre of a friend who attends the political meetings on Sunday afternoons, all these activities continued unabated. But, more significant, the comadres' visitations to Arturo's home doubled during this time. Furthermore, all of the comadres attended the meeting on February 24, when the final preparations for the visit to the governor were made.

Between 7 and 10 P.M. on February 24, Valenzuela explained both the circumstance and the details of the March 3 visitation to the governor in Toluca. He explained that he had arranged for bus transportation with the Líneas de México ("Mexico Buslines"), for a norteño[9] group to play, and for one of the local folk-dancing groups to perform. In addition, he would arrange for all to have their taquitos and frijoles in front of the governor's palace. Few questions were asked by those present while Valenzuela noted that there were several reasons for their visit to the governor: first, he wanted to demonstrate that the organization of colonos was still strong; second, he thought it would be propitious, at that time, to demand the punishment of land developers; and third, this would formally initiate his new organization, clearly distinguishing it from the CRC. Thus, all those present, including the press, would note that the Coalición was in no way associated with Mondragón's CRC.

There was little discussion of these articulated public goals and, following the meeting, four subcommittee heads were made responsible for gathering as many supporters as possible. Doña Carmen stated that she would make sure that as many persons as possible from the old subcommittee 20 would be present. This statement of commitment verified that the comadres would again be present, and that these women represented the backbone of this subcommittee and whatever network of supporters they could gather (even those who were not then participants in the field but with whom these women had established relations in other contexts).

During the week, all arrangements were readied. Manuel Verdugo, Arturo's righthand man in political organizing, was directed by Arturo to ensure that his gente ("people") were ready; he called the governor's office from the Public Works Department numerous times to settle last-minute details on arrival time, projected number of persons, and so on.

By March 2, 1974, all the arrangements had been made. At 7 P.M., as Verdugo and three others were readying the transport of two loudspeakers, a microphone, and amplifiers, a man named Salgado walked into Arturo's yard and asked him to call the secretary of governance in Toluca immediately for further instructions concerning the planned demonstration for the governor. He was asked to go to the local community waterworks station and from there, call the governor's secretariat.

An hour and a half later, Arturo returned to his home despondent. The secretary had told him that the demonstration would have to be cancelled because a sudden problem had occurred that necessitated the governor's presence in another part of the state. As Arturo related the account to Verdugo and the others, Verdugo began to curse and suggested that this was no way to treat them after they had made all the arrangements. Arturo responded that they had little choice but to follow the governor's instructions, and that there was little reason for any more discussion of the matter. The debate went back and forth for two and a half hours, until it was much too late for undoing all the preparations. It ended with Verdugo arguing strongly to go ahead with the demonstration; Arturo disagreed.

Arturo's physical appearance manifested symptoms of anxiety. During the discussions with Verdugo, Arturo walked in circles and gestured with both arms in the air. His lips quivered, his voice cracked, and he licked his lips frequently. In addition, he drank four glasses of water and two glasses of soda during the hour and a half. He smoked heavily and seemed quite nervous. During the discussion, he would lower his head and bite his lower lip, cross his legs and make kicking motions with his right foot. Occasionally, he would dismiss Verdugo's argument with a brush of his hand, and when he finally became exasperated with Verdugo's opposition, he began to curse loudly. Verdugo then told Arturo that as far as he was concerned, they were going to go to Toluca, and that if Arturo did not want to go, that was his decision. Arturo then sent out for a bottle of brandy and sat down to discuss the problem with the two males who had stayed in the room. They both agreed with Arturo that they should follow the governor's orders, and that little was to be gained in going to Toluca if the governor was not present.

The next morning men and women had begun to gather at Arturo's home by 8 A.M. Arturo had not yet awakened, and his decision had not yet reached them. Among the first to arrive were the *comadres*, dressed in ordinary clothes (not in their "Indian" clothes utilized in confrontation, demonstration, or power display). In addition, relatives, friends, other *comadres*, and neighbors and visitors of these *comadres* also were present. Moreover,

Gamboa's subcommittee had arrived, as well as three other sub-committees. "Bigotes," García's brother, seven of his pals, and two other relatives also arrived at approximately the same time.

At 8:30 those present were given the news that the demonstration for the governor's benefit was going to be called off; various persons, including the *comadres*, appeared to be disgusted. Several of them commented that this would not have happened a few years previously, that it was unbelievable that Arturo would have accepted the governor's decision, and that it seemed that they would all be made to look like fools (*pendejos*, literally "pubic hairs") if they did not go. In the meantime, the *norteño* music-and-dance group arrived aboard a flatbed truck, dressed in Stetson hats, black western wear, and cowboy boots.

A few minutes later, Arturo appeared and told the crowd around him that the governor had been called out of town and that the secretary had told him not to come to the governor's palace. Since so many had arrived, however, he said he would try to get through to the secretary to receive permission to go anyway. This was greeted with hoots by some of the women, who laughed at Arturo and asked why he needed permission to do something, especially since it was the governor and people like him who were responsible for the conditions they were forced to live in. Arturo did not respond but instead went quickly into his home, washed, changed clothes, and with one of the drivers, went to the Fide-comiso offices, where he could use the telephone. In his absence, those who were present began to comment. It was from the *co-madres* that the most volatile and emotional commentaries came, and it was they, with Verdugo, who affected the outcome.

Forty-five minutes later, Arturo was left on the corner of the street a block and a half from his home. Simultaneously, the *co-madres*, Verdugo and twenty or so others walked toward Arturo. In the middle of the street, they met—a half-block from the Municipal Palace, twenty meters from the main street, and ten meters from one of Arturo's *compadres*, Juan Limón, who had been one of Arturo's closest supporters since 1969 and with whom he had exchanged *compadrazgo* (see chapter 7).

Juan, who had a small shoe store fronting the street, walked toward Arturo with his daughter and wife. The daughter was Arturo's godchild, and, therefore, a close affective relationship existed between the two. Mrs. Limón was also an intimate friend and *comadre* of Julieta. Thus, the presence of Juan and his family was an extremely important ingredient in the playing out of this event. Arturo stood silently as the group gathered around him. Verdugo stood facing him; the *comadres* formed an arc around him. Juan's daughter and wife stood to the left of Verdugo, Juan at his right. Arturo stared at Verdugo and then said that the secretary had repeated that they should not go to the governor's palace. Verdugo, who had consistently been one of Arturo's strongest supporters, asked Arturo:

Verdugo (V): Bueno, ¿qué pasó? ("Well, what happened?").

Arturo (A): Lo mismo, no quieren que nosotros vayamos, se me hace por lo que pasó con Mondragón ("The same. They don't want us to go; I think because of what happened with Mondragón").

V: ¿Cómo con Mondragón? ("What do you mean with Mondragón?").

A: Sí, no quieren hacerle política a Mondragón después de lo que pasó aquí ("Yes, they do not want to act politically against Mondragón, especially after what happened" [referring to the shootings at Valenzuela's house]).

V: Mira, a mi no me importa de eso. ¿Qué somos nosotros? ("Look, that does not matter to me. What are we?").

Comadres: Sí, Sí—¿Qué tiene que ver? ("Yes, yes, what does that have to do with it?").

A: ¿Cómo que nosotros? Si el gobernador no va a estar, no más vamos a ir de intrusos y no nos van a recibir ("What do you mean us? The governor will not be there; we are only going as intruders, and they will not receive us").

Juan (J): Oye compadre, ¡qué extraño se me hace esto! Desde cuándo está preocupado de que nos reciban. No le quiero decir nada, compadre, pero se me hace que Gamboa tiene razón. ("Hey, *compadre*, how strange this is to me. Since when have you become concerned that they receive you? I do not wish to say anything, *compadre*, but it seems to me that Gamboa has a point").

Arturo did not respond but instead stared down at the ground. Doña Carmen said that she too thought it strange that they would need permission to do what they had planned to do. Then she shouted out:

Apenas acabamos de enterrar a un compañero y luego nos dices que
ahora no podemos hacerlo. El otra día en frente de todos dijiste que
íbamos a seguir luchando juntos contra ellos. A mi no me importa si
vemos al pinchi ladrón o no, pero ¡chingado Don Arturo! ¿desde
cuándo hacemos lo que nos dicen? Si nos esperamos hasta que nos
den permiso no hacemos nada nunca. Todos estamos bien encabro-
nados con esto. Nosotras vamos a ir sin ti si no vas tú ("We just finished burying a comrade, and then you say that we will not do this.
The other day [at the ritual] you said that we would continue the
struggle against them. I don't care if we see the son-of-a-bitching
thief, but what the fuck, Don Arturo, since when do we do what
they say? We are all angry about this. We are going to go without
you if you don't go").

Doña Carmen, in this instance, used the second-person formal to
reinforce her comments; this usage did not imply deference but
was used in formal declarative statements.

A: ¿Pero, y qué chingado quieren que haga? ¿Quieren que las autoridades nos peguen una paliza no más porque sí? Eso se me hace una
babosada. Si quieren ir está bueno, pero lo que tienen que saber es
que ellos nos pueden chingar muy fácil ("What the fuck do you want
me to do? Do you want them to beat us for nothing? If you go, fine,
but you have to know that they can fuck us very easily").
     Doña Carmen: Eso es lo que digo. ¿Qué chingado nos importa? Si
así fuéramos pensado cuando nos agarramos con los coyotes hace
dos años, aquí todavía estuviéramos hablando. ¡Qué chingaderas,
Arturo! ("That is what I mean, Arturo. What the fuck do we care? If
that is the way we would have thought when we fought against the
coyotes two years ago, we would still be talking. What fucking
things, Arturo!").
     A: Bien, bien, está bien—Vámonos a la chingada ("All right, all
right, let's go get fucked" [spoken resignedly]).

Within the next half hour, three buses had arrived, and 200 men,
women, and children packed into them and into ten cars. Two
hours later, the troupe arrived in Toluca. Except for judicial
police, who infiltrated the assembled crowd asking their intentions, and the secretary of governance, who hurriedly conferred
with Arturo about their intentions, the festivities proceeded on
schedule.

First, Arturo stood in front of those assembled on the patio of the governor's palace and addressed the governor's secretary with a flourish of friendly language, asserting that the governor had accomplished great public works in Netzahualcoyotl and that he had brought more stability to the lives of its citizens. But he also proclaimed that many citizens were still concerned that, in spite of these accomplishments, there were groups of persons, led by the likes of Mondragón, who would damage these accomplishments and in fact worked in contradiction to the governor's objectives. He stated that although these concerns were not resolved, he was sure that the governor would take steps to remedy *"el terror de los Mondragonistas"* ("the terror of the Mondragonistas"). Arturo then looked around and said:

> Sr. Secretario aquí le presento a la gente de Cd. Netzahualcoyotl que sigue luchando contra la opresión de pocos por el beneficio de ellos mismos. Aquí le presento a la gente con quien el gobernador puede contar en su lucha contra los que no quieren que tenga éxito en sus obras humanitarias. Aquí estamos todos para servirle, Sr. Secretario, como compañeros, como amigos ("Mr. Secretary, I present you with the people of Netzahualcoyotl, who continue struggling against the oppression of a few who profit at the people's expense. Here are the people who the governor can count on in his fight for humanitarian works. Here we are, all of us, to serve you, Mr. Secretary, as a friend, as comrades").

The secretary then approached Arturo and embraced him in the traditional Mexican style. Smiling to the gathering, he stated that it was a great honor for him, on behalf of the governor, to thank them for their spontaneous display of genuine affection and support, and that he was positive that the governor would greatly appreciate their efforts in the future. He knew that in spite of those who wished to destroy the governor's public works in their city, as long as the governor had their warm affection, all conditions in the city could be resolved.

Those present then applauded, and the musicians began to play Mexican *rancheras*, while the dancing troupe performed a northern folk dance. The festive occasion continued until 3 P.M., at which time the passengers boarded their buses, packed themselves into the cars, and sped back to Netzahualcoyotl.

The next day the press reported how once again the people of Netzahualcoyotl showed their appreciation for the governor's efforts to make a better life for them by appearing at his palace and paying tribute to his works. The *comadres, compadres,* and Arturo's pals, however, never again attended a meeting called by Arturo. They remained friends and kin, but never again would they politically support Arturo, unless he divorced himself from the "coyotes" at all levels. He had not understood that the rituals of the locality were in total opposition to those of domains above it. The cohort of men and women, however, did know this, and they withdrew their support from one who had been enmeshed in domains where he did not belong.

This cohort knew and understood this fact, and by forcing Arturo to visit the governor's palace, they forced themselves upon domains unaccustomed to such treatment and countered the repetitive rituals of marginality by upsetting the pattern of "proper" relations of submission and dominance. The "rebellion" was short-lived, but memory of the experience will always remain, as will the autonomous social power inherent in the locality.

MICROCULTURAL CHANGE

The visit to the governor helps illustrate that "microcultural" change did occur in Netzahualcoyotl, as events in 1979 and 1980 have confirmed. For the period in question, it is necessary briefly to review the events leading to the visit to the governor, and then discuss its aftermath, on a social, political, cultural, and behavioral level. It is only then that an understanding of more recent events, in which persons in Netzahualcoyotl participated in direct action circumventing the usual rituals of marginality, can be explored.

The Visit

Prior to Emilio's death, Valenzuela's political status was relegated to that of broker without portfolio. His entanglement had not led to "integration," as had been true for Mondragón and his cohorts. The reason is simple: Valenzuela had not been willing to acquiesce in the sale of lots by members of the CRC, and he therefore opposed Mondragón publicly. Mondragón, in contrast, relied on land squatters and the illegal sale of lots as the basic sources of his support. Such support could be manifested for the state in the "intermediate" rituals of marginality, when called for by state elites. As an "integrated" councilman of the city, Mondragón had access to the state and municipal regularizing processes and legal machinery by which lots could be sold or bought, without the interference of municipal authorities, of which he was one. Valenzuela, however, had refused a portfolio, had remained outside of the institutionalized graft system, and had thus been effectively disposed of politically through various gambits affecting the composition of the Fidecomiso, and through negotiations affecting the payments to land developers, the state, and the Chase Manhattan Bank.

Everything appeared under control in Netzahualcoyotl by 1974, with the population effectively structurally marginalized, its political leadership coopted or ineffective, and the basis of political support shifted from legitimacy to coercion. Valenzuela had been culturally "delocalized" of support, authority was delegated from above, not allocated from below, and vertical, unequal, and single-interest relations had been firmly established with regularized exchanges of "favors." For persons like Mondragón, it was untimely that there emerged once more a small, localized, and legitimate support network of *"viejas chingonas"* and *compadres* after the death of Emilio. It was especially untimely since rituals of marginality had been once more well entrenched.

The processes that made such an emergence possible had nothing to do with a political strategy as such, but rather with the untimely death of Emilio García López. It was his death that brought former supporters together once more in various rituals. These rituals, which expressed sentiments about Emilio, also contained specific social statements about the nature of support for Valenzuela. The rituals surrounding Emilio's death provided reinforcement to the sentiments that bound this cohort of political activists together. His death activated the old networks of supporters and their underpinning of social relations.

It must be recalled that in the pre-Novena rite, which was held the day before the cemetery ritual, the network of *comadres* had attended, in addition to various pals who had been in the CRC during Valenzuela's tenure. The reaction against the two persons who received communion was one of mocking disagreement; it was not the communion rite that the *comadres* mocked but rather that women who had not been part of their political activities were putting on airs by receiving communion on this occasion. They did not share in the sentiment of this political cohort of women, and by receiving communion, they intruded in that sentiment. While it could be understood that family members would receive communion, all others were part of the political networks activated to support Valenzuela, and such networks had little to do with the religious content of the service.

On the following day and before the departure to the cemetery, once again this division among supporters appeared and was manifested in the verbal dueling between Doña Beatriz and Graciela. In fact, Graciela and her friends had been expelled from their immediate circle. Graciela had joined Arturo only recently, and then only to receive assistance concerning a lot that Mondragón had sold her. Yet she had received communion the day before. She represented the sort of support that was in complete opposition to that generated by the various rituals in which the *comadres* and *compadres* participated. Once assembled at the cemetery, these sentiments came to be closely associated with Valenzuela's political fortunes. In fact, the physical environment itself provided a setting in which such sentiments were easily activated. The cross with the inscriptions symbolized and reintroduced their collective political cultural identity.

Even Valenzuela's proximity to Padre José, and the priest's brief but impassioned sermon concerning "the fight of men and women," provided additional sentiment and impetus for Valenzuela to regain his support. In turning to Valenzuela at the close of the ritual, the priest also provided him with an association to a sacred ritual, useful in conducting political activity. Such an association was further reinforced when one of the *comadres* began to pass out religious literature and Doña Mariana received communion.

It was at this juncture that Valenzuela regained legitimate political support of the most intense sort—that based on the shared sentiments of communally based relationships and ties. It was at this point that the *comadres* once again joined with Valenzuela. Their participation in the activities in Toluca was not based on their relationships with the governor but rather only on their ties with Valenzuela and the sentiments he represented communally.

They entered the ritual at Toluca because they wanted to meet in the governor's palace to show their political power and to demonstrate that, once again, they were a force to be reckoned with. Theirs was not an act of obeisance, although the form of the ritual was the same. The celebration was to be *their* celebration of social autonomy, once more expressed communally in front of the governor, but with the greatest of irony. The governor would not realize what was occurring, and everyone would think that the ritual signified the opposite of what was meant. For a Mexican, this sort of display represents the pinnacle of autonomy and power, and is the ultimate show of scorn: when what is experienced seems like what it is but, in fact, is its opposite. Women especially have long practiced such cultural sleight of hand.

What followed has already been detailed: Valenzuela's hesitation, the reaction of his *comadres* and *compadres*, and their eventual appearance in Toluca. Yet their reaction to Valenzuela was not as important as the fact that they were all willing to go without him, recognizing that the "coyote" elites were being legitimized by Valenzuela, who in turn was legitimized by the elites. Their demonstration in Toluca, unknown to the governor or to Valenzuela, became a demonstration, for themselves, of even greater irony. The governor would perceive it as an act of obeisance; Valenzuela would perceive it as an act of support for him; and the public would perceive it as an indication of appreciation for the governor on behalf of the population of Netzahualcoyotl, as indeed the newspapers reported later. Their demonstration was a farewell celebration for Valenzuela, for his crude attempts to use their sentiments politically, and for his retreat when opposition emerged; a farewell to the governor; and a celebration of autonomy in social power. They would never return to the governor's palace in Toluca, and never again would they return to Valenzuela as political supporters, although they would continue to play the guitar, drink beer, tell jokes, and cooperate with him in other contexts.

For this small network of men and women, the "microcultural" change consisted of recognizing the myths of universal access and representation. When occasions arose—as in late fall 1979, when prices of staples went up too quickly; in January 1980, when the state implemented a value-added tax; and in February 1980, when bus fares doubled—these networks did not turn to Valenzuela or to the governor. Instead, they sacked stores, formed large-scale demonstrations, and overturned and burned buses, so that police had to be sent in from the state. They had tested and refuted the myths.

Such reactions are not supposed to occur among migrants, according to the most recent literature, given that most migrants are "deferential, nonthreatening [in their] approach to negotiating with public officials" (Cornelius 1975:185). Yet they do occur and can best be understood as the residue of microcultural changes, after which such populations are no longer willing to accept the fiscal and political dictates of the formal public, private, or labor sectors. The myths that these sectors represent have slowly but surely been recognized as elaborate rationalizations to maintain the cult of lies they compose. As such, rationalizations continue to be recognized, but the rituals expressing such rationalizations will tend to shift, if not in form at least in major function.

The great irony is that even when rituals of marginality are performed by populations in "appropriate" and equivalent contexts, like that described here, the form may be the same but the meaning and intent (lost upon the audience but not the performers) very different. In time, the audience of elites will be able to depend on neither what the performance expresses nor the relations it represents. By that time, "microcultural" changes will have reached "macrocultural" proportions.

The tragedy for Arturo Valenzuela Cisneros was that, unlike his *comadres* and *compadres*, he never did recognize the myths for what they were, the rituals as performances, and the changes around him as real. He still does not.

THE "INTEGRATION" OF ARTURO VALENZUELA CISNEROS AND THE AFTERMATH: 1979

In 1979, Arturo Valenzuela Cisneros became the "elected" delegate to the Mexican federal Congress. As a federal deputy to the Congress, he occupied the seat allowed to the PPI (Partido Popular Independiente) by the Mexican government. He also continued his broker role within the city, state, and Agrarian Department. But he was without the local support that had marked his political activities in the past. Instead, he was dependent on Mr. X—his leftist connection who ensured his "election" as a federal deputy. This was the same Mr. X who had been so invaluable to the state and federal authorities, and to the land developers, in their overall supralocal strategy to create the Fidecomiso and ultimately to further the structural marginalization of the population of Netzahualcoyotl (see chapters 5 and 8).

Arturo Valenzuela Cisneros's living room, where in the past his political supporters had gathered, is now adorned with hammer-and-sickle posters and a bust of Lenin, prominently displayed. Yet, in this case, ideology had little to do with the display. Arturo had never read or in fact understood the most basic assumptions of the Marxist or Marxist-Leninist positions.

Arturo rambled through intoxicated accounts of how he was going to demand the punishment of land developers, right the wrongs of the Mexican Constitution, and ensure that the crimes committed in Ciudad Netzahualcoyotl were never again repeated, now that he was legitimately elected to the federal congress.

Meanwhile, the former governor of the state of Mexico, who from 1976 to 1982 would serve as the mayor of Mexico City, was awarded the "Outstanding Urban Innovator" prize in Switzerland for his work in urban development in Netzahualcoyotl and for his development of urban infrastructures in communication and transportation in the federal district and the metropolitan zone of Mexico City. He, in fact, made it easier for populations like those of Netzahualcoyotl to more speedily search for work.

The secretary of governance became the head of the research section of the PRI. Loya, the former mayor of Netzahualcoyotl, became a federal senator and will sit in Congress at the same time Arturo will take his seat in the House of Representatives (Cámara de Diputados). Mondragón is now being groomed and prepared for high state office and has become a prominent PRI official.

As Roberto López Cobos stated in his description of supralocal "formal" domains: "What happened will happen and continue happening." Yet the *comadres* and Roberto's pals did not allow it to happen for a very brief moment. Such moments are expressions of deep cultural change that have little to do with elective or appointed office, as Valenzuela believed. Elected offices or appointed offices have more to do with the national, state, and local myths of marginality. The encompassing ideology for such myths benefit the elites of the public and private sectors. In contrast, the deep microcultural changes that the *comadres* and *compadres* forged have more to do with fellowship, with moral considerations of reputation and communality, and with maintaining social identity within the locality, and hence with preserving the possibility of a sense of self. This emergent self, as Valenzuela's tragic political demise showed, is often apprehended by elites and power holders and transplanted to contexts outside of those important to its continued survival and growth. This is the essential characteristic of any ritual of marginality. As for the networks of *"viejas chingonas"* and *compadres*, they need not fear becoming the "property" of the formal elites so long as they continue to engage those elites. When such control can no longer be exerted effectively in Mexico, the basis of larger patterns of cultural change will have taken hold.

10
Conclusions: Sociocultural Dynamics and Culture Change

I HAVE ARGUED that the marginalized population of Ciudad Netzahualcoyotl is the creation of elite policies designed to promote capital-intensive technology. I have stated that, in economic terms, large parts of the population of the city were economically marginalized, but that I did not anticipate this population becoming "demarginalized." Furthermore, that this population is politically marginalized is amply illustrated in the ethnographic analysis of the CRC. Various rituals of marginality have been devised at the community level to ensure that such marginality continues, including brokerage, political friendship, and political exchange-relations.

Environmental conditions and lack of contractual fulfillment by land developers, combined with the conflict between land invaders and lot owners, led to the creation of conditions in which the CRC could develop. Established rituals of marginality proved insufficient to satisfy the needs of the population, and heterogeneous persons joined together to seek results with political action. After a great deal of physical confrontation, political organizing, schisms within the CRC, and sophisticated elite strategies ensuring the private sector's "protection" from its obligations, the public sector "integrated" the CRC leadership, except for Arturo Valenzuela Cisneros. The population thereby became further marginalized and further excluded from the benefits of the system, although the

239

costs of this entanglement continued to be their burden. A few individuals benefited, but those who refused to become part of illegitimate institutionalized processes were left out or relegated to old rituals of marginality, such as political brokerage. These were the rituals in which Valenzuela participated prior to his "election" as a PPI representative. This "election" was the culminating ritual, for the national government provides seats to such parties, and few votes are actually counted for such "elections."

I have argued that political activities in Mexico inevitably result in such outcomes—"entanglement" in the networks of elites who control access to and resources in the public, private, and labor sectors. This is a social-structural condition, not simply a strategy. *Individuals* will be "integrated," but the mass of the population will be further pauperized and excluded, as happened in Ciudad Netzahualcoyotl.

I have shown that such processes have profound unintended consequences for the lives of human beings. For Arturo Valenzuela Cisneros, the basis of his sense of self was rooted in his primary and secondary localities. He eventually lost his local support, and this led him to his final "integration," accompanied by a number of hysterical episodes and great quantities of ethanol. These were the behavioral consequences of the stress accompanying Valenzuela's changed roles, the loss of his intimate support, and the inevitable loss of his sense of self-worth, which had been rooted in social and cultural referents. His temporary political dormancy was interrupted only when his primary and secondary "localities" entered into the political field after the death of Emilio. Valenzuela's misuse of these localities contributed to his ultimate marginalization.

POLITICS, PROCESS, AND CULTURE CHANGE

Despite the further marginalization of the population and the process of "integration," there were other forces that resulted in microcultural change in Netzahualcoyotl. This change came in the form of networks of men and women projecting their sense of social autonomy by defying the power of the state and, perhaps as important, defying "one of their own." Arturo came to be recognized as too enmeshed in elite domains to represent the two bases of their political power: mutual trust and a sense of communal identity. To not have defied the governor and Arturo after the rituals surrounding Emilio's death would have amounted to a denial of their communal existence. For women who had braved the cudgels of police and for men who had been beaten, shot, and abused by authority, defiance of Arturo was a public statement of cohort identity, and an experience by which such an identity is validated.

It is in such acts that fundamental cultural change is manifested, and it is manifested in the formation of an identifiable cohort of networks of men and women who scorn the various "rituals of marginality" that have traditionally crosscut sector and class cleavages throughout Mexico. For this cohort, "politics cannot be *as usual.*"

The coalescence of these networks of women and men into an identifiable cohort was a consequence of their mutual experiences, and these experiences provide the central elements and characteristics of their cohort. Among the most important are:

1. An intensive experience of social and ecological contexts, as described in chapters 2 and 3. This shared experience pushed these networks to rely on self-help and mutual protection as a means of survival. These recourses were manifested in the invasion of land, the mass protection of lots, the daily social exchanges between neighbors and fictive kin, and the economic and business exchanges, such as *tandas* and cooperatives. The less the access to the formal sector, the greater the reliance on reciprocal networks of exchange and *confianza* for survival.

2. An intensive experience as part of an economically and politically marginalized informal sector. The experience of competition, within a surplus-labor market, for redundant and largely wasteful occupations that waste the potential of human growth is a particularly degrading experience. Coupled with an overriding economic ideology in the formal sector proclaiming that all persons have equal access to resources and opportunities "to make it," the expe-

rience of having to work for nothing in order to gain access to possibilities of employment created great contradictions for the population, which either overtly or covertly became part of the general experience of inequality and scarcity.

3. An intensive experience in trying to fulfill the basic cultural goals of land ownership, security, and *confianza*, but being constantly thwarted, exploited, or denied the resources, access, or permission to do so, until political activities finally moved elites to respond. This single experience, regardless of outcome, was a positive one. Even police response and suppression can be looked upon as a useful reaction, for it signaled that protest had reached and vibrated the networks of power holders. People as a whole became disillusioned and frightened, but this cohort faced down even the worst repression, and from that confrontation emerged the basis for the "glue" of their common cultural heritage.

4. An intensive experience of cultural congruency of goals, objectives, language, dress, reciprocity, residential affinity, and belief systems with leaders willing to express them in private or in political domains. While the total population of participants in the CRC was very heterogeneous, the political activities of these networks of men and women became the means and mechanism by which commonality and mutuality were formed. With such a formation, cultural congruence could also be formed at the most basic primary and secondary "localities." Arturo's misperception was in not recognizing such congruence and opting for alien localities.

5. An intensive experience in generating multiple-interest and multiple-stranded social relations that transcended political activities. Based on kinship, residence, fictive kinship, and intimate friendship, these relationships of reciprocity and mutuality were the unintended consequences of political action that in time became of greater import to these men and women. These were the bases of social life, social identity—public and private—and the localities from which a sense of self emerged. This emergence was perpetuated through constant exchange and interaction in a variety of contexts, including, for women, the household, across fences in lots, and in the ritual, visitation and political activities— all as part of the extensive communication networks. For men, similar contexts were present, but interaction was expressed most

commonly at night in recreation and visitation. The two networks came together in political activities, but the experience will always remain regardless of whether these networks are called into action or not.

6. An intensive experience, for women, participating in the tactics and strategies of political activity and successfully using such networks for defense and offense. This experience provided women with a sense of political autonomy based on residential networks of peers. In addition, it provided women with the experience of confronting men collectively and confronting institutions (judicial and private) of great power. Their willingness to engage in violence is an experience that, in and of itself, illustrates the intensity and profundity of collective and communal identity, which in turn is symbolized by their "Indian" dresses. In the context of the environment, the risks of engaging in such violence were great, indeed, given the record of repression and suppression on the part of police and municipal authorities. It is significant that the initial stimulus for violent confrontations between the CRC and police was the incarceration of a woman—Maria Cruz— who had been arrested in an earlier altercation (see chapter 4). Women, as was shown, controlled much of the CRC activity during the day and provided valuable organizational, political, and social power in their efforts.

7. An intensive experience in the defense of property, perceived rights, and expectations, by physical means if necessary, by men and women. For the *comadres* and *compadres*, their "place in the sun" was always in jeopardy to the vagaries of climate, politics, economics, and fraud by land developers, municipal authorities, other residents, and certainly by elites in domains above them. Their willingness to defend their small, miserable lots, their rights to these lots and the *jacales* on them, and their sense of entitlement to such lots and homes at whatever cost, created a perception of strength and power. This consensus was demonstrated in their determination to "visit" the governor.

8. An intensive experience of being manipulated by "formal" sectors and becoming entangled within the confines of state and federal elites. The use of the Fidecomiso for the benefit of the private sector was among the most important experiences for these

cohorts of men and women, for it validated their mistrust of elites and resulted in pessimistic and realistic evaluations of the likelihood of resolving their grievances. The parameters for seeking resolution were defined by the state, federal authorities, municipal officials, and the segment of the CRC that illegally sold lots. The experience of becoming further marginalized reinforced their reliance on themselves rather than on the rituals used to exploit their marginality.

9. The intensive experience of "losing" political leaders through entanglement and "integration," while the population became further marginalized. Whether it was Mondragón, Valenzuela, or Maldonado, their inevitable "cooptation" confirmed the workings of the larger system of entanglement. As *compadre* Juan described it: *"Es un revoltijo de huevos"* ("It is scrambled eggs"). If any new organizational movement takes place, these cohorts will very carefully scrutinize and evaluate the means, tactics, and goals of its leadership. They will assume a critical position toward any organizational movement.

10. An intensive experience of seeing through the myths of "universal" integration and participation advanced by political elites, and the tendency of elites to pursue their particularistic interests and benefits at others' expense. The underlying myths of the cult of elites that punctuate the rituals of marginality at the national, state, or municipal levels are recognized as rationalizations to maintain inequality and scarcity. Doña Carmen's clear statement regarding the governor of the state as a "son-of-a-bitching thief," the *comadres'* and *compadres'* pressuring of Arturo to participate in the visit to the governor, and the forcing of the state authorities to receive them are behavioral indicators of their recognition of the underlying myths of elites. For them, ideology had little merit, and the left end of the political spectrum was as much a participant in their marginalization as were the governmental authorities. Arturo's Mr. X, who participated in so many of the strategies that eventually led to the CRC's entanglement at the expense of the population, was particularly recognized as a valuable ally of the "coyotes" in the Agrarian Department. They also viewed Arturo's final "election" by the government through the PPI as supported by Mr. X.

11. An intensive experience of revitalizing local meanings, contexts, and sentiment through local rituals and, at the same time, activating their networks for political purposes. Their purpose was to celebrate their own sense of social autonomy vis-à-vis the rituals of marginality by participating in the governor's "state of the state" rituals of obeisance. This ability to manifest scorn for the ritual by participating in it is an expression of autonomy and power. By participating, it seemed that the networks were acquiescing to standard rituals of marginality, but in fact their participation meant the opposite—nonparticipation. Soon after, they withdrew from all such rituals, and when basic needs did arise, they did not seek brokerage, political friendships, or political exchanges.

12. An intensive experience of social autonomy and social power expressed through networks of persons refusing to utilize national, state, or municipal rituals of marginality to meet basic biosocial needs. These networks will not seek to resolve basic needs of living; the means by which this is accomplished will be quite different. As events of 1979 and 1980 have shown, such networks will not accept the explanations provided by elites for their increasing difficulties in surviving nor will they accept the mechanisms usually offered as the means of resolving the reality of inequality and scarcity.

When these various experiential dimensions are combined, they form a very different cohort from those willing to accept "business as usual," the broad myths of national "integration," and the mechanisms for such integration. These cohorts will prove increasingly important as greater portions of the population of Mexico concentrate in greater and greater numbers in the urban central valley of Mexico.

WITHDRAWAL OF LEGITIMACY FROM NATIONAL MYTHS AS ADAPTIVE BEHAVIORS

The formation of cohorts such as exist in Netzahualcoyotl would seem to be especially problematical to the traditional means by which political actions become diffused in Mexico. Insofar as rituals of marginality are largely understood to be repetitive means by which cultural and political elites maintain, dominate, and expand their domains of privilege, such cohorts can be seen as withdrawing their allocation of legitimacy to the underlying myths and the authorities representing such myths. As Adams (1975:45) has stated: "They are arguing that it is possible to seriously weaken powerful organizations, even nation-states, by withholding this [allocative] power." I would add that they are arguing that they *must* not only withhold allocative power from nation-states but also deny the underlying myths that define the nation as a "universalistic" entity. Adams (1975:45) continues: "The question is open. The withdrawal to isolation from the larger society may weaken the superiors by loss of some allocated power. But the subordinates also lose the benefits, the delegated power, of the larger society." I would suggest that such cohorts would argue that the question is indeed open as to whether they will seriously weaken the state by withdrawal. The capacity of their withdrawal to initiate the collapse of the state depends on how widespread it becomes. For these cohorts, however, "entanglement" in the system of political and economic relations comprising the nation-state, as occurred in Netzahualcoyotl, is too costly an expedient. Entanglement pays for the *individual* mobility of leaders and provides the means by which governors, secretaries of governance, mayors, and councilmen can ascend in the public sector. For the population of marginalized persons, entanglement even included payment to the Chase Manhattan Bank and to an American university for courses in administration.

Therefore, the nation-state's "delegated" powers come with a very high price tag. For such cohorts to withdraw their allocated support from the national state, and to withdraw their belief in the myths proclaiming the nation as a "universalistic" entity, is in reality a *very adaptive strategy*. It is the sort of strategy that seems to be increasingly distributed throughout Central America and, most recently, Mesoamerica. It is a maximizing strategy that is much more cost-effective than continuing to believe, as Arturo Valenzuela did, that somehow public sectors are accessible to the population, that private sectors, given "hard work," are accessible to the population, and that labor sectors are representative of their membership. For selected individuals, these cohorts would argue, the "open society" is a reality; for the masses of the population, it is not. Therefore, such populations would argue that depriving the nation-state of legitimacy by withholding allocated power (Adams:1975) is no longer a question of choice but rather a logical means of more efficiently meeting survival needs.

On a rational basis, such a strategy seems valid. To continue to allocate support and legitimacy to an organizational system that ensures one's exploitation and inequality, and to provide resources for the enrichment of a few, would be behaviorally maladaptive. To continue to support the myths that underpin the organization of the nation-state, in light of events that disprove such myths, would seem tantamount to a sort of cognitive dissonance in which two opposing beliefs occupy the same pattern of thinking. The greatest dissonance would appear to be generated when information negates the one belief and validates the other, and yet the opposing beliefs are maintained. Arturo Valenzuela Cisneros seemed to express both behavioral maladaptation and cognitive dissonance. From a rational point of view, then, the strategy of withdrawal for such populations would seem to be a *must* rather than a *choice*. If this is so, then it would seem that the validity of the myth of the nation, and the sectors comprising it, would be open to question throughout Mexico by the cohorts of women and men who undergo the kinds of intensive social, economic, political, cultural, and psychological experiences described in this work.

There seems to be little reason to believe that such experiences will not continue to occur with the same unintended consequences, since no fundamental social-structural or urban-policy changes are apparent for much of urban central Mexico, or for Mexico as a whole. It is probable that increasing numbers of the Mexican urban population will arrive at the same conclusions regarding the myths sustaining their marginality, and such conclusions would become especially strengthened by national or international economic crises.

Appendix A

SPANISH VERSION OF LETTER FROM EX-PRESIDENT
CÁRDENAS

Andes 605
Mexico 10. D.F.

Prof. _____
Gobernador Constitucional del Estado,
Palacio de Gobierno,
Toluca, Mex.

Estimado y fino amigo:

Para tu conocimiento y efectos te ruego la consideración que en justicia proceda a los señores portadores de la presente que han traído carta del Senor Lic. José G. Zuno, fechada en Guadalajara, Jal. y que en esta misma me permito transcribir.

"... Una comisión de auténticos mexicanos, representando a Ciudad Netzahualcoyotl, del municipio de Texcoco, va a visitarte y a pedir ayuda para que se salven de la explotación de inhumanos fraccionadores que indebidamente están disponiendo de las tierras que,

248

Appendix A

ENGLISH VERSION OF LETTER FROM EX-PRESIDENT
CÁRDENAS

Andes 605
Mexico 10. D.F.

Prof. _____
Constitutional Governor of the State
Government Palace
Toluca, Mexico

My dear and fine friend:

For your knowledge and action, I ask that you give consideration to
the justice of the appeal that the bearers make who have brought a letter
from Lic. José G. Zuno, dated in Guadalajara, Jal., and from this I have
permitted myself to transcribe.

"... A commission of authentic Mexicans, representing
the city of Netzahualcoyotl, of the municipality of
Texcoco, will visit you to ask your help to save them
from the exploitation of inhuman land developers who
purposely despoil these lands, which since Lic.

249

desde el gobierno del Lic. Alemán, están reservadas
para ellos. Son familias que suman más de seiscientos
mil habitantes.-Yo ya escribí a _____
y esperamos que también tú, con tu alto sentido de servicio, les des tu apoyo, por lo que ellos y yo te lo
agradecemos muchísimo [sic]."

Muy cordialmente.

Lázaro Cárdenas del Río

Alemán's administration, have been reserved for them.
The families total more than 700,000 persons.
I have already written _____
and I hope that you, with your high regard for service,
will give them your support, which they and I will
greatly appreciate."

Very cordially yours,

Lázaro Cárdenas del Río

Appendix B

LAND DEVELOPMENT COMPANIES AND OWNERS

Land Development Companies	Owners
1. El Sol	Cesar Hahn Cárdenas
	Javier Muñoz Anaya
2. Estado de Mexico	Justino López Herrera
3. Agua Azul—Grupo A	Salvador Oriard
4. Romero	Raul Romero
5. Land Developers	
Aurora, S.A.	Bernardo Eckstein Sals
(a) La Aurora Oriente	Carlos Mimbel
(b) Esperanza	Lic. Horberto Kanner
(c) La Aurora, S.A.	Bernardo Eckstein Sals
(d) La Aurora Sur	Abraham Eslonick
6. Villada (Seccion I)	Cenobio y Jesús Ortíz González
7. Villada (Seccion II)	Elsisa López Almasin
8. Evolución y Ampliación	
Villada	Victor Manuel Villasenor
9. Inmobiliaria Valle, S.A.	Vicente Castañeda Guido
(a) Evolución—Grupo A	
(b) La Perla	
10. Metropolitana	José Lorenzo Zallany
11. Las Aguilas	Alejandro Romero L.
12. Ampliación de Las Aguilas	

252

13. Constitución del 57
14. Lotes Santa Martha
15. Terrenos M. Islas   Salvador Oriard y Socios
16. Pantitlán   Mercedes Martínez del Campo
17. Reforma   Ing. Rodolfo Elvia y Jorge Ramírez

The following companies have been developed clandestinely:
1. Las Flores
2. Maravillas
3. San Juan
4. Los Volcanes
5. Mexico
6. Modelo
7. Atlacomulco
8. Loma Bonita
9. Porfirio Díaz
10. Pirules
11. Las Fuentes
12. Las Virgencitas

Appendix C

¡ ATENCION !

COLONO:

Una vez más la Propaganda Impresa del CONGRESO RESTAURADOR DE COLONOS, A.C., llega a tus manos y pone a consideración tuya sus puntos de vista.

LOS FRACCIONAMIENTOS DE CD. NETZAHUALCOYOTL

¡FRAUDE CRIMINAL!

¿SERVICIOS? .... ¡TODOS! (AGUA, LUZ, DRENAJE, MER-CADOS, ESCUELAS, ETC. ETC.) .... PERO en el CON-TRATO.

¿AGUA? ...... NO Recomendable para el uso HUMANO, Analizada por La Secretaría de Salubridad y Asistencia.

Conforme al Artículo 27 Constitucional, el dominio de la Nación sobre el Ex-Lago de Texcoco es INALIENABLE, INNEGOCIABLE E IMPRE-SCRIPTIBLE.

254

Appendix C

ATTENTION!

COLONIST:

Once again the News Press of the CONGRESO RESTAURADOR DE COLONOS, A.C. is in your hands and places its points of view before you for your consideration.

THE LAND DEVELOPERS OF CD. NETZAHUALCOYOTL

CRIMINAL FRAUD!

SERVICES? . . . . ALL OF THEM (WATER, LIGHT, SEWAGE, MARKETS, SCHOOLS, ETC. ETC.) . . . . BUT IN THE CONTRACT.

WATER? . . . . . . NOT recommended for HUMAN consumption, analyzed by the Secretariat of Health and Welfare.

In accordance with Article 27 of the Constitution, the dominion of the former lake of Texcoco is not ALIENABLE, NEGOTIABLE, OR PROSCRIPTIBLE.

Los Fraccionadores, Verdaderos Delincuentes Internacionales y los Desvergonzados, Traidores y Antipatrióticos Presta-Nombres, Vendiendo lo que no es suyo, robando al Pueblo y a la Nación.

Con una publicidad mentirosa caímos en las garras de estos bandoleros de profesión. Los anuncios de ventas de terrenos invitan a las familias a vivir ¡FELICES! en las colonias de CD. NETZAHUALCOYOTL. ¡NADA MAS FALSO Y VIL!

. . . las familias que Sí viven felices son las de los fraccionadores, Eckstein, Stern, Kreimerman, Zlotnick, Kaner, Holzer, Zakany, Romero, etc. etc. Extranjeros, perniciosos, pillos de la peor calaña.—¡Muy Felices! —¡Sí!—con miles de millones de PESOS que los hizo ricos ilícitamente: a costa del sacrificio de los HUMILDES.

COMPAÑERO COLONO:—NO DEBES SEGUIR PAGANDO POR NINGUN CONCEPTO AL FRACCIONADOR.

No hagas caso de sus amenazas terroristas porque sólo busca intimidarte para seguir robándote tu dinero.

¡Defiende el Patrimonio de tu Familia!

UNETE AL   CONGRESO RESTAURADOR DE COLONOS

The Land Developers, Real International Delinquents without Shame, Traitors, Unpatriotic, Lender of Names, Selling what is not theirs, Stealing from the Community and the Nation.

With false publicity we fell into the paws of these bandits-by-profession. The advertisement selling lots invites families to live HAPPILY! in the colonias of CD. NETZAHUALCOYOTL. NOTHING MORE VILE AND FALSE!

. . . the families that do live happily are those of the land developers— Eckstein, Stern, Kreimerman, Zlotnick, Kaner, Holzer, Zakany, Romero, etc. etc. Foreigners, pernicious rogues of the worst indolence.— Very Happy!—Yes!—with thousands of the pesos that made them rich illegally at the cost of the sacrifice of the poor.

Comrade Colonist:—YOU SHOULD NOT CONTINUE PAYING THE LAND DEVELOPER FOR ANYTHING!

Do not pay attention to the terroristic threats, because they only seek to intimidate you in order to continue stealing your money.

Defend the Legacy of your Family!

UNITE WITH THE CONGRESO RESTAURADOR DE COLONOS

Appendix D

ESTIMATE OF CRC MEMBERSHIP IN CIUDAD
NETZAHUALCOYOTL, BY NEIGHBORHOOD (N = 39,424)

50	1.	el sol	0	20.	san mateito
250	2.	estado de mexico	0	21.	aurorita
350	3.	maravillas	0	22.	formando hogar
0	4.	el barco I	0	23.	joyita
0	5.	el barco II	0	24.	amipant
0	6.	el barco III	0	25.	mi retiro
0	7.	netzahualcoyotl I	100	26.	pavon
0	8.	netzahualcoyotl II		27.	pavon secc. silvia
0	9.	netzahualcoyotl III	0	28.	mexico I
0	10.	porvenir		29.	mexico II
0	11.	perete		30.	mexico III
0	12.	volcanes		31.	central
0	13.	martinez de llanos	4,000	32.	tamalipas
0	14.	xochitenco		33.	tamalipas secc. virgencitas
100	15.	juarez pantitlan		34.	tamalipas secc. las flores
	16.	nueva juarez pantitlan I		35.	tamalipas secc. el palmar
	17.	nueva juarez pantitlan II	200	36.	agua azul grupo a super 4
	18.	nueva juarez pantitlan III		37.	agua azul grupo c
0	19.	angel veraza			

	38.	agua azul grupo b		60.	aurora oriente
		super 4		61.	aurora seccion a
	39.	agua azul grupo b		62.	aurora romero
		super 23	2,000	63.	ampliacion villada
500	40.	pirules			super 43
	41.	las fuentes	4,000	64.	ampliacion villada
	42.	porfirio diaz			super 44
	43.	modelo		65.	ampliacion villada
	44.	romero			poniente
	45.	atlacomulco	1,324	66.	vicente villada
50	46.	metropolitana I		67.	ampliacion villada
	47.	san lorenzo			oriente
0	48.	metropolitana II		68.	las aguilas
0	49.	metropolitana III		69.	ampliacion las aguilas
3,500	50.	evolucion poniente		70.	constitucion de 1857
	51.	evolucion super 24		71.	sta. martha
	52.	evolucion super 43		72.	manantiales
	53.	evolucion super 22		73.	loma bonita
	54.	evolucion	4,000	74.	la perla
16,000	55.	ampliacion evolucion	2,000	75.	reforma b
	56.	aurora sur		76.	reforma a secc. I
	57.	aurora I		77.	reforma a secc. II
	58.	aurora II	1,000	78.	esperanza
	59.	aurora III			

NOTE: The *colonias* listed here are all that existed in 1971 and 1974. In 1971 there was a total of fifty-eight *colonias* and fifty-eight subcommittees, but there was not a subcommittee in each *colonia*. Next to the number of each *colonia* is an estimate of the number of supporters. Those *colonias* with zeroes have no subcommittees; those without estimates following *colonias* with estimates are regarded as part of the preceding *colonia*.

Appendix E

MEDICAL REPORT FOR ARTURO VALENZUELA CISNEROS
(MARCH 12, 1974)

This is a thirty-four-year-old married Mexican male who is, at present, a political leader.

CC: 1. Chest pain and shortness of breath.
     2. Intermittent weakness and blurry vision.

Subjective:
   1. For several months, the patient has noted pain in the left precordial area, sharp in character, lasting minutes to hours, usually associated with shortness of breath. Often there is concomitant pain in the back of the neck and numbness of both arms, mostly in the left arm.
   This usually occurs when the patient is under emotional stress, often during a stress-laden situation and sometimes when "nervous" although at rest. It does not occur upon exertion, although his usual work does not require great physical effort. He has recently been able to do very strenuous physical exercise without chest pain or shortness of breath.
   The chest pain is relieved by drinking an alcoholic beverage or by lessening of the emotional stress. He denies associated diaphoresis.
   There is no history of heart disease or heart murmur, and there are no symptoms of congestive heart failure.
   2. At times for several years, the patient has noted intermittent blurry vision and intermittent weakness of arms and legs. In 1969, the first episode of blurry vision occurred, such that he had to be assisted in

getting about for approximately four weeks. This occurred following a severe blow to the back of the head, reportedly resulting in one day of total blindness. Other episodes, usually lasting hours or days, involve numbness of both legs and weakness of both legs.

The last major episode of leg weakness occurred in February 1974, following a particularly frustrating event concerning an emotionally laden political crisis.

He denies speech difficulty, double vision, ataxic symptoms, or severe recurrent headaches (although he has privately admitted having headaches, and I have noticed considerable differences in fluidity of speech and a marked tendency to stutter).

Past Medical History:
Usual childhood diseases and diphtheria (typhoid two months previous, as diagnosed by Mexican physician)
Surgery: none
Injuries: none, except for blows
Allergies: none known
Medications: none

Habits:
Tobacco: one pack daily
Ethanol: one-half quart daily weekdays; intoxicated most weekends, at night

Occupational History:
Main function is that of a political leader in his community, a figure somewhat like a mafia godfather, respected and beloved. But this work includes the ever-present danger of assassination by neighboring political enemies. The patient admits to insomnia and morning wakefulness when situations are particularly difficult.

Family History:
Father: age seventy-eight, well
Mother: age seventy-six, arthritis
Four siblings died in infancy
Two siblings (brothers) living, ages twenty-eight and thirty-seven
Six children; only female child (age six) suffers from speech impediment
Wife: age thirty-two, appears to suffer also from nervous tension but in generally good health

Review of Systems:
General: weight loss of ten kilos in past two years, not undesired; concerned he has heart disease
ENT: negative
Respiratory: normal
Cardiovascular: see present illness
Gastrointestinal: normal
Genitourinary: treated successfully for gonococcal nephritis many years ago
Musculoskeletal: normal
Neurologic: see present illness
Psychiatric: see present illness and occupational history. No history of hallucinations or persistent delusions. A certain degree of concern about his safety is probably based on fact, not delusion.

Objective: Physical Examination:
Temperature: 98.6   Pulse: 80   Resp.: 12   Blood P.: 125/75
General: A normally developed thirty-four-year-old man appearing somewhat older than chronological age.
Skin: clear
EMT: pupils: equal, round, reactive to light and to accommodation
    fundi: normal
    tympanic membranes and hearing: normal
    nasal mucosa: normal
    oral mucosa: normal
    teeth in excellent condition, without dental repairs
Neck: myroid gland: normal
    no lymphadevopathy
    carotid and venous pulses: normal
Thorax: normal configuration. Some tenderness of second to fourth costochondral functions, bilaterally.
Lungs: clear
Heart: P in I at fifth intercostal space at mid-claircular line. No murmur; heart sounds normal. S3 and S4 absent. No precordial thrills.
Abdomen: Soft, flat, nontender; liver normal size; edge felt one fingerbreadth below right costal margin.
    Spleen not palpable
    No abnormal abdominal masses
    Bowel sounds normal
    Rectal examination not performed

External genitalia: normal
Peripheral pulses: normal
Neurologic: oriented well
  cranial nerves: II-XII, normal
  motor: normal
  sensory: normal
  deep tendon reflexes: very brisk, 4 + bilaterally, no clonus
No pathologic reflexes present
Cerebellar function tests: Finger-to-finger testing reveals mild intention, tremor bilaterally. No tremor at rest; heel to shin performed normally. Romberg normal. Gait and stance normal. (I still consider my
subjective evaluation valid because of my familiarity with subject.)

Assessment:

1. *Chest pain and shortness of breath:*
   The physical examination did not reveal any evidence of organic
heart disease. His history was also not consistent with organic heart disorder. The costochondral tenderness may be responsible for part of the
symptomatology related to his chest, but it is much more likely that his
chest pain and shortness of breath are symptoms of emotional stress, i.e.,
psychogenic or psychosomatic.
   It is doubtful that laboratory data such as x-rays, EKG, or other special laboratory data would reveal evidence of organic cardiovascular
disease.
   Indeed, his symptoms occur with great frequency in the general population, oftentimes under the term *neurocirculatory asthenia.*
   It is important that the patient recognizes the emotional origin of his
symptoms and realizes that proper therapy includes lessening of tension.
This awareness is of significance, since it is not likely that he will suffer
severe disability as a result of his symptoms, as long as he truly under-
stands the emotional origin of his symptoms.
   It is also noteworthy that a relatively unsophisticated or relatively
uneducated person should have this insight, which is often absent in people of higher educational levels. It is likely that this reflects capability of
rather high intellectual capacity.
   It should also be noted that after examination and after the reassurance
was given that heart disease was not present, the patient's outlook, general behavior, and demeanor changed considerably. He became active
and cheerful, and that afternoon he went about his business efficiently
and with enthusiasm. He was noted to be clever, witty, and voluble. This

attitude and behavior was in marked contrast to that which was pre-
dominant earlier. He himself said that simply knowing that he was not ill
made him feel like a different person.

It is encouraging to observe that his somaticization was not clung to
rigidly.

2. *Intermittent Weakness and Blurry Vision:*
The first occurrence of visual difficulty in 1969 followed an
injury to the occiput. Injuries to this area may be accompanied by usual
symptoms because of the presence of important optical nerve pathways
in the immediate underlying cerebrum. It is possible that there was, at
least in that first injury, a modicum of organic brain injury, and that this
served as the basis for his visual symptomatology.

It is overwhelmingly probable, however, that the disabling visual
symptoms are also psychosomatic in origin, as are the episodes of weakness and temporary paralysis.

For the sake of completeness, mention should be made of the unlikely
possibility of underlying early multiple sclerosis (MS). In MS there may
be intermittent sensory and motor defects as well as transitory visual
problems associated with hyperactive deep-tendon reflexes and intention
tremor. These were all present during this examination, but are not likely
to be indicative of MS in this case.

Progression of increasingly frequent and increasingly severe neurologic symptoms and signs with the passage of time is about the only true
diagnostic parameter of MS. We did not feel it proper to attempt tests
that might point to this diagnosis and that are also dangerous.

End of report.

Notes

INTRODUCTION

1. This and most other proper names referring to people and organizations are pseudonyms.
2. *Lonchería* is borrowed from the American "lunch." It probably came into use after the bracero movement of the 1940s, when workers were served sack lunches (*lonches*)—thus, *lonchería*.

1: THE USE OF MYTH IN MARGINALITY

1. For empirical and theoretical discussions in opposition to the notion of marginality, see Peattie (1974); Perlman (1975, 1976); Roberts (1978); and Levine (1979:176).
2. For works in opposition to the characterization of populations as behaviorally marginal, see Roberts (1973, 1978); Perlman (1975); Lomnitz (1977); and Vélez-Ibañez (1978a). Portes (1976) emphasizes that such populations are not apolitical in any intrinsic sense.
3. "Fictive friendship" is an interpersonal relationship in which the idiom describing the relationship is "friendship" but the relationship is specific only to contexts such as clubs, institutions, and periodic events. These relationships lack density, continuous reciprocity, and real affect. Such relationships are more likely to exist among urban peoples for whom mobility and flexibility are required as a consequence of complex wage structures (Vélez-Ibañez forthcoming).

2: MARGINALITY IN QUANTITATIVE TERMS

1. According to Tamayo (1971) of 1,026 sampled responses of general satisfaction with economic and social conditions, 51 percent of the male heads of households expressed satisfaction with their present level, whereas 33 percent expressed dissatisfaction; 15 percent of the females indicated satisfaction with their present level, whereas 13 percent expressed dissatisfaction; 72 percent did not respond. My own sample indicates a much higher degree of dissatisfaction among adult females than among males in a given household. Seventy percent of the females expressed dissatisfaction; 40 percent of males expressed satisfaction.

2. *Palanca*, or "leverage," is especially useful in tight labor markets where kinship, friendship, or reciprocal favors are actively used. Qualifications are usually set aside, especially in elite sectors.

3. The Social Security Health System is not a social security program but rather a national health service provided by federal medical clinics at low fees to eligible workers.

4. The national average was computed by averaging the literacy rates of twenty-nine national states, two territories, and the federal district. The range varies from a high of 90.9 percent for the federal district to a low of 55.4 percent for the state of Guerrero, with a median of 76.7 percent (*IX censo general de población:* 1970: vol. 1, pp. 3, 27, 47, 87, 105, 157, 175, 365, 499, 605, 725; vol. 2, pp. 3, 67, 305, 383, 535, 547, 585, 697; vol. 3, pp. 3, 85, 115, 131, 223, 315, 437, 467, 597, 617, 763, 811).

5. These percentages are based on the deduction of 82,227 persons who had not had any formal instruction from the 298,062 figure, for 30 percent; the 25 percent figure was arrived at by subtracting 62,114 persons who had completed grades one or two from the 298,062 figure.

6. This figure was computed by considering persons of both sexes, ages eleven through nineteen ("Censos de población" 1970:67, Q-3):

				Ages				
11	12	13	14	15	16	17	18	19
14,963	15,864	13,967	13,116	11,537	10,776	11,377	11,423	9,725

3: THE ETHNOGRAPHIC CONTEXT

1. Porras and Segal (1976:11) report that the infant mortality rate is 125 per 1,000, two times the national level, malnutrition among children is endemic, and respiratory diseases seriously spread throughout the city.

2. Between 1971 and 1974, twenty-one new *colonias* were added by subdividing those already in existence. Thus, in 1971, fifty-seven *colonias* were listed by the *municipio;* by 1974, they numbered seventy-eight.

3. The term *pepsi-coatlization,* according to Mexican literary figures, describes the introduction of North American values of conspicuous consumption and such object-artifacts as refrigerators, television sets, radios, and nonutilitarian objects into the Mexican cultural stream. Eric Wolf (1959:254) points to this process as culminating in what he calls *"pocho"* culture, derived from Julio de la Fuente's *Cambios Sociocultu-rales en Mexico* (1948). Wolf states that *pocho* culture is a hybrid consisting of the premises of unlimited vertical mobility reached by and measured by increased income, and the goods such income can purchase; further, those in control, control only temporarily, and the physical trappings of such elites and the tastes of those in control are distributed among the general population through an efficient, automatic distribution system. Eternally unlimited production of goods and new, Madison Avenue-like, ever-changing consumption are values in their own right, with moral dimensions dividing those who adhere from those who do not. Both *pocho* and *pepsi-coatlization* refer to the cultural diffusion of meanings, symbols, and object dimensions of the North American brand of open society—in short, conspicuous consumption. The irony, of course, is that in the United States a dialectical reaction against such a cultural process has ensued at different periods in American history, but never quite as reactive as during the sixties through the seventies. Carlos Fuentes, in his work *Todos Los Gatos Son Pardos* (1970), coined *pepsi-coatlization* and Wolf described *pocho* culture. Neither, however, deals with the process of synthesis with traditional cultural patterns.

4. *Tolvaneras* are sandstorms that sweep across the lake bed and onto Netzahualcoyotl, blowing contaminated fecal dust particles and inorganic matter into homes and streets. Between January and May, such *tolvaneras* cover the inhabitants with a fine, tan dust.

5. For the sake of simplicity, maps 1, 3, and 4 are divided into eastern, central, and western sections, and each map has a letter key with which east-west and north-south streets can be located. Maps 1, 3, and 4 are all

from before 1971. Map 2 (1974) is difficult to use because of the way *colonias* have been demarcated; it was thought that some accuracy should be sacrificed for the sake of clarity. When numbers are used to refer to maps, these will be found on map 2 and refer to *colonias*; when letters are used to refer to maps, these will be found on maps 1, 3, and 4 and refer to streets.

6. The Cali-Max is a modern supermarket located on the corner of boulevards Puerto Central Aéreo and Ignacio Zaragoza, approximately five kilometers from Netzahualcoyotl. Access to the Cali-Max from Netzahualcoyotl can be accomplished in one of two ways: by bus, directly from Netzahualcoyotl, or by a combination of bus and subway. For the most part, women who shop in the Cali-Max use the direct-bus method rather than the combination. The subway, although probably one of the most modern and efficient in the world, is nevertheless packed in the early hours with city-bound workers and is inconvenient for persons with packages. Generally, shopping for staple items in the federal district is much more convenient for persons living in the eastern part of Netzahualcoyotl than those living in any other section of the city.

7. The study in question is entitled "Resumen de la investigación efectuada en la Colonia del Sol," and was done between March 2 and March 13, 1970, by the Department of Psychology of the Universidad Nacional Autónoma de Mexico (National Autonomous University of Mexico), under the aegis of the Instituto de Acción Urbana e Integración Social (AURIS, for short). For the most part, this study was based on questionnaires provided to informants without previous informal contact or participant observation. In addition, some data taken during the course of this study by an anthropologist was accomplished by the "rocking-chair method," in a government office.

8. This population figure for the western section is probably considerably undercounted; nevertheless, it is the best estimate for 1968. Given population influx to the northeastern parts of the eastern section in 1972 and 1973, the 196,612 figure may very well be doubled by 1975. The southernmost sections, from Avenida Perules (C, map 3) to Avenida Texcoco, would largely have remained stable because of the mostly finished urbanization process in this area. Figures used here were taken from the *Estudio de Factibilidad Técnica, Financiera, Economía, y Social Para la Instalación de las Obras de Alcantarillado en el Municipio de Netzahualcoyotl* (1969:88).

9. *Rites de passage* for fifteen-year-old girls.

10. A *jucio de amparo* is a writ calling for a stay of government action.

Padgett writes of the *amparo*: "*Amparo* has some elements of the writ of injunction and some of habeas corpus as known in Anglo-American law. Cases in *amparo* rise from acts of government agencies at any level which are claimed to infringe constitutionally guaranteed rights. *Amparo* can also arise from the claim that a national law has invaded the sovereignty of a state, or that state laws have invaded national jurisdiction. Perhaps most important with regard to *amparo* are the personal procedural rights which it is designed to protect, although these do not reach to political matters as the courts define political matters. To a certain extent precedent operates in the case of *amparo*, since five similar decisions on a point of law by the Supreme Court create a fixed application in *amparo* proceedings" (1966:148, n. 12). I would disagree with Padgett that the *amparo* does not arise from or touch upon political matters. If anything, the *amparo* is a powerful political resource and tool utilized widely in Mexico.

11. I have said elsewhere (Vélez-Ibañez 1978b) that brokering is a worldwide phenomenon found among nations, groups, and individuals whenever there are "gaps" in communication for economic, political, social, or cultural reasons. Brokering emerges from a variety of contexts, among which the most important are political. "In the United States political machines directed by political bosses is one traditional form of brokerage. Machines generally 'get in the middle' between local-level clients and city, county, and national administrations which serve as patrons. Generally such machines ensure that particular decisions regarding personnel, contracts, and administration of laws are favorable to a host of clients in return for support at the polls (see Wolfinger 1974). In India, Bailey (1969) has long analyzed the manner in which 'face-to-face' communities intersect with national political structures through middlemen and has elaborated their various functions, as did Fallers (1965) in Africa when he noted the middleman position of the then 'modern African chiefs.'

"As a general notion then, and as a worldwide phenomenon, such middlemen or brokers appear anywhere communication channels between groups and cultures need bridges. As Boissevain (1974:149) has indicated, brokers or middlemen get people in touch with each other while occupying a host of statuses: '... from connecting relatives who direct the communication between kinsmen and whose profit motive is more latent than manifest, through political middle-men whose medium of exchange is services, information and votes, to such specialists as marriage and real estate brokers whose relations approach the commercial as their tariff is largely paid in cash.' Whether for maximizing profit directly or for some future reciprocal 'favor' middlemen play crucial roles in the daily lives of people in varying localities around the world. From *Mafiosi* (Blok 1974) to national patrons (Gonzalez 1972), persons and nations play middlemen roles even though their ascribed or achieved status are decidedly different from those acted out during 'brokering' activities" (p. 368).

12. The *azules* of 1971 retained their everyday brown shirt and trousers, were given a gun and a billy club, and then were turned loose on the populace. By 1974, however, *azules* were obliged to undertake a training program within the Municipal Palace for a period of a few weeks, and then were turned loose, now with dark-blue uniforms and plastic helmets.

13. The first elementary school in the section, Lic. Isodro Fabela, opened on February 16, 1966. For the principal and teachers, it was evidently a traumatic event. According to Javier García Martínez, the school's first principal: "The school is a constructed building without name, whose school rooms measure six by four cubic meters, with one small office and two small rooms for bathrooms; all this without anything else but four walls and a desolate panorama. And on this day of our arrival, there was a veritable sandstorm, indescribable to such a degree that some of our colleagues wanted immediately to abandon this place named Ciudad Netzahualcoyotl" (Monroy 1969:31; translation mine).

14. On March 24, 1975, the supplemental deputy, Angel García Bravo, was accused of destruction of private property, assault, illegal arrest, and assault with intent to do bodily harm, in a charge signed by 500 inhabitants of the Colonia del Sol. In addition, the mayor of the city, Oscar Loya Ramírez, was accused of ordering the arrest of those who protested Bravo's alleged illegal activities in the colonia (*Excelsior* 1975: 1).

15. "CRC" are the initials of the Congreso Restaurador de Colonos, whose evolution will be described in chapter 4. For the purposes of clarification at this point, however, in 1974 the CRC was part of the support resources for the third councilman, Mondragón, and consisted mostly of persons who held lots and homes illegally.

16. The tamale sellers have a particularly strange and marvelous set of attention-grabbing devices. Since their tamales are carried in steam containers on hand-pushed, two-wheeled carts, the operators are able to let off steam via a regulator that makes a loud, screeching noise, much like

the high-pitched steam whistles at noon in a factory. They combine this whistle with their "call," which sounds more like a loud, deep-throated moan. The word *tamale* is barely decipherable. When I first heard this, I thought that someone had been attacked by a screeching band of dogs, and the moans were the victim's response.

17. Every year at midnight on September 15 the president of the republic repeats, from the main balcony, the supposed words of Miguel Hidalgo proclaiming Mexico's independence from Spain. This is referred to as the Grito de Dolores, supposedly first uttered in Dolores, Guanajuato.

18. The traditional view of *caciquismo* holds that it is an informal method of political control by a small association of individuals under one leader (Friedrich 1965:190). Reliance on violence and verbal persuasion, and use of collateral relatives, are principal methods of political control. *Caciquismo* is also considered a transitional urban phenomenon restricted to evolving, low-income settlements (Cornelius 1973:150). I find that this type of leadership is not endogenous to low-income areas, nor is it transitory (see Vélez-Ibáñez 1978b). In Netzahualcoyotl the role of the *cacique* is primarily one of broker and leader of land-squatting movements rather than revolutionary leader.

19. The *toreo*, or bullfight arena, was built in 1967. Bullfights featuring *novilleros* or unknown *matadores* are held there.

4: THE CRC AND ITS EMERGENCE

1. Talacingo is a town of 3,500 persons, 64 percent of whom are agricultural workers. Surrounding *congregaciones* ("nucleated settlements"), which are considered part of Jalacingo but have their own names, range in population from 100 to 3,500 persons. Persons in these settlements are primarily engaged in subsistence agriculture (the percentage ranges from 79.6 to 99.6).

2. The Popular Socialist party was founded by Lombardo Toledano after his expulsion from the Partido Revolucionario Institucional (PRI) in the late 1940s; however, by 1958 it was highly factionalized (Padgett 1966:75).

3. See Appendix A for the text of the letter in Spanish and in English.

4. The author possesses the numbers of the warrants.

5. A self-regulating body of five persons who ensured that conflicts between members were settled within the organization itself.

6. The CNOP is one of three sections of the PRI, with labor and the

agrarian sector represented by the *Confederación de Trabajadores Mexicanos* (CTM) and the *Confederación Nacional Campesina* (CNC), respectively. The CNOP, according to its constitution (*Bases Consitutivas,* art. 2, in Padgett 1966:124) is composed of "(a) small agriculturalists; (b) small industrialists; (c) small merchants; (d) artisans; (e) members of cooperative enterprises; (f) professional men and intellectuals; (g) youth groups; (h) women's clubs; (i) diverse groupings." According to Padgett (1966:125), the CNOP is composed of heterogeneous groupings representing the Mexican middle class and the popular sector. Control is in the hands of professional persons who function to present petitions to governing circles on behalf of its dues-paying members. As Padgett (p. 127) suggests, the CNOP is largely a broker's organization, mediating between its membership and the federal government. Support is gauged by the number of persons the government requests for public demonstrations. The payoff, which Padgett does not deal with, is coercive and, as will be seen, similar to that expected of the CRC in its dealings with the governor of the state.

7. At the rate of exchange of 12.50 pesos per dollar, the actual amount was $56,640.

8. There are no accurate records that can be utilized for empirical evidence, but my best estimate is based on data collected by the agency Fidecomiso in 1974 regarding registration of land titles. Between December 1973 and February 1974, weekly registrations numbered into the hundreds. In the two-month period (December 10, 1973, to February 10, 1974), 1,675 of the 2,322 registered titles either had from two to four owners or had not been registered by the land developers. Taking January 30, 1974, as typical, 78 land titles were registered, and of these, 10 had two owners, one had three, and one had four.

9. The expression *"vamos a trabajar"* ("we are going to work"), in reference to a particular *colonia*, meant that that *colonia* would be saturated with leaflets and presented with speakers.

10. According to the secret police-reports, the pilot was unaware of the "roots of this movement, felt totally disciplined, and vowed allegiance to the federal government, state government, and to the party (PRI)." Neither the source for the reports nor the reports themselves can be revealed. The text of this fragment in Spanish follows: "Capitán Piloto _____ quien manifestó que él había actuado en esa forma porque no conocía la raíz de este Movimiento, pero que se encuentra totalmente disciplinado, tanto al Gobierno del Estado Federal como al del Estado de México, como al Partido (PRI)."

11. Emiliano Zapata was a mestizo born in Anencuilco, Morelos, on August 8, 1879. He led the Army of the South against the Porfirio Diaz regime (1879-1910) and later against Victoriano Huerta. Zapata, like most intransigent revolutionaries in Mexico, was later shot, on April 10, 1919, as the result of a betrayal (Millon 1970:12, 36).

12. *Corridos* are epic songs that probably originated in south Texas.

13. The text of the song in Spanish follows.

> "El Corrido del Estudiante por Jesús Gómez" (pseudonimo)
> Voy a cantar el corrido del año '68.
> Mataron 1,000 estudiantes en Ciudad de Tlatelolco.
> Ya el estudiante se oculta en su montaña secreta
> Ya el campesino se acerca para tomarle la oferta
> Porque los pueblos cansan de que les pisen sus leyes.
> Vamos a darles batalla a estos malditos burgueses.
> Vámonos para Chihuahua. Vámonos para Guerrero
> Vamos a darle en la chapa a este bandido gobierno
> Ya la fogata se enciende, como pidiendo batalla
> ¡Qué viva Genaro Vásquez! ¡Qué viva Lucio Cabañas!
> Que han ofrendado el valor a mi patria mexicana.

14. The total number of *registered* supporters was 39,424. This is a remarkably large number of dues-paying persons (see also Appendix D).

5: ENTANGLEMENT, FISSION, AND REORGANIZATION OF THE CRC

1. See note 8 in chapter 4 for a description of La Confederación Nacional de Organizaciones (CNOP). What the particular transaction between Maldonado and the governor was, and what the specifics of the *arreglos* between Maldonado and the mayor were, are not known. But Maldonado did become one of the "elected" PRI councilmen for the city in 1973, and in fact he did keep the CRC label for his own political organization after the fission of 1971. Including the minor schism of 1970, which has not been detailed, after a second major fission in 1973, there were four CRCs in existence.

2. Although this is a pseudonym, it reflects that she did not use her married surname while holding the office of president of the Accion Femenil ("Feminine Action").

3. This estimate was based on interviews with forty-seven of the subcommittee presidents. I have concluded that the fraction leaving was probably substantially higher, for two reasons: first, my own *confianza* had not yet been established with them in 1971; and second, they under-

estimated in order not to look too bad to the *"antropófago"* ("cannibal" —a play on the word *antropólogo,* meaning "anthropologist") from the United States.

4. The Confederación Nacional Campesina ("National Agrarian Confederation"), or CNC, is one of the tripartite sectors of the PRI and includes a number of small farmer, rural labor, and peasant leagues. It functions to mobilize rural support for the PRI and represents itself as a defender of the interests of rural persons vis-à-vis the government and large private landholders (Johnson 1971:65).

5. For example, subcommittee 22 had a total of 427 persons paying contributions in June 1971; in July, 231; and in November, 374. This dramatic increase was the result not only of new members but also of old ones returning. This increase was verified by fourteen subcommittee presidents in 1972.

6. The real name of Mr. X, the periodical for which he works, and the party in which he is active will not be revealed, nor will pseudonyms be used, for the sake of protecting this person and others who contribute to, participate in, and support the goals of this party. Although it is likely that this political party will become a legal entity by the time this book is published, in 1974 it was not. I do not wish to endanger the line between Mr. X and the Agrarian Department director, who has many such *arreglos* from Left to Right on the political spectrum.

7. The amount of 30 million pesos was reported in *El Imparcial* (July 17, 1971). The 600-million-peso figure was provided by an employee of the Inter-American Fund in 1972. The secretary of governance for the state of Mexico made several trips to Washington, D.C., and New York City to secure the loan. The total amount expended on the urban infrastructure up to 1976 was approximately 100 million dollars (Porras and Segal 1976:10).

8. The central square adjoining the presidential palace in Mexico City.

9. *El Día* gave almost daily coverage to the CRC and its activities during 1972-1973, primarily because of relations Valenzuela had established when he worked there as a security guard. *Excelsior* and the locals also participated in the coverage. A national periodical, *Punto Crítico,* had a four-page article on the CRC during this period.

6: ONE DAY IN THE LIFE OF THE VALENZUELA FAMILY

1. Thirty-three of these thirty-four persons Julieta recognizes as consanguine full or half-siblings. Her father, an Oaxacan politician, is said to

have sired eighty or so children. He was married three times and maintained three *casas chicas* (polygamous arrangements) until his death in 1974.

2. The road and the sidewalk are really one and the same. Electric light poles along the streets define the area on which cars may travel. Pedestrians use the protection of the space between the light poles and the front of the lots of homes as sidewalks.

3. A *charro* costume is usually worn on festive days and consists of elaborate decorated or plain wool trousers flared at the cuffs, a cotton shirt, usually embroidered in greens and reds, a vest and matching bolero jacket, and a silk scarf, all topped with a broad-rimmed sombrero as plain or as elaborate as the rest of the costume.

4. Fifty-nine percent of households do have inside plumbing; 22.1 percent have outside water sources on their lots; the rest have neither. Inside plumbing, however, does not guarantee access to water, because of breakdowns, repairs, and a low water-table.

5. Usually, Carnation condensed milk from a buffet-sized can is used.

6. Mexico has federal, state, and municipal schools; thus, a city like Netzahualcoyotl may have all three types within the same municipality.

7. Among the names mentioned previously in chapter 3, the Municipal Palace is known also as the *"zoologíco"* for two reasons: first, honest persons are locked in jail and treated as animals; second, politicians in the palace are thought of as "animals"—*lobos* and *coyotes*—in their "zoo."

8. The text of Julieta's statement in Spanish: "Desde la mañana uno está en apuros. No se sabe si se puede acabar una cosa cuando surge otra. Cada uno pide atención, cada uno pide algo y no hay acabo. Como madre sé que la responsabilidad es mía pero lo que me ocupa más es tener que constantemente estar en guardia de lo que no se espera."

9. Ecatepec is not where this person really lives.

10. The text of Arturo's statement in Spanish: "Si no fuera por mi mujer y madre en ese tiempo fuera sido solo en la lucha. Después, de que sí, después de que les dimos la revolcada, después de que ya los funcionarios nos escuchaban, después de que me hice amigos de los coyotes, después de que me conocieran en 'Los Pinos,' después que les convenía, entonces sí y no pagaron. Eso no se me olvida."

11. Over a period of three years, this average shifted with Arturo's political fortunes. At one time, when he had been forced into hiding, his contacts were extremely limited.

12. *Cuidadosa* means "guarded," but in this context Julieta means that her mother-in-law is too exact and meticulous.

7: BROADER NETWORKS OF SUPPORT AND SOCIAL IDENTITY

1. A rotating credit association is a lending, borrowing, and savings practice in which individuals have access to relatively large amounts of money or valued resources and participate in the "rotation" of these resources. Thus, "a leader organizes among friends, neighbors, relatives, and/or fellow workers an association in which four other persons agree to contribute a set amount of ten dollars a week. The rotation of resources is decided by lot or by the order in which persons agreed to join. Each person receives forty dollars once from the association. Each person will have contributed a total of forty dollars to the others at ten dollars per week. The total 'life' of the association is five weeks" (Vélez-Ibañez forthcoming). Roberto generally provides Arturo with the first number, thus allowing him to receive forty dollars from the other members on the very first turn (see also Vélez-Ibañez 1982).

2. This is a double entendre since *huevos* colloquially means "gonads"; therefore, mixing or becoming enmeshed with supralocal officials eventually results in the dilution of power, symbolically represented by gonads.

3. "Bigotes" means literally "mustache," but Anastasio did not have one. When I inquired about why he was so nicknamed, the response included a very wry smile and an allusion to the *chuparosa* ("hummingbird"). The word is derived from *chupar* ("suckle") and *rosa* ("rose"). In this case, *bigotes* refers to Anastasio's reputation as a ladies' man and his expertise in certain amorous techniques.

4. Ecatepec, though nearby, is not the actual community referred to here.

5. This expression is a several-layered proposition. First, green wood burns very slowly and creates a lot of smoke. Hence, persons undergoing the torture of being burnt in green wood would burn slowly and painfully. Second, even the most observing of males commit faux pas in regards to marriage fidelity. Third, it is unfortunate that women have to live with men but even a greater misfortune that women cannot live without them. There is a tongue-in-cheek element to this expression and to the meanings involved.

8: THE MYTH OF POLITICAL INTEGRATION

1. I have practically no information on Serrano since it was only shortly before I left the field that I became aware of his important role within the CRC. In 1975 he was still the head of a splinter organization

called Federación de Obreros y Campesinos de Mexico ("Federation of Workers and Peasants of Mexico").

2. See note 8, chapter 4.

3. A federally sponsored corporation designed to negotiate, consider, and resolve contending interests of political importance. Usually such corporations include a financial, judicial, and public-works section.

4. Felipe Carranza was President Echeverria's personal counselor and chief of the judicial branch of the Agrarian Department. He was also a former justice of the Supreme Court (see chapter 4).

5. Mr. X, described in chapter 4, was responsible for introducing Valenzuela to the director of the Agrarian Department.

6. The candidate had been, in June 1970, one of the original commissioned state judicial agents, sent by the state of Mexico, to investigate the CRC. His name appears on two different secret police-reports as one of two agents commissioned to undertake the investigation of the CRC.

7. The new organizational name, the Coalition for Renewal of Netzahualcoyotl, is fictitious, but it is similar to the actual name. In 1974 Valenzuela changed the organization's name once again when he became a broker for others outside of Netzahualcoyotl and Chimalhuacán. The new organization was called the Coalición de Obreros y Colonos del Valle de México ("Coalition of Workers and Settlers of the Valley of Mexico").

8. See Vélez-Ibañez (1978b) for a full description of this case.

9. I arranged a medical examination by two close friends who are M.D.s. See Appendix E for a detailed report of the medical examination.

9: LOCAL-LEVEL RITUALS AND RITUALS OF MARGINALITY

1. The INJUVEN (Instituto Nacional Juvenil, or "National Juvenile Institute") is the youth section of the PRI. The CTM (Confederación de Trabajadores Mexicanos, or "Confederation of Mexican Workers") represents the industrial "formal" labor sector and is part of the national government party—the PRI.

2. Following is the Spanish version of Padre José's opening statement: "Mis amigos, compañeros, y familia de Emilio—todos estamos aquí en la casa de Emilio para prestar homenaje a Emilio García—padre de hijos, querido esposo, amigo y compañero de muchos de ustedes aquí. Este homenaje no lo hacemos con tristeza porque eso, estamos seguros, no le gustaría a Emilio; pero más importante porque sabemos que El Señor en Su gran juicio, le ha conseguido su puesto a Emilio cerca de Su mano.

Estamos unidos todos aquí para celebrar—todos sus amigos, todas sus amistades—todos esos que vivieron juntos con Emilio, todos esos que comieron y tomaron de la vida con Emilio—todos esos que sufrieron y lucharon con Emilio—todos—celebrando este día con él y para él. ¡Claro que le hace mucha falta a sus hijos y a su mujer! y sin embargo la vida aquí es suficiente dura sin mas tragedia. Pero, mis queridos hermanos, todos aquí tienen la oportunidad de ayudar, de aconsejar a los hijos y proteger a la viuda. Claro que los parientes, los hermanos, hermanas, compadres lo harán, pero además todos los compañeros y compañeras que lucharon con él tienen la responsabilidad de ayudar, de aconsejar—igual que los demás. Sabemos que aquí el que no se ayuda el uno al otro, no puede sobrevivir estas condiciones. Todos hemos luchado—todos—Emilio también luchó como padre, como marido, para darle de comer a su familia—pero también luchó por muchos de nosotros—Entonces vamos a celebrar esta misa en su honor, pero antes, por favor, es necesario que yo no más hable—que ustedes, miembros de su familia, sus compadres, sus amigos, sus compañeros, digan cómo se sienten de su amigo Emilio."

3. Following is the Spanish version of Padre José's statement: "Estamos seguros después de esta Santa Misa que todos estamos de acuerdo en que cada uno de nosotros tenemos que contribuir moralmente, o económicamente al beneficio de la familia de Emilio. Todos saben que la vida aquí es muy difícil, que la mayoría de nosotros estamos en dificultades de vivienda. Pero, mis hermanos, tenemos la responsabilidad—y esto no lo puedo repetir demasiado—de ayudar a esta mujer y a los siete hijos de Emilio. Tenemos que sacrificar un poquito para asegurar que la familia de Emilio esté bien—no la abandonen y no abandonen a sus hijos. Estoy seguro que Dios en un modo o otro los va a asistir."

4. One of the more gruesome ramifications of this is that people may bury their dead in the immediate environs of Netzahualcoyotl, such as under their homes or close to the water- and sewage lines. Dreams of children, according to one local psychiatrist, are filled with cannibalistic symbols and nightmares.

5. The allusion to WS (Graciela) whoring with Mondragón reflects that she had, until recently, been part of Mondragón's sphere of influence. She had switched her allegiance to Valenzuela after a dispute with a fellow Mondragonista, in which she lost a house lot. Resentment over her taking communion, her complaint of having to wait, and her presence in the yard combined to create the causes for this dispute.

6. Following is the Spanish version of the gold-lettered epitaph on

Emilio's cross: Emilio García López, padre y querido esposo. Luchó contra los poderosos y ganó para siempre el respeto de sus compañeros. Valiente, honesto, y al frente de nuestro movimiento, Emilio siempre será acordado un puesto de honor en nuestra lucha.
De parte de todos sus compañeros de
la Coalición de Obreros y Colonos
del Valle de México.

7. Following is the Spanish version of Padre José's concluding statement at the February 17 ritual: "Se acabó la misa pero la lucha de Emilio, y de hombres y mujeres como él no se ha acabado. Es necesario que todos nosotros aquí estemos unidos únicamente para ganar el patrimonio para nuestros hijos, para el beneficio de nuestras familias. Tenemos que acabar con la explotación de la gente de Netzahualcoyotl, y el único modo de pelear los fraccionadores es pelear juntos, como una comunidad debe. Todos sabemos que la lucha no se puede hacer solo. Uno solo no puede ganar—a uno solo se lo comen en un modo o el otro—se lo comen comprándolo deshonestamente o con fuerza y amenazas. Uno solo no tiene poder. Uno solo no es nada. Pero unidos, juntos ayudándonos unos a los otros—se puede ganar la lucha."

8. Following is the Spanish version of Valenzuela's statement at the February 17 ritual: "Mis compañeros—todos nosotros—todos—no hay ninguna persona aquí que no haya luchado en una forma u otra contra las fuerzas del estado, contra las fuerzas de los fraccionadores. Todos nos acordamos cuando andabamos juntos y las palizas que nos daban las autoridades del municipio. Pero todos aquí, todos aquí luchamos a veces con fuerza brusca, con piel contra arma, con piedras contra rifles, hondas contra carabinas. Esa valentía, esa fuerza, se estableció por el trabajo de hombres y mujeres como el valiente Emilio. Todos tenemos el deber de no rechazar los sacrificios, tan inmensos y tan dolorosos que Emilio pasó con nosotros. Todavía sigue la lucha contra los fraccionadores y con partes del gobierno—no con él...[excitado] sí, lo voy a decir, ¿para qué andar de chismoso?...con él, con el gobernador del estado—para qué andamos con cosas?—Ese señor y los coyotes de los fraccionadores tienen la culpa de todo esto [implica la muerte de Emilio]. Pero, mis compañeros, esa culpa, justamente no se puede pagar sin que nosotros nos apoyemos unos a los otros y, con esta fuerza, la constitución se cumple. Todos nosotros los mexicanos del país tenemos el deber de vivir tranquilamente, educando a nuestros hijos, viviendo en casas limpias, con comida que nos alimente, con protección judicial, sin temor, con trabajo que nos pague lo que nos merecemos—pero ¿qué ha pasado? Los coyo-

tes, los políticos, grandes y chicos, nos traen como esclavos, como si nosotros fueramos sus peones. No señor, no es justo—nunca será justo. Y por esa justicia Emilio siempre peleó y por eso murió. Tenemos que seguir luchando todos juntos, tanto los hombres como las mujeres—tenemos que hacerlo—no hay remedio.

"Y ahora, de parte de la Coalición de Obreros y Colonos del Valle de México, les damos las gracias por haber venido para dedicarle este día a nuestro compañero-Emilio. Gracias."

9. *Norteño* means "from the north." Here it is used to indicate folklore music and dance from the northern region of Mexico.

Bibliography

Abu-Lughod, Janet, and Richard Hay Jr., eds. *Third World Urbaniza-tion*. Chicago: Maaroufa Press, 1977.

Acedo Mendoza, Carlos. *America Latina, marginalidad y subdesarrollo*. Caracas, Venezuela: Fondo Editorial Comun, 1973.

Adams, Richard N. *Crucifixion by Power: (1963-1967). Essays on Guate-malan National Social Structure*. Austin: University of Texas Press, 1970.

————. *Energy and Structure*. Austin: University of Texas Press, 1975.

————. "The Structure of Participation: A Commentary." In *Politics and the Poor. Political Participation in Latin America*, vol. 2, edited by M. A. Seligson and J. A. Booth. New York: Holmes and Meir, 1979.

Alonso, José Antonio. *Sexo, trabajo y marginalidad urbana*. Mexico D.F.: Editorial EDICOL, 1981.

Anderson, Bo, and James D. Cockroft. "Control and Cooptation in Mex-ican Politics." *International Journal of Comparative Sociology* 7 (1966): 16-22.

Annuario estadistíco comediado de los EUM, 1968. Tasa demográficas del país por entidades federativas, 1965-1968. Mexico D.F.: Departa-mento de Estadisticas, 1968.

Bailey, F. G. *Strategems and Spoils: A Social Anthropology of Politics*. New York: Schocken, 1969.

Bando de policía y buen gobierno: Ciudad Netzahualcoyotl. Mexico D.F.: Editorial 'America,' 1971.

Blok, Anton. *The Mafia of a Sicilian Village, 1860-1960*. New York: Har-per and Row, 1974.

Boissevain, Jeremy. *Friends of Friends: Networks, Manipulators, and Coalitions.* New York: St. Martin's Press, 1974.

Bonilla, Frank. "Rio's Favelas: The Rural Slum within the City." In *Reports Service, East Coast of South America Series, No. 3, Brazil.* New York: American Universities Field Staff, 1961.

Butterworth, Douglas. "A Study of the Urbanization Process among Mixtec Migrants from Tilantongo in Mexico City." In *Peasants in Cities,* edited by W. Mangin. Boston: Houghton-Mifflin, 1970.

——— . "Two Small Groups: A Comparison of Migrants and Non-Migrants in Mexico City." *Urban Anthropology* 1 (1972):29-50.

Butterworth, Douglas, and John K. Chance. *Latin American Urbanization.* New York: Cambridge University Press, 1981.

Cain, Glen G. "The Challenge of Segmented Labor Market Theories to Orthodox Theory: A Survey." *Journal of Economic Literature* 65 (1976):16-22.

Carlos, Manuel L., and Bo Anderson. "Political Brokerage and Network Politics in Mexico: The Case of a Representative Dominance System." In *Networks, Exchange, and Coercion: The Elementary Theory and Its Application,* edited by David Willer and Bo Anderson. New York: Elsevier, 1981.

"Censo de poblacion." Unpublished data gathered from quartos (*cuadros*) 1, 3, 11, 12, 14, 16, 18, 22, 28, and 33. Mexico D.F.: Departamento de Censos, 1970.

Chance, John. "Recent Trends in Latin American Urban Studies." *Latin American Research Review* 15 (1980):183-188.

Cohen, Abner. *Custom and Politics in Urban Africa.* Berkeley and Los Angeles: University of California Press, 1969.

——— . *The Politics of Elite Culture: Explorations in the Dramaturgy of Power in a Modern African Society.* Berkeley, Los Angeles, London: University of California Press, 1981.

Cohen, Robin, and David Michael. "The Revolutionary Potential of the African Lumpenproletariat: A Sceptical View." *Bulletin of the Institute of Developmental Studies* 5 (1973):31-42.

Collier, David. *Squatters and Oligarchs: Authoritarian Rule and Policy Change in Peru.* Baltimore: Johns Hopkins University Press, 1976.

Cornelius, Wayne. "A Structural Analysis of Urban Caciquismo in Mexico." *Urban Anthropology* 1 (1972):234-261.

——— . *Political Learning Among the Urban Poor: The Impact of Residential Context.* Comparative Politics Series, edited by H. Eckstein, T. R. Gurr, and A. Zolberg. Beverly Hills, Calif.: Sage Publications, 1973.

————. "Urbanization and Political Demand-Making: Political Partici-pation among the Migrant Poor in Latin American Cities." *American Political Science Review* 68 (1974):1125-1146.

————. *Politics and the Migrant Poor in Mexico City.* Stanford, Calif.: Stanford University Press, 1975.

Cornelius, W. A., and H. Dietz. "Urbanization, Demand-Making, and Political System Overload: Political Participation among the Migrant Poor in Latin America." In *Frontier of Urban Research,* edited by R. Stiefbold. Coral Gables, Fla.: University of Miami Press, 1976.

Cornelius, W. A., and F. M. Trueblood, eds. *Anthropological Perspec-tives on Latin American Urbanization.* Latin American Urban Re-search, vol. 4. Beverly Hills, Calif.: Sage Publications, 1974.

————. *Urbanization and Inequality: The Political Economy of Urban and Rural Development in Latin America.* Latin American Urban Re-search, vol. 5. Beverly Hills, Calif.: Sage Publications, 1975.

de la Fuente, Julio. *Cambios socioculturales en Mexico.* Acta Antropo-logica, vol. 3, no. 4 (1948). Mexico D.F.

de la Rosa, Martin Medellin. *Netzahualcoyotl: un fenómeno.* Mexico D.F.: Fondo de Cultura Ecónomica, 1974.

————. *Promoción popular y lucha de clases: análisis de un caso.* Cd. Netzahualcoyotl, Mexico D.F.: Servicios Educativos Populares, A.C., 1979.

Dietz, Henry A. "The Office and the *Poblador*: Perceptions and Manipu-lations of Housing Authorities by the Lima Urban Poor." In *Authori-tarianism and Corporatism in Latin America,* edited by J. M. Malloy. Pittsburgh, Pa.: University of Pittsburgh Press, 1977.

División municipal de las entidades federativas. Mexico D.F.: Secretaría de Industria y Comercio, Dirección General de Estadísticas, 1969.

Eames, Edwin, and Judith G. Goode. *Urban Poverty in a Cross-Cultural Context.* New York: Free Press, 1973.

Eames, Edwin, and Judith Goode. "The Culture of Poverty: Misapplica-tion of Anthropology to Contemporary Issues." In *Urban Life,* edited by G. Melch and W. P. Zenner. New York: St. Martin's Press, 1980.

Eckstein, Susan. *The Poverty of Revolution: The State and the Urban Poor of Mexico.* Princeton, N.J.: Princeton University Press, 1977a.

————. "The State and the Urban Poor." In *Authoritarianism in Mex-ico,* edited by J. L. Reyna and R. S. Weinert. Philadelphia: ISHI Publi-cations, 1977b.

Estudio de factibilidad técnica, financiera, economía, y social para la in-stalación de las obras de alcantarillado en el municipio de Netzahual-coyotl. Mexico D.F.: Sociedad de Recursos Hidraulicos, 1969.

Excelsior, 25 March 1975, p. 1.

Fagen, Richard R., and William S. Tuoy. *Politics and Privilege in a Mexican City*. Stanford, Calif.: Stanford University Press, 1972.

Fallers, Lloyd. *Bantu Bureaucracy: A Century of Political Evolution among the Basoga of Uganda*. Chicago: University of Chicago Press, 1965.

Fanon, Franz. *Wretched of the Earth*. London: MacGibbon and Kee, 1965.

Freedman, Marcia K. *Labor Markets: Segments and Shelters*. Montclair, N.J.: Allanheld, Osmun, 1976.

Friedrich, Paul. "A Mexican Cacicazgo." *Ethnology* 4 (1965):190-209.

———. *Agrarian Revolt in a Mexican Village*. Englewood Cliffs, N.J.: Prentice-Hall, 1970.

Fuentes, Carlos. *Todos los Gatos son pardos*. Mexico D.F.: Siglo Vientiuno Eds, 1970.

García, Martínez Javier. *Memoria de trabajo, Netzahualcoyotl*. Puebla, Estado de Mexico: Direccion de Educacion Publica, 1969.

Garza, G., and M. Schteingart. "Mexico City: The Emerging Megalopolis." In *Latin American Research*, vol. 6, edited by W. A. Cornelius and R. V. Kemper. Beverly Hills, Calif.: Sage Publications, 1978.

Geisse, Guillermo. "Income Inequality and Spatial Arrangements in the Latin American City." In *Current Perspectives in Latin American Urban Research*, edited by H. L. Browning and A. Portes. Austin: Institute of Latin American Studies and University of Texas Press, 1976.

Ginzberg, Eli. *Labor Market: Segments and Shelters*. Washington, D.C.: Government Printing Office, 1976.

Glade, W. P., and S. Ross. *Criticas constructivas del sistema politico Mexicano*. Austin: Institute of Latin American Studies and University of Texas Press, 1973.

Gluckman, Max. *Politics, Law, and Ritual*. Chicago: Aldine, 1965.

Gonzalez, Nancie L. "Patron-Client Relationships at the International Level." In *Structure and Process in Latin America*, edited by A. Strickon and S. M. Greenfield. Albuquerque: University of New Mexico Press, 1972.

Grindle, Merilee S. "Policy Change in an Authoritarian Regime: Mexico under Echeverria." *Journal of International Studies* 19 (1977):523-555.

Handelman, Howard. "The Political Mobilization of Urban Squatter Settlements." *Latin American Research Review* 10 (1975):35-72.

Hansen, Robert. *The Politics of Mexican Development*. Baltimore: Johns Hopkins University Press, 1971.

Houghton, Neal D. "What Price Development for Mass-Poverty Areas?" *Western Political Quarterly* 22 (1969):774-789.

————. "A Case for Essential Abandonment of Basic U.S. Cold War Objectives." *Western Political Quarterly* 23 (1970):384-410.

Iglesias, Maximiliano. *Netzahualcoyotl: Testimonios Historicos (1944-1957)*. Cd. Netzahualcoyotl, Mexico: Servicios Educativos Populares, A.C., 1978.

Johnson, Kenneth F. *Mexican Democracy: A Critical View*. Boston: Allyn and Bacon, 1972.

Kapferer, Bruce. "Structural Marginality and the Urban Social Order." Mimeographed. Los Angeles: University of California, Los Angeles, 1980.

Kaufman, Robert R. "The Patron-Client Concept and Macropolitics: Prospects and Problems." *Comparative Studies in Society and History* 16 (1974):284-308.

Kemper, Robert V. "Migration and Adaptation of Tzintzuntzan Peasants in Mexico City." Ph.D. dissertation, University of California, Berkeley, 1971.

Kurtz, Donald F. "The Rotating Credit Association." *Human Organization* 32 (1973):49-58.

Leach, Edmund. *Political Systems of Highland Burma*. 2d ed. Boston: Beacon Press, 1979.

Leeds, Anthony. "The Anthropology of Cities: Some Methodological Issues." In *Urban Anthropology: Research Perspectives and Strategies*, no. 2, edited by E. Eddy. Athens: University of Georgia Press, 1968.

————. "The Significant Variables Determining the Characteristics of Squatter Settlements." *America Latina* 12 (1969):44-86.

————. "The Culture of Poverty—Conceptual, Logical, and Empirical Problems with Perspectives from Brazil and Peru." In *The Culture of Poverty: A Critique*, edited by E. Leacock. New York: Simon and Schuster, 1971.

————. "Urban Anthropology and Urban Studies." *Urban Anthropology* 1 (1972):5.

————. "Locality Power in Relation to Supralocal Institutions." In *Urban Anthropology*, edited by A. Southall. New York: Oxford University Press, 1973.

Levine, Daniel H. "Urbanization in Latin America: Changing Perspectives." *Latin American Research Review* 14 (1979):171-183.

Lewis, Oscar. *Five Families: Mexican Case Studies in the Culture of Poverty*. New York: Basic Books, 1959.

————. *La Vida: A Puerto Rican Family in the Culture of Poverty.* New York: Random House, 1965.

Lomnitz, Larissa. *Networks and Marginality: Life in a Mexican Shantytown.* New York: Academic Press, 1977.

————. "Mechanisms of Articulation between Shantytown Settlers and the Urban System." *Urban Anthropology* 7 (1978):185-205.

————. "Horizontal and Vertical Relations and the Social Structure of Urban Mexico." Translated by Cinna Lomnitz. Mimeographed. Mexico D.F., Universidad Autónoma de Mexico.

Mangin, William. "Latin American Squatter Settlements: A Problem and a Solution." *Latin American Research Review* 2(1967):65-98.

————. "Poverty and Politics in Cities of Latin America." In *Power, Poverty, and Urban Policy,* edited by W. Bloomberg, Jr. and H. L. Schmandt. Beverly Hills, Calif.: Sage Publications, 1968.

McGee, T. G. *The Persistence of the Proto-Proletariat Occupational Structures and Planning for the Future of Third World Cities.* Comparative Urbanization Series, no. 4. Los Angeles: School of Architecture and Urban Planning, University of California, Los Angeles, 1974.

Meyer, Lorenzo. "Historical Roots of the Authoritarian State in Mexico." In *Authoritarianism in Mexico,* edited by J. L. Reyna and R. S. Weiniert. Philadelphia: ISHI Publications, 1977.

Mills, C. Wright. *The Power Elite.* 2d ed. New York: Oxford University Press, 1959.

Monroy, Orranta Luis. "Investigación urbanística que justifica el estudio y proyecto de un mercado municipal para Ciudad Netzahualcoyotl del municipio de mismo nombre, en el estado de Mexico." M.A. thesis. Mexico D.F., School of Engineering, Universidad Autónoma de Mexico, 1969.

Moore, Joan W. *Homeboys: Gangs, Drugs, and Prison in the Barrios of Los Angeles.* Philadelphia: Temple University Press, 1978.

Moore, Richard J. "The Urban Poor in Guayaquil, Ecuador: Modes, Correlates, and Context of Political Participation." In *Politics and the Poor. Political Participation in Latin America,* vol. 2, edited by M. A. Seligson and J. A. Booth. New York: Holmes and Meier, 1979.

Nader, Laura. "Up the Anthropologist—Perspectives Gained from Studying Up." *Reinventing Anthropology.* 2d ed., edited by D. Hymes. New York: Vintage Books, 1974.

Nicholas, Ralph. "Rules, Resources, and Political Activity." In *Local-Level Politics,* edited by Marc J. Swartz. Chicago: Aldine, 1968.

IX censo general de población: Localidades por entidad federativa y municipio, algunas de su características de su población y vivienda. Mexico D.F.: Secretaría de Industria y Comercio, 1970.

Nun, José. "Superpoblación relativa, ejército industrial de reserva y masa marginal." *Revista Latino-Americana de Sociología* 5 (1969): 178-236.

Nun, José, Juan Carlos Marín, and Miguel Murmis. *La marginalidad en América Latina.* Working Paper, no. 2. Santiago, Chile: ILPES/DESAL, 1967.

Padgett, Vincent L. *The Mexican Political System.* Boston: Houghton-Mifflin, 1966.

"Panorama económico." *Bimestral del sistema de bancos de comercio.* 21 (May-June 1971).

Paz, Octavio. *The Labyrinth of Solitude.* New York: Grove Press, 1961.

Peattie, L. R. "The Concept of 'Marginality' as Applied to Squatter Settlements." In *Anthropological Perspectives on Latin American Urbanization,* edited by W. A. Cornelius and F. B. Trueblood. Beverly Hills, Calif.: Sage Publications, 1974.

Perlman, Janice. "Rio's Favelas and the Myth of Marginality." *Politics and Society* 5 (1975):131-160.

―――. *The Myth of Marginality: Urban Poverty and Politics in Rio de Janeiro.* Berkeley, Los Angeles, London: University of California Press, 1976.

Porras, Augustin, and Aaron Segal. "The Urban Satellite: Colonizing Mexico City's Outer Space." *People* 3 (1976):9-11.

Portes, Alejandro. "The Economy and Ecology of Urban Poverty." In *Urban Latin America: The Political Condition from Above and Below,* edited by A. Portes and J. Walton. Austin: University of Texas Press, 1976a.

―――. "The Politics of Urban Poverty." In *Urban Latin America: The Political Condition from Above and Below,* edited by A. Portes and J. Walton. Austin: University of Texas Press, 1976b.

―――. "The Informal Sector and the World Economy: Notes on the Structure of Subsidized Labor." *IDS Bulletin* 9 (1978):35-39.

Portes, Alejandro, and Harley L. Browning. *Current Perspectives in Latin American Research.* Austin: University of Texas Press and the Institute of Latin American Studies, 1976.

Portes, Alejandro, and John Walton. *Urban Latin America: The Political Condition from Above and Below.* Austin: University of Texas Press, 1976.

"Resumen de la investigación efectuada en la Colonia del Sol." Mimeo-

graphed. Mexico D.F., Department of Psychology, Universidad Auto-
noma de Mexico, 1970.

Roberts, Bryon R. *Organizing Strangers: Poor Families in Guatemala City.* Austin: University of Texas Press, 1973.

———. *Cities of Peasants: The Political Economy of Urbanization in the Third World.* Beverly Hills, Calif.: Sage Publications, 1978.

Rocco, Raymond A. "Lo Mexicano? Culture, Ideology, and Marginal-ity." Mimeographed. Los Angeles: University of California, Los An-geles, 1981.

Rosaldo, Renato. *Ilongot Headhunting: 1883-1974. A Study in Society and History.* Stanford, Calif.: Stanford University Press, 1980.

Ross, Marc H. *The Political Integration of Urban Squatters.* Evanston, Ill.: Northwestern University Press, 1973.

Seibel, Mark. "Mexican Outskirt Suffering Growth Pains." *Los Angeles Times*, 20 April 1980, p. 8.

Seligson, Mitchell A., and John A. Booth, eds. *Politics and the Poor. Political Participation in Latin America*, volume 2. New York: Holmes and Meier, 1979.

Serron, Luis A. *Scarcity, Exploitation, and Poverty.* Norman: University of Oklahoma Press, 1980.

Smith, Peter H. "Does Mexico Have a Power Elite?" In *Authoritarianism in Mexico*, edited by J. L. Reyna and R. S. Weinert. Philadelphia: ISHI Publications, 1977.

Stavenhagen, Rodolfo. *Sociología y subdesarrollo.* Mexico D.F.: Edi-torial Nuestro Tiempo, 1971.

Stone, Judy. "Babenco's Real People, Brazilian Style." *Los Angeles Times*, 8 November 1981, p. 26.

Strickon, A., and S. M. Greenfield. *Structure and Process in Latin Amer-ica.* Albuquerque: University of New Mexico Press, 1972.

Swartz, Marc J. Introduction to *Political Anthropology*, edited by M. J. Swartz, J. V. Turner, and A. Tuden. Chicago: Aldine, 1966.

———. Introduction to *Local-Level Politics*, edited by M. J. Swartz. Chicago: Aldine, 1968.

———. "Processual and Structural Approaches in Political Anthro-pology: A Commentary." *Canadian Journal of African Studies* 3 (1969):53-59.

———. "Area Studies, Theory, and Cross-Cultural Comparison." *Afri-can Studies Review* 13 (1970):63-69.

———. "The Processual Approach in the Study of Local Level-Politics." Mimeographed. La Jolla, Calif.: University of California, San Diego, 1972.

Swartz, Marc J., V. Turner, and A. Tuden, eds. *Political Anthropology.* Chicago: Aldine, 1966.

Tamayo, Jorge, et al. *Encuesta definitiva en Cd. Netzahualcoyotl.* Mexico D.F.: Contratistas Oaxaqueños, 1971.

Tuohy, William. "Psychology in Political Analysis: The Case of Mexico." *Western Political Quarterly* 27 (1974):289-307.

Turner, Victor. *Schism and Continuity in an African Society: A Study of Ndembu Village Life.* Manchester: University Press, 1957.

Uzell, Douglas. "Bound for Places I'm Not Known to: Adaptation of Migrants and Residence in Four Irregular Settlements in Peru." Ph.D. dissertation, University of Texas, Austin, 1972.

Van Velsen, J. "The Extended-Case Method and Situational Analysis." In *The Craft of Social Anthropology,* edited by A. L. Epstein. London: Tavistock Publications.

Vélez-Ibañez, Carlos G. "Youth and Aging in Central Mexico: One Day in the Life of Four Families of Migrants." In *Life's Career-Aging: Cultural Variations in Growing Old,* edited by B. G. Myerhoff and A. Simic. Beverly Hills, Calif.: Sage Publications, 1978a.

————. "Amigos Políticos o Amigos Sociales: The Politics of Putting Someone in Your Pocket." *Human Organization* 37 (1978b):368-377.

————. "Social Diversity, Commercialization, and Organizational Complexity of Urban Mexican/Chicano Rotating Credit Associations: Theoretical and Empirical Issues of Adaptation." *Human Organization* 41 (1982):107-120.

————. *Bonds of Mutual Trust: The Cultural Systems of Rotating Credit Associations among Urban Mexicans and Chicanos.* New Brunswick, N.J.: Rutgers University Press, forthcoming.

Villareal, Rene. *The Policy of Import Substitution, 1929-1975.* Edited by J. L. Reyna and R. S. Weinert. Philadelphia: ISHI Publications, 1977.

Wallace, A. F. C. *Culture and Personality.* 2d ed. New York: Random House, 1970.

Walton, John. "Urban Hierarchies and Patterns of Dependence in Latin America: Theoretical Bases for a New Research Agenda." In *Current Perspectives in Latin American Research,* edited by A. Portes and H. L. Browning. Austin: University of Texas Press and Institute of Latin American Studies, 1976.

————. *Elites and the Politics of Development: A Comparative Study of Four Cities.* No. 4. Austin: Institute of Latin American Studies, University of Texas, 1977.

Ward, P. M. "The Squatter Settlements as Slum or Housing Solution: Evidence from Mexico City." *Land Economics* 52 (1976):330-346.

Weaver, Thomas, and Douglas White. "Anthropological Approaches to Urban and Complex Societies." In *The Anthropology of Urban Environments*. Monograph no. 11, edited by T. Weaver and D. White. Boulder, Colo.: Society of Applied Anthropology, 1972.

Wolf, Eric R. "Aspects of Group Relations in a Complex Society: Mexico." *American Anthropologist* 58 (1956):1065-1078.

――――. "The Virgin of Guadalupe: A Mexican National Symbol." *Journal of American Folklore* 71 (1958):34-39.

――――. *Sons of the Shaking Earth*. Chicago: University of Chicago Press, 1959.

――――. "Kinship, Friendship, and Patron-Client Relations in Complex Societies." In *The Social Anthropology of Complex Societies*, edited by M. Banton. London: Tavistock, 1969.

Wolfinger, R. E. *The Politics of Progress*. Englewood Cliffs, N.J.: Prentice-Hall, 1974.

Worsley, Peter. "Franz Fanon and the 'Lumpen-proletariat.'" *Socialist Register* (1972):193-230.

Zeitlin, Irving M. *Ideology and the Development of Sociological Theory*. Englewood Cliffs, N.J.: Prentice-Hall, 1968.

Index

Designer: University of California Press Staff
Compositor: Janet Sheila Brown
Printer: Maple-Vail Book Mfg. Group
Binder: Maple-Vail Book Mfg. Group
Text: 11/13 Paladium, Compuwriter II
Display: STOP/Paladium